REDEEMING THE CITY

REDEEMING THE CITY

Theology, Politics, and Urban Policy

RONALD D. PASQUARIELLO
DONALD W. SHRIVER JR.
ALAN GEYER

THE PILGRIM PRESS
NEW YORK

Scripture quotations are from the *Revised Standard Version of the Bible*, copyright 1946, 1952 and © 1971 by the Division of Christian Education, National Council of Churches, and are used by permission. Scripture quotation marked KJV is from the King James Version of the Bible. Scripture quotation marked NEB is from the New English Bible.

Excerpt from "Choruses from 'The Rock' " is in COLLECTED POEMS 1901–1962 by T.S. Eliot; copyright 1936 by Harcourt Brace Jovanovich, Inc.; copyright © 1963, 1964 by T.S. Eliot; reprinted by permission of Harcourt Brace Jovanovich, Inc. Excerpts from *Is There Hope for the City?* by Donald W. Shriver, Jr. and Karl A. Ostrom are copyright © 1977 The Westminster Press; used by permission. Excerpts from *The Meaning of the City* by Jacques Ellul are copyright © 1970 Wm. B. Eerdmans Publishing Co; used by permission. Excerpts from *The Secular City* by Harvey Cox are reprinted with permission of Macmillan Publishing Co., Inc.; copyright © Harvey Cox, 1965, 1966. Excerpts from *The Home of Man* by Barbara Ward are copyright © 1976 W.W. Norton & Company, Inc; used by permission. Excerpts from THE URBAN WILDERNESS: A HISTORY OF THE AMERICAN CITY by Sam Bass Warner, Jr. are copyright © 1972 by Sam Bass Warner, Jr; reprinted by permission of Harper & Row, Publishers, Inc. Excerpts from The New York Times (October 21, 1979) and The New York Times Book Review (September 16, 1979) are copyright © 1979 by The New York Times Company; reprinted by permission. Excerpt from "Save Youngstown: Save America" is from the January 1978 issue of *Grapevine* and is reprinted by permission of the Joint Strategy and Action Committee, Inc., a New York-based ecumenical agency, and of *Grapevine*.

The Publisher is grateful for permission to quote the various church statements located in Appendix B of this volume. Credits are given on the first page of each statement.

Library of Congress Cataloging in Publication Data

Pasquariello, Ronald D.
  Redeeming the city.

Bibliography: p. 214
  1. Urban policy—United States. 2. City churches—United States. I. Shriver, Donald W.
II. Geyer, Alan F. III. Title.
HT123.P365   1982   307.7'64'0973   82-12383
ISBN 0-8298-0626-1 (pbk.)

THE PILGRIM PRESS, 132 WEST 31 STREET, NEW YORK, NY 10001

CONTENTS

68655

We build in vain unless the LORD build with us,
Can you keep the City that the LORD keeps not with you?
A thousand policemen directing the traffic
Cannot tell you why you come or where you go.
A colony of cavies or a horde of active marmots
Build better than they that build without the LORD.
Shall we lift up our feet among perpetual ruins?
I have loved the beauty of Thy House, the peace of Thy sanctuary,
I have swept the floors and garnished the altars.
Where there is no temple there shall be no homes,
Though you have shelters and institutions,
Precarious lodgings while the rent is paid,
Subsiding basements where the rat breeds
Or sanitary dwellings with numbered doors
Or a house a little better than your neighbour's;
When the Stranger says: What is the meaning of this city?
Do you huddle close together because you love each other?
What will you answer? 'We all dwell together
To make money from each other'? or 'This is a community'?
And the Stranger will depart and return to the desert.
O my soul, be prepared for the coming of the Stranger,
Be prepared for him who knows how to ask questions.

T.S. Eliot, "Choruses From 'The Rock,' " *Selected Poems*.

"The way to the Celestial City lies just through this town, where this lusty fair is kept; and he that will go to the City, and yet not go through this town, must needs go out of the world."

John Bunyan, *The Pilgrim's Progress*

FOREWORD

THIS BOOK began in the work of the Urban Policy Panel of the Churches' Center for Theology and Public Policy. The Center was established in 1976 as an ecumenical study center with these objectives:

1. To muster the intellectual resources of the churches for sustained study of the bearing of Christian faith on political life and thought.
2. To develop humane perspectives on policy issues and processes, with special concern for justice to the poor, the powerless, and the oppressed and for the peace of the whole human family.
3. To affirm and nourish the ministry of the laity among politicians, bureaucrats, diplomats, judges, lobbyists, and activists.
4. To empower church leaders and groups for competent and credible action in the policy arena by a thorough grounding in research and reflection.
5. To assess the attitudes and behavior of the churches as they affect public life, with particular concern for integrity between pronouncements and practice.

The Center established the Urban Policy Panel of church leaders, public policy practitioners, academics, and church activists, as a permanent body with a long term commitment to American urban policy. A substantial portion of chapter two was based on a chapter from the Ph.D. dissertation submitted to the Fletcher School of Law and Diplomacy by Dr. Keith D. Martin. Participants in the panel who made substantial preliminary contributions to this book are: Dr. Lewis G. Bender, Department of Political Science, Eastern Michigan University; the Rev. Lon Dring, Director, Montgomery County Community Ministry, Maryland; Dr. Norman Faramelli, a member of the Urban Mission Conference of the Episcopal Diocese of Massachusetts and Director of Planning, Massachusetts Port Authority; Ms. Elizabeth Haselden, Metropolitan Program Director, Church Women United; the Rev. Kinmoth W. Jefferson, Director of Urban Ministries, United Methodist Church; the Rev. Stanley F. Knock, Jr., Washington Representative, Interreligious Coalition for Housing; Dr. Keith Martin, Director, National Capital Semester for Seminarians, Wesley Theological Seminary, Washington, D.C.; Doug Mitchell, Pittsburgh, PA; Dr. Charles Moore, Birmingham, AL; Walter Rybeck, Special Assistant to the Chairperson, House Committee on Banking, Finance, and Urban Affairs; the Rev. John Steinbruck, Pastor, Luther Place Church, Washington, D.C.; Dr. Gibson Winter, Professor of Christianity and Society, Princeton Theological Seminary.

The Church's Center for Theology and Public Policy,
4500 Massachusetts Ave., N.W., Washington, D.C. 20016.

REDEEMING THE CITY

Introduction

CITIES CAN be beautiful. Cities can be the cultural magnets of civilizations where art and architecture and science and industry flourish. Cities can be neighborly communities where the most diverse peoples care deeply for one another, for their own heritage, and for the common good. Cities can be the habitat of a good and abundant life. Cities can be places where God is known and loved and praised by joyful multitudes.

But something else is happening in American cities in the 1980s. We see it in the windowless hulks of abandoned buildings and in the weedy rubble of bulldozed blocks. We smell it in cluttered gutters, littered alleys, and rotting railroad stations. We hear it in the relentless sirens of police cars racing to the latest scene of violence or of fire trucks speeding to another flaming arson. We are jolted by it in the potholed streets. We recoil from the look of it in the faces of thousands of jobless twenty-year-olds loitering on street corners.

Many of America's central cities seem lost in a downward spiral of decay and death. New skyscrapers may rise, but so does unemployment. The urban infrastructure groans with age and neglect. The social fabric tears apart in despair and cynicism and terror. There is a domestic arms race between fearful haves and desperate have-nots.

As government preoccupation with and spending for "national security" escalates, the existential security of citizens in their own communities declines. Long caught between mortality and bankruptcy, older cities are now being deprived of federal funds and programs in the name of national defense, anti-inflation, and local initiative.

This book is a plea for a new urban policy for America and for a vital role for the churches in the genesis of that policy. It is inescapably a political book—but hardly less theological on that account. Its authors assume that the most searching political analysis can only deepen the quest for religious truth. We also assume that the churches are inescapably involved in the fate of American cities, for good or for ill. There is a long and troubled history of the churches' implication in the forces of urban change. We seek to bring candid historical perspectives to this study, but our overriding concern is for the future—hence our hopeful emphasis on redeeming the city.

A generation ago, governmental and religious leaders were serious about the renewal of cities. Indeed, "renewal" was the key word of both urban planners and church activists. There were radiant visions of what cities could become. Many good things were done. In retrospect, it is clear that many renewal programs, at best, lacked staying power and, at worst, aggravated the problems they sought to overcome.

Urban Action in the 1960s: In the decades following World War II, church leaders took initiatives in urban ministry parallel to the initiatives of government and sometimes in advance of government. By the early 1960s, inner-city ministries recognized their interdependence with other church structures and had begun to develop metropolitan strategies. Church organizations and leaders became involved with the civil rights movement and the war on poverty. Inner-city black churches demonstrated to their white suburban counterparts the interconnections between personal and social salvation, churchly and political ministry, justice for poor people and obstructions to justice in the unequal opportunities of American society. The incorporation of white Christians into the civil rights movement, rooted in the black churches, was a major breakthrough for white consciousness of these very connections. It was natural for some white and black churches, for example, to support the War on Poverty of the Lyndon Johnson years and to sense, with Martin Luther King, Jr., the incompatibility of that war with the one in Vietnam. Sargent Shriver, then Director of the Office of Economic Opportunity, considered the churches an important ally in the fight against poverty. That office, in the late 1960s, funneled an estimated $90,000,000 annually through the churches for community action programs.[1]

Moreover, during the late 1950s and early 1960s the Catholic Church established offices of urban affairs or social action within diocesan structures. Camaraderie developed among priests and other religious leaders working in social action. Early social action movements such as the Catholic Interracial Councils, the Catholic Rural Life Movement, the "labor priests," the Catholic Worker, Catholic Charities, the Christian Family Movement, and the Young Christian Workers and Students developed. All of these groups were consonant with the emerging social teaching of the Catholic Church, especially found in the social encyclicals of Popes Leo XIII, Pius XI, and John XXIII.

Nonetheless, the social activism that invigorated churches during the 1960s was not translated into organized and integrated attacks on urban problems in the 1970s. By 1972, national denominational efforts to fight poverty, racism and other urban problems had all but died. Ecumenical ministries, too, became victims of the lethargy infecting the nation and the churches. Ecumenical approaches to church ministries suit urban environments, but when program cutbacks come to the churches of America, the ecumenical usually suffers disproportionately.

As national interest waned, the responsibility for urban mission reverted to local congregations with little or no support from national or judicatory offices. In most cases, efforts to grapple with urban problems consistently simply stopped. In many churches, the fight against poverty and racism gave way to the struggle to survive as a congregation.

Today, some churches are still involved in most facets of urban life: meals for the elderly, job assistance for the unemployed, housing renewal, education and training for the under-employed, assistance for the handicapped, outreach to prisoners, and social and psychological counseling for distressed persons. But most of these worthy programs are bound to the financial and social limitations of local congregations. Meaningful support (especially financial) for urban social programming does not extend to the hierarchies of most denominations. Except for organizations such as the Catholic Campaign for Human Development few national church resources have been brought to bear on the problems of the inner city.

Urban Policy in the 1970s: If the needs of the urban poor are to be addressed in a meaningful way, the churches must find ways to relate the wealth of suburbia to the problems of the inner-city. Church efforts must extend beyond the inner-city congregation and beyond church structures. The most effective way to proceed is through involvement in public policy change, at the municipal, state and federal level. By their participation in these struggles, some church leaders learned this principle and issued a rousing "Call to Commitment to the City" in 1978. The "Call" commended repentance as a proper Christian starting point for the reform of society. The behavior of church people, says the document, is at the heart of our national urban crisis. Church members are the ones who have

> abandoned the cities in pursuit of a more comfortable and affluent lifestyle. We have benefited from government highway, tax, mortgage and development policies which have created suburban sprawl for the haves and the prison of the ghetto for the have-nots. We stood idly by and watched the dismantling of the antipoverty

programs of the 60's. In our own congregational life we have contributed to and blessed the white exodus from the city, and the resulting disinvestment, by moving our churches . . . to greener pastures and by looking 'beyond the Beltway' for the location of new houses of worship. Even those middle-class congregations which have remained in the city have, with far too few exceptions, exhibited a greater concern for protecting their own real estate and searching out larger and more convenient parking lots than in risking a commitment to the poorest of the poor who live at their doorsteps.[2]

The "Call to Commitment," while expressing some dissatisfaction with the formal urban policy of the Carter Administration announced on March 27, 1978, commended this effort as "the first time an American President has attempted to forward a comprehensive and coherent national policy for cities." The church document implicitly commended such a comprehensive approach to the churches, too. It admitted, however, that to date the religious community had "made no serious organized attempt to influence the direction of this policy as it was being formulated," despite an elaborate process of hearings and discussion in which some Christian laity vainly sought input from the churches. No body of Christians had been mandated to address urban policy at the national governmental level. Urban policy remains a peripheral item in church bureaucracies and theological seminaries, if it gets any attention at all.

In sum, while the churches have had substantial influence in reinforcing and even stimulating historic urban trends in America, their influence has hardly been exercised in formulating urban strategy or as intentional political action—at least not in the work of most pastors, laity, and church executives.

The practical purpose of this book is to help stimulate this long overdue concern and action.

Assumptions Concerning the Churches' Role: Americans long ago agreed that no one human institution—political, economic, religious, or social—will dominate our national society. No person, organization, idea, or institution has total responsibility for the country: it is so basic a cultural dogma for Americans that we hardly discuss it.

This book assumes that government, business, churches, synagogues, voluntary associations all have a role in reshaping American urban life. None has the sole responsibility. Only some pattern of collaboration among all of them is likely to yield genuine, whole, and humane reshaping of our common life. To say this is to ward off any accusation of imperialism on the part of the churches when they propose to take overdue initiative here. Economic perspectives and economic organizations come closest to dominate the perspectives preferred by many Americans in their thinking about cities. Capitalists and communists alike are wedded to this economism, an empirical mistake. We mean to avoid that mistake in the church-related strategies that are the heart of our final chapter.

At the outset, we propose the biblical notion of *shalom* as a basic image of what the church seeks, expects, yearns for in human society. Beyond mere strategy, *shalom* governs our sense of what strategy aims to bring about, and under what criteria of continuing reformation the strategic plans of humans should be judged. In the Hebrew–Christian perspective, *shalom* is both a gift from God the Creator and a task for responsible human beings.

This biblical concept means

- communal well-being rather than possessive individualism.
- a special bias in ethics towards the needs of poor people, the powerless, and other marginal folk of society.
- empowering persons to join together in common pursuit of peace, justice, and compassion in society.
- a divine challenge to human beings to look at their life together, as a whole, in an expanding sense of responsibility for a neighborhood that ultimately includes all humanity and the created world.

This all-embracing religious and ethical concept may be impossible to reduce to a set of policies for any combination of human institutions, but it provides a basic orientation to those heirs of the biblical vision who participate in policymaking with neighbors oriented by other visions.

At the end of this book we propose church strategies for urban policymaking in the United States based on our observations, conclusions, and presuppositions. We claim that:

- The U.S. is now an urban nation; what affects the lives of people in the metropolitan complex ultimately affects the life, strength, and integrity of the nation.
- Human need is not confined to the urban areas but the urban situation, particularly in the older inner cities, lends more desperation to the problems.
- Most of the issues affecting the quality of urban life are interrelated and require an integrated approach.

- Action on *national* urban policy cannot be isolated from involvement in those concrete issues of *local* community life which national policy affects.
- The development of this policy has direct bearing on the national budget and the priorities for the allocation of national funds.
- Any allocation of funds, human energies, and institutional resources reflects a culture, an interconnected set of attitudes and beliefs as well as combinations of power and influence. Anti-urban and anti-poor attitudes get structured into programs and policies by human decision; in turn, such programs and policies reinforce these very attitudes. One aim of policy change is to break this vicious circle.
- A just national urban policy will benefit all the people of the nation, and not only people who happen to reside in large cities.
- The churches should not regard their role as only one of monitoring and critiquing urban policy. The churches must be actively engaged in developing policy and initiating those strategies and projects that will address the issues and the institutions which can affect it.
- Religious people need education about the many complex issues being addressed, and a new understanding of the role of advocacy and empowerment in Christian service.
- Strategies will have to be directed toward systemic change in the political and economic spheres. Most social problems are simply not amenable to individual or private sector solutions.
- The urban problem calls for the cooperation of a wide body of possible partners in the religious community itself. It is an ecumenical task. It also requires other partners outside formal church structures. It is a broadly political task.
- A strategy inspired by *shalom* means accentuating the potentialities and capabilities of people. It means participating in the making of the tools, structures, organizations, and institutions required for rebuilding the fabric of a truly human community. It requires human action in response to the gifts of God in creation and in history.

NOTES

[1]James Adams, *The Growing Church Lobby in Washington* (Grand Rapids: Eerdmans, 1970), p. 45.

[2]"A Call to Commitment to the City," Washington, D.C.: Churches' Center for Theology and Public Policy, *Center Circles*, no. 2, November, 1978, p. 2.

1.

Vision and Visibility:

The Peace of God for Human Cities

PEOPLE USED to talk about the cities as places of adventure and excitement, as centers of culture, government and religion. More and more people talk as though the city is a machine running by itself. Cities, in fact, are networks of people, meshed in a variety of structures. For many people those structures are sources of pain and hardship. Here is the way John Steinbruck and Lon Dring, pastors of the inner city and suburban Washington, D.C., encounter that pain from day to day.

THE HOUSING PINCH

Washington is an expensive city. The median price for a new home in the Washington metropolitan area was $88,990 in January, 1980; nationally, it was $60,000.[1] There is a desperate lack of affordable housing in the Washington Metropolitan Area. On the average, a family would require an annual income of about $35,000 to get a mortgage on an $88,990 house.

Renters fare no better. In 1978, in the District of Columbia, sixty thousand renter households were eligible for housing assistance. By 1980, only twenty-five thousand households were in subsidized units. Non-subsidized rental housing is vanishing. Rental vacancies are 3.6% or lower in the various jurisdictions. Many of these vacancies are in marginal neighborhoods and buildings. A renter can expect to pay 35% of his income for rent.

Rent control has become a two-edged sword. Where it has remained in effect, it has contributed to the decrease in the number of rental units as landlords, unable to meet rising operating costs or seeking greater profits, either abandon their property to decay, or convert it to condominiums.[2]

Where rent controls were lifted, rents rose rapidly, and the poor were driven out of their homes. Few had places to go.

Condominium conversions mean trauma, rejection, and displacement for the elderly, persons on fixed incomes, and young married couples. Yet, conversions will continue as a way for owners to liquidate their holdings at substantial capital gain. At the same time, they pass on their operating costs to the purchasers of individual apartments. The new owners also benefit, through tax savings and potential capital gains, on the resale of their units.

Families who are seeking a hedge against inflation by purchasing their own homes can expect to pay about 40% of their income in mortgage payments. To maintain such an investment, both parents need to work.

While the housing pinch is a question of unaffordable housing and rents, it is also a matter of decay, waste, and confusion. Within blocks of new office buildings and stately old churches are apartment complexes, empty and slowly falling to ruin. Old brownstones and row houses are in dismal states of disrepair. Sixty-five thousand households were reported in need of assistance because of crowding, excessive rent, or lack of bathroom and kitchen facilities in the District of Columbia at the end of the 1970s. The suburbs are facing the same kinds of problems due to rapidly aging housing.

In instances where government has stepped in to help, the cure has sometimes been worse than the disease. In one case, efforts to form a partnership of local residents, business, and governments to rehabilitate a building for the benefit of the community were scuttled because of federal bureaucratic ineptitude, confusion, and red tape.

This is an oft-told tale. For too many city dwellers, urban renewal has meant urban removal as the poor were moved from family and community networks to public assistance in strange parts of the city.

Whatever else a city is, it is a place where people live close by many other people. The cost of such living is rising. Is the cost worth paying? Who will pay it?

THE UN/UNDER-EMPLOYMENT PINCH

Recently the largest mortgage lender in the Washington area, squeezed by a prime interest rate approaching twenty percent, was facing bankruptcy. He closed fourteen branch offices, laying off hundreds of people.

Unemployment is a peculiar phenomenon in the Washington metropolitan area. The unemployment rate, about 9% in 1979, does not give the whole picture because of the economic structure of the area. Government is the backbone of its economy, employing 32% of all workers. This means the area has a higher proportion of skilled workers than elsewhere. There are few entry-level jobs and unskilled workers have fewer opportunities than in other cities.

There are high levels of unemployment in geographic pockets within the region. In 1978, the District of Columbia, for example, had an unemployment rate which was almost twice as high as the regional unemployment rate. One-fifth of the area's labor force is located in the District, while nearly one-third of the region's unemployed live there. The picture is the same for geographic pockets in suburban Maryland and Virginia.

High levels of unemployment are found among certain groups: women, young persons of both sexes, and blacks. Unemployment for young black males (ages 16 to 19) ran to nearly 50% in the District. At the same time, upper-income employment expanded, out of the reach of the groups mentioned above. Population pockets of high unemployment are caused by a history of victimization: discrimination, inadequate job skills because of poor training and preparation, educational tracking into low job levels, employment in jobs affording little or no career advancement.

Unemployment is a spiritual as well as an economic problem. It attacks a person's sense of worth and wholeness. It destroys hope and produces despair. Despair is infectious; it can spread beyond individual and family to a whole community. Underemployment more subtly generates the same spiritual malaise. An underemployed person is working at a job which is below his or her ability. This aspect of the pinch squeezes women and minorities in particular.

The high cost of urban living has made employment itself a problem. Men and women are pressured to work long hours, often at unfulfilling jobs, to climb the career ladder. The toll on the family due to working fathers and mothers still has to be measured.

Unless the city is also a place to work, it is not a human place to live. Can jobs be found for all American city residents who want to work?

THE PINCH OF SOCIAL ALIENATION

In an informal survey, when asked where they hurt, Washington area suburbanites consistently complained of the "lack of community." Mitch Snyder, who works with the very poor in the heart of the District of Columbia, has denounced time and time again the sin of "distancing" or "isolating" which he sees eating at the heart of society.

This is grass roots recognition that along with food, shelter, health, work, there is another fundamental human need: social participation. This is the need to be recognized by the society at large and to be engaged directly in making those decisions which touch on one's present life and future.

Social alienation seems endemic to urban society. Mother Teresa of Calcutta, when accepting the Nobel Prize for Peace, said that the deepest pain of the poor was not the lack of material goods, but "rejection and loneliness." Philosopher Lawrence Haworth, author of *The Good City*, has suggested that specialization, despite its many benefits to society, contributes to the fragmenting of community, leaving individuals little way to experience their wholeness.

One meets the homeless everywhere in Washington. More and more abused children and wives, runaways and transients are appearing on the streets. There are no figures to measure the size of the problem, but local governments have appealed to churches to help provide emergency shelters to respond to this growing and overwhelming need. Few, unfortunately, have responded.

Prejudice, and its more virulent form, racism, are types of social alienation. They are the rejection of a person or persons because of external factors of cultural difference, like the color of a person's skin, or the way a person socializes, or the way a person organizes his or her work life. A study of a suburb north of the District of Columbia has shown that a dollar in the hand of a black person will not purchase on the housing market what the same dollar would bring a white person. Steering—directing certain groups of persons to particular areas to buy homes—and redlining—disinvesting neighborhoods on the basis of arbitrarily determined racial, ethnic, or physical characteristics—still occur.

Displacement is another face of social alienation. Attracted by the many opportunities urban living offers, middle class people are moving into central city neighborhoods. The poor who live there are forced out by skyrocketing rents, taxes, and property values.

Even where school boards have made a sincere effort to end *de jure* segregation, housing patterns in the Washington metropolitan area have maintained *de facto* segregation. In 1979, the schools in the District of Columbia had a student population of 106,156. Of those, 100,300 were black. Black and white students work well together in structured classroom situations, but, when the bell rings, they go in opposite directions, still deeply separated by geographical, social, economic and cultural class differences, as well as racial prejudice.

These are signs of what may become a basic crisis facing Washington area schools: the loss of a broad commitment to public education. The quality of education is being hurt by budget cuts. Those whites and upwardly mobile blacks who live in the city are increasingly sending their children to private schools.

It is not enough, for human fulfillment, that people should live and work in the same location. Not geography but community determines the quality of human life in a city. Are American city-dwellers, in all their diversity, capable of affirming each other as members of a community?

THE WELFARE PINCH

The number of welfare recipients and the size of welfare households have both decreased in the Washington metropolitan area. Welfare expenditures by local governments have leveled off. Welfare families have not benefited from this turn of events.

Welfare payments have not kept pace with inflation. The average Aid to Families with Dependent Children (AFDC) payment per household was $230 per month in the metropolitan area in 1978. This represents an increase of 13% from the 1970 level. During the same period of time, the Consumer Price Index—the measure of the cost of food, shelter, health care, energy—increased for the metropolitan area by 68%.

Plainly, inflation has devastated welfare families. In 1979, a family of four needed $12,398 a year to live (as defined by the U.S. Department of Labor, Bureau of Labor Statistics) in the Washington metropolitan area. A welfare family of four received an average of $5,100 in AFDC and food stamp payments in the same year.

How do they cope? Wherever they can, they are accumulating debts to pay expenses. Some are not paying their rent, utility, and food bills. That situation cannot continue forever.

"The American Dream" once nourished the belief that this was a land of opportunity for the poor. But the welfare system is nourishing an underclass of permanently poor people. Shall we revise the dream or change the system?

OTHER PLACES, OTHER PINCHES

There are other places people are hurting: the energy pinch—electric bills have quadrupled in the past few years; the transportation pinch—becoming more costly, available to the well-to-do; the nuclear pinch—

the holocaust we have all feared for years may not be caused by a bomb, but by a nearby utility plant; the health care pinch—thousands are without means to cover their medical costs or take steps toward preventive health care. The shoe is pinching everywhere, and it is getting tighter.

The lesson in all this is that it is not enough to take care of these problems individually. It is not enough to ease the pain. If the shoe is pinching, one can look for ways to stop the pinching here or there. But perhaps what one should do is to have the manufacturer design a better shoe.

That is what the churches need to be doing, working with the designer to come up with a better shoe. They need to dig down and get to the structures that are causing the pinch on all classes and types of city dwellers, particularly the poor. This means looking at the city as a whole. It means dealing with the policies that give rise to the structures. It means social change by political action at the policy level.

VISION AND VISIBILITY

Large cities offer many examples of what one sociologist called urban villagers—groups of people who seldom stray outside the few blocks where they live, and who perceive the rest of the city as alien territory. New York, it is said, is not one city but a collection of such neighborhoods whose ties to each other loosen by the year. Social workers in Chicago tell us that there are children living within the Loop who have never seen Lake Michigan, three or four blocks away. These are the children who grow up never really "seeing" the life-world of people who live in Oak Park and Cicero, not to speak of Evanston. Doubtless there are Evanstonians who have never seen the slums of the Loop, either. Psychologically, neither the slum dwellers nor the suburbanites reside in a place so large as Chicago. They have no image of the city as a whole.[3]

Students of the psychology of perception assure us that more than beauty may be in the eye of the beholder. Almost every human assertion that *"this* is *that"* contains a complex interaction between something externally viewable and something internal to the viewer. It is believed that the structures of human nerves and brain cells are conditioned by experience so that certain perceptions are possible or impossible, to the viewpoint of the mature adult. Past experience shapes future experience systematically, inexorably.

This open and closed condition of human "vision" is an old concern of some religious traditions: "Where there is no vision, the people perish,"

(Proverbs 29:18 KJV). For the Jewish tradition, "vision" was not some divinely-inspired dream but a perception of mundane events, interpreted through some larger framework than others might bring to the same events. The prophets in the Hebrew tradition did not deal with different historical data than did their critics. They saw the data differently. In this sense, they participated in a quest for a truth that engages the minds of modern scientists on terms not altogether different. Progress in science is often not a matter of getting more facts but of seeing alleged facts in a new perspective, a new theoretical framework that enables the scientist to assert new truth.

The authors of this book are committed to the quest of seeing, evaluating, and acting in the human community as a whole, especially in the context of American urban life. To "see things whole" is an enormous, perhaps a pretentious ambition. But its source is in the Hebrew-Christian tradition itself. In the following pages, we attempt to describe briefly how this tradition sees human cities through images—or perceptual filters—such as *shalom*. In reverting to the Bible as a start on describing our perception of contemporary American urban life, we do so with no sense that a biblical beginning permits us to commend our view of the modern city as a "revelation." Other views, with other starting places, may duplicate, supplement, or contradict our way of viewing. No viewpoint on human affairs is automatically privileged over others, but no viewpoint can claim to be value-free, either.

Every medium, time, and place of human perception is conditioned by a viewpoint as well as by things viewed. This is true of every image on the television screen, every newspaper headline, every social-scientific study, every analysis of the urban crisis from a government bureau, and every proposal for urban policy change in this book. The last few pages, on "pinches" in the lives of people in American cities, have a perceptual viewpoint. In the pages to follow, we examine this point of view—its roots in the Bible, its curiosity about certain capacities of human beings, and its hopes for a certain kind of human future.

The Bible is not the only source to which Jews and Christians turn for giving such an account of themselves and their points of view. But it is a peculiarly important source, for it records the earliest surviving memories of these religious communities. The past we celebrate pre-enacts the future we hope for.[4] It predisposes us to be open to certain "facts" in our own time and place. This is not mindless delusion on our part but a participation in the human condition, where mind, memory, and perception are inextricably connected.

THE CITY IN THE BIBLE

The interpretation of the Bible itself is subject to the above critique. In different periods of Western history, Christians have understood the biblical tradition from various points of view. As an introduction to the authors' own late-twentieth-century view of this tradition, we do well to remember certain other contrasting views.

Dwight L. Moody, for example, had a fundamental insight about the cities of America which motivated his evangelistic activities. He is reported to have said, "If we can stir them, we shall stir the whole nation." Throughout his life, however, he stayed aloof from the material suffering and problems of urban dwellers, concentrating his efforts on his own individualistic style of revivalism. But Moody recognized the cities as the centers of national life.

Reinforcing his religious individualism, and reinforced by it, was the economic individualism of classical capitalism, whose heyday in American life was Moody's own era. In the urban context, economic individualism has often meant that the key to the solution of social problems should be economic opportunity for individuals. Combined with an individualistic, contractual system 'for the buying and selling of land and other property, the cultural forces of theology and economic ideology have had a drastic impact on the shaping of life in American cities.

A parallel influence, stemming from a certain way of reading the Bible, has come from church preachers and teachers who underscore the negative estimates of "city" in the Bible and skip lightly over its positive estimates. Ever since Augustine's great work, *The City of God*, theologians have been well aware that the murderer Cain is credited with being the builder of the first mundane city, while Abel, a farmer, "built none." One way of reading all the rest of the Bible is to highlight the judgments and the destructions that God brings upon human cities—Babel, Sodom, Gomorrah, Jericho, Nineveh, Babylon, Rome. Each of these cities is famous in the biblical narrative for its idolatry against the true God and its oppression of the people of God. Each becomes a symbol of the dangers of city life to the life of fidelity to the Kingdom of God. In this part of the biblical perspective, cities are sinful places. Prophets like Amos condemn them as places where the poor are oppressed, commerce supplants community, and the old life of the desert people gives way to the settled life with all its temptations to idolatry. Among modern biblical interpreters, none has pursued this negative view of the city as one theme of the Bible with more drastic consistency than Jacques Ellul. His book, *The Meaning of the City*, sets out to discover "what the Bible reveals concerning the city." He concludes from his study, "From the first book in the Bible to the last there is the same judgment of the city"—the same negative judgment.[5] Everywhere in the Bible Ellul finds the human city as the place of idolatry, oppression, and opposition of human power to the power of God. Typical of the Ellulian reading of the urban theme in the scriptures are the following exerpts from the book:[6]

> The very fact of living in the city directs a man down an inhuman road.

> It was in slavery that Israel and the city were bound together . . . Never again will the cities built by the chosen people be an act of the chosen people . . . And the prophesies of those long-haired prophets who were a constant reminder of the innocence of the nomadic life as opposed to urban life were based on that first apprenticeship: Israel bound herself to slavery, and even more, to the land of sorrow and sin by the cities she built, cities that were always the imitation of what she had learned in Egypt . . .

> The spiritual power of the city must . . . clash with the spirit of grace. Such is the central problem that the city represents for Israel. Such is the problem for every man who wants to live by the grace of Christ.

> All that is said about Babylon can be applied to every other city, to today's cities even more than to any cities known by the seer . . .

> The Scriptures affirm that the agent of war is the great city. There is no such thing as a great agricultural war. A rural people is never a ravenous people.

> All the inhabitants of the city are destined sooner or later to become prostitutes and members of the proletariat.

> If the prophets and Revelation presented the city as the place on earth where the conflict between God and the earth is carried to its highest pitch, where all the powers in revolt gather together, where God's victory is assured, it must be because the cities—our cities—are a sign of the world's destiny, because these cities bear in their bosoms all the hopes of man for divinity! . . . The city is without doubt the product not only of man's effort, but even more, of his good will . . . It is the engineer's bright eye, the urbanist's broad sweep of mind, the hygienist's idealism which determine its course. Yet look at the results: even more slavery . . .

> The message of the cross must be carried to the center of man's autonomy. It must be established where man is most clearly a

wild beast . . . Christ's sending his disciples out into the cities of Israel is their most dangerous mission, for it is directed against the heart of the world's power and betrayal.

Jesus Christ in no way modifies the Old Testament message . . . [He] has no conciliatory or pardoning words for the cities . . . When he speaks to the cities, he never has anything but words of rejection and condemnation.

In Matthew's text we see Jesus speaking differently to the multitude than to the city. The multitude, the crowd! Such is the form of life in the city. Man can be nothing but a crowd in the city . . . He has no silent zone, he lives in a perpetual noise that eliminates any isolation, any meditation, any authentic contact.

No man will change the city—first of all because he will never use it for good.

Can anyone change the evil city? Yes, says Ellul; the God who brings judgment and grace to all the earth in Jesus can change all the earth, including the city. Such a change is a divine miracle. The death and resurrection of Jesus in Jerusalem resulted in a drastic reduction of human pretension represented in all urban life but especially in the claim of historic Jerusalem to be a "holy" city. Only the resurrection of Jesus keeps the Bible's whole message about the city from being unrelieved pessimism. Ultimately God promises a New Jerusalem, a new creation where humans at last are delivered from their idolatry. The old urban vision of humans has been abolished, the new City of God has been established in Jesus in anticipation of the End-Time. In the meantime,

. . . it is no holy world. Let there be no confusion: there is no use expecting a new Jerusalem on earth. Jerusalem will be God's action, absolutely free, unforeseeable, transcendent . . . from this very city [God] is going to make the new Jerusalem. Thus we can observe God's strange progress: Jerusalem becomes Babylon, Babel is restored to the status of a simple city, and this city becomes the city of the living God.[7]

Jews and Christians who read their Bibles through the spectacles of Jacques Ellul will be looking from an angle of vision different from the one employed in this book. We attempt no reasoned refutation of his vision here. Simply, our problem with his approach to the Bible is its one-dimensional insistence on shaping its message to his theological predispositions. Absent from his reading is an appreciation for the mixed righteousness and corruption in David, the founder and first king of Jerusalem; the combination of judgment and hope for historic eighth-century Jerusalem in the prophecies of the First Isaiah; the almost-physical hope for restoration of his beloved city in the later prophecies of Jeremiah; the meaning of the contrast between the prophet Nahum (gleeful over the destruction of Nineveh) and Jonah (who is required by God to preach repentance to that same city); the fact that the early church begins in Jerusalem, that the early churches were primarily urban in location, that Paul put a high value upon his Roman citizenship and his vocation for preaching the gospel in Rome; and the possibility that theological ambivalence towards human cities is a better summation of "the" biblical view than theological condemnation.

We believe that ambivalence is the better summation. We resist Ellul's penchant for a dialectic that verges on dualism—God's grace over against the constructs of humans. We read the Bible as a book full of the same confusing mixture of good and evil that we detect every day in cities where we live. *Empirically* claims like: "The very fact of living in the city directs a man down an inhuman road" and "A rural people is never a ravenous people" are absurd. Jews who left the ghettoes of Russia in the late nineteenth century to come to America left a rural culture dominated by "ravenous" anti-semitism; and they found, even in the steaming East Side of New York City, a degree of blessing that was not in absolute contrast to the ancient liberation from Egypt. The world of human cities, and God's relation to them, is more complex, less single-dimensioned than Ellul's account of the Bible permits. We need not be captive to his way of interpreting the Jewish and the Christian heritages.

On the other hand, we would not want our angle of vision to be mistaken for typical, liberal American confidence in the goodness and the promise of human achievement as represented in the city. A tendency towards this confidence was evident in the 1965 book by Harvey Cox, *The Secular City*. In one important point of theological and biblical interpretation, Cox agrees with Ellul: from the Exodus to the cross of Jesus, God was at work "secularizing" the traditional "holy times and places" of human culture. After the Exodus and after the resurrection of Jesus, no one has an excuse for worshipping in an urban temple as the holy place to find God or living on a rural patch of earth as the only place to remain human.

The modern secular city, says Cox, is an embodiment and a celebration of change, mobility, open human futures. In resonance with the experience of many Americans, Cox points out that rural and small town living has its own slaveries. Even the anonymity of city life can be a stage in the loosening of old, suffocating identities imposed by small town culture upon its inhabitants.

The contemporary urban region represents an ingenious device for vastly enlarging the range of human communication and widening the scope of individual choice. Urbanization thus contributes to the freedom of man.

> The Gospel . . . means a summons to choice and answerability . . . In the historical process itself man meets the One who calls him into being as a free deciding self, and knows that neither his past history nor his environment determines what he does. In the anonymity of urban culture, far from the fishbowl of town life, modern man experiences both the terror and the delight of human freedom more acutely . . . The God of the Gospel is the One who wills freedom and responsibility, who points towards the future in hope. The Law, on the other hand, includes any cultural phenomenon which holds men in immaturity, in captivity to convention and tradition. The Law is enforced by the weight of human opinion; the Gospel is the activity of God creating new possibilities in history . . . From this perspective, urbanization can be seen as a liberation from some of the cloying bondages of preurban society. It is the chance to be free.[8]

Cox would also agree with Ellul that out in the wilderness the Israelites were closer to their Lord than when they flirted with the "lords" (the Baalim) of Canaan. The latter were stationary gods-of-the-land. They were immobile, but Yahweh "went before" his people. "He moved wherever he wanted to."

> This was a crucial victory for the Yahwist faith, since the historical character of Israel's vision of life depends on Yahweh's stalwart refusal to be a hearthgod of some home-sweet-home.

Similarly, and more radically, the early Christians believed in the ascension of the resurrected Jesus, with the implication that now "Jesus is mobile." The Spirit that raised him from the dead still "goes before" the faithful disciples, who on earth have "no lasting city" (Hebrews 13:14). "They were essentially travellers." As such, they often founded their earliest churches in the cities rather than the less mobile rural countryside of the Roman Empire. "Mobile man," in Cox's view,

> . . . is less tempted than the immobile to demote Yahweh into a baal. He will usually not idolatrize any town or nation. He will not be as likely to see the present economic and political structure as the unambiguous expression of how things always have been and always should be. He will be more open to change, movement, newness. There is no reason why Christians should deplore the accelerating mobility of the modern metropolis. The Bible does not call man to renounce mobility, but "to go to a place that I will show you." (Genesis 12:1) Perhaps the mobile man can even hear with less static a Message about a Man who was

born during a journey, spent his first years in exile, was expelled
from his own home town, and declared that he had no place to
lay his head. High mobility is no assurance of salvation, but
neither is it an obstacle to faith.[9]

On the whole, the contrast between the Ellul and the Cox perspectives
on the biblical "meaning of the city," is stark. Rather than a symbol of
human idolatry, the secular city for Cox is a symbol of a human step of
obedience to God, the on-the-move ruler of history. Rather than being
an inhumane oppressor of individuality and community among humans,
the city is "the commonwealth of maturity and interdependence."[10] Rather
than deluding humans about their capacity to live with no thought of their
Creator, the modern city is a summons from the Creator to the responsible
use of God-given powers. Rather than being an occasion for new enslave-
ment of the weak by the powerful, the city can be understood as the context
of a great gospel summons to new human effort "to come to terms with
the new historical reality" of urban, secular society and with "the formulation of ways to live more equitably with other human beings in a
system of increasing reciprocity."[11]

The authors of this book would not encourage any reader to side with
one or the other of two such contrasting ways for reading the Bible and
the experience of modern humans in their cities. Each such perspective
calls our attention to something real, and from each we have important
truth to learn. On the whole, we would warn against the danger of one-
sided exegesis, of which we suspect Ellul to have been guilty, or lopsided
emphasis on the liberating side of the modern urban experience, into
which Cox sometimes fell. Indeed, the Bible's contribution to our understanding is richer, more complex, and more illuminating than any of
our interpretations, including the one to follow here. That is why we are
all well-advised to keep reading this ancient book, in the confidence shown
by John Robinson as he bade farewell to the America-bound Pilgrims in
1620: "God has yet more light to break forth from his Holy Word."

Our "light," in the following, is derived from a view of the Bible and
the views of those Bible scholars that accentuate two-sided ambivalence
concerning human cities in relation to the City of God. This ambivalence
is found in the Bible itself, in our experience of cities, and in our own
disposition to entertain hope rather than despair for them. We are sym-
pathetic, for example, with the views of an Old Testament scholar like
Bernhard Anderson, who has concluded that the story of the Tower of
Babel is not about the city, but about unity and diversity. The story needs
to be understood in terms of the creation theology that precedes it. Humans

are not condemned for their pride and creativity, but because of their intention to gather the people into a centralized location, thereby resisting God's purpose that they should multiply, fill the earth and subdue it. [12] Anderson claims that to see the city, on the basis of the Babel story, as the locus of evil in human history is an insufficiently contextual interpretation.

Sodom and Gomorrah, on the other hand, were condemned for a sin much worse than the homosexuality that is often associated with their name. They were condemned for inhospitality towards strangers, perhaps the greatest moral offense in desert countries. In Bedouin cultures, the desert was the common enemy. Survival was always at stake. Among Bedouins, even one's enemy was to be protected and treated with hospitality while he was within a host's tent. Prophets like Amos demanded that Israel remember the abiding principles of fidelity to its Lord and its own humanity revealed in the Exodus-liberation of the nation. Here was no romantic longing for a rural lifestyle but an insistence that neighborliness to strangers belonged in cities, too.

Babylon is frequently criticized in the Bible, no doubt because its rulers dominated the Middle East for long periods of biblical history. While Babylon is accused of all types of urban immorality, the underlying evil is her worship of false gods. The essence of Israelitic identity is the worship of the one, true God, Yahweh. Babylon's blandishments to idolatry cause its condemnation. (See Isaiah 46: 1-13)

Babylon appears again in the Book of Revelation, where it is a symbol of Rome. Here, as in the prophets, it is criticized for its pride and immorality, but it is ultimately condemned for its cult of emperor worship, a case once more of setting up false gods before the one true God. (See Revelation 17: 1-14)

Throughout the Bible, God's love for the city is never in doubt: "On the holy mount stands the city he founded; the Lord loves the gates of Zion more than all the dwelling places of Jacob." (Psalm 87: 1-2) Even in judgment, always tempered with a vision of redemption, God's love is present. God is at work in the city throughout history, redeeming creation.

The following series of urban biblical images inform our attitude and behavior toward the city. We have emphasized positive images of the city in the Bible because we see the church of America as desperately needing positive guidance for shaping urban life in our country. Neither negative nor positive biblical views must be suppressed, but the positive is our best clue to what the Lord requires of us in the future.

THE CITY AS GIFT, AS CENTER OF A NEW CREATION

In Deuteronomy, where the laws by which God's people are to live in their new land are laid down, are these words:

> And when the Lord your God brings you into the land which he swore to your fathers, to Abraham, to Isaac, and to Jacob, to give you, with great and goodly cities, which you did not build, and houses full of all good things, which you did not fill, and cisterns hewn out, which you did not hew, and vineyards and olive trees, which you did not plant, and when you eat and are full, then take heed lest you forget the Lord, who brought you out of the land of Egypt, out of the house of bondage. (6:10-12)

The prophetic hope for city life is first of all an earthly, not a heavenly, promise. The city, particularly Jerusalem, played a central role in the life of the people of Israel. By bringing the ark to Jerusalem, David made the city. He made it the focal point for his people's spiritual life, more than a convenient commercial and economic center.

In the minds of the Hebrews, "spiritual life" implied a much more wholistic concept than privatized religion. Jerusalem, as well as other biblical cities, was seen as the center of culture and learning where the great social, economic, political, and theological questions of the day were explored and debated.

To be sure, the conviction that God's special favor rested upon the city of David conflicted now and again with the prophetic conviction that nothing could protect Jerusalem from the judgment of God for its sins. Jeremiah struggled all his life against the blithe confidence of his critics that no harm would ever come to the city of "the temple of the Lord. . . ." Yet even Jeremiah (ch. 32) foresaw the time when exiles would return to Jerusalem, and, in token of that faith, he even purchased a piece of land in the Jerusalem suburbs!

Because the city is a gift from God it must be a home for those for whom God has a special concern: the poor and the outcast. Cities of refuge were an early form of courts of appeal, where those involved in unintentional murder could find sanctuary. There are elaborate legal descriptions of how certain cities are to serve as a refuge for the manslayer:

> When you cross the Jordan into the land of Canaan, then you shall select cities to be cities of refuge for you, that the manslayer who kills any person without intent may flee there. The cities shall be for you a refuge from the avenger, that the manslayer may not die until he stands before the congregation for judgment. (Numbers 35:10-12)

Deuteronomy commands that roads be built to make it possible for a fugitive to reach the city of refuge (19: 1-3). Here is an example of the transformation of a tribal revenge-ethic by an appeal to the intertribal law of Moses with its base in the mercy and compassion of God in the Exodus from Egypt.

THE CITY AS A PLACE OF MINISTRY AND MISSION

Refuge for the manslayer offers us one vision of the city's mandate to minister to people in distress, but the biblical story extends well beyond this. In the New Testament, in particular, the city is the scene of much of Jesus' preaching, teaching, and healing. He instructs his disciples to go into the cities and towns of the land, and he moves between city and country. In Luke, Jesus says, "I must preach the good news of the kingdom of God to the other cities also; for I was sent for this purpose [4:43]."

Paul's mission is essentially an urban one, and the welfare of the city church is a theme which runs throughout the Book of Acts and the Pauline epistles, most of which bear the names of particular cities of the Empire. The prophets Isaiah, Jeremiah, and Ezekiel saw their mission as centered in what happened in one city, Jerusalem, whose destruction could be understood as divine judgment only in the context of a divine promise of reconstruction. And, in contrast to the prophet Nahum, who exulted over the downfall of wicked Nineveh, Jonah boldly asserts Israel's missionary obligations towards the Ninevites. God loves the people of pagan cities, too, however much such ecumenicity may annoy a prophet!

THE CITY AS AN ARENA OF GOD'S JUDGING ACTIVITY

Few horrors of twentieth century American cities cannot be found in the Bible. Famine, pestilence, death, violence, and personal immorality of all sorts are part of the biblical urban scene. They usually are understood by the biblical writers as either a provocation for or result of God's judgment and wrath.

The most persistent theme linking the urban environment to God's judging activity is social justice and the failure of the city to live up to this divine mandate. Several biblical passages attribute the destruction of Sodom and Gomorrah to a lack of justice. Ezekiel says, "Behold, this was the guilt of your sister, Sodom; she and her daughters had pride, surfeit of food, and prosperous ease, but did not aid the poor and needy [16:49]."

This vision of the city as a place where the poor and the needy are to receive justice is also captured in the Psalms:

> Some wandered in desert wastes, finding no way to a city to dwell in; hungry and thirsty, their soul fainted within them. Then they cried to the Lord in their trouble, and he delivered them from their distress; he led them by a straight way, till they reached a city to dwell in. (Psalm 107:4-7)

THE CITY AS AN ARENA OF GOD'S REDEEMING ACTIVITY

Hope and redemption are the final words in the biblical narrative. The prophetic indictment of the city and society does not stand alone; it is coupled with God's promise of mercy, forgiveness, and new life.

Jeremiah, for example, links judgment and redemption in both word and deed. While advocating the fall of Jerusalem, he buys land at Anathoth, just outside the city, as a sign that he and his people will some day return.

> Now therefore thus says the Lord, the God of Israel, concerning this city of which you say, "It is given into the hand of the king of Babylon by sword, by famine, and by pestilence": Behold, I will gather them from all the countries to which I drove them in my anger and my wrath and in great indignation; I will bring them back to this place, and I will make them dwell in safety. And they shall be my people, and I will be their God. I will give them one heart and one way, that they may fear me for ever, for their own good and the good of their children after them. I will make with them an ever-lasting covenant, that I will not turn away from doing good to them; and I will put the fear of me in their hearts, that they may not turn from me. (Jeremiah 32:36-40)

Redemption follows judgment in Ezekiel also, where the high dramatic moments in Israel's life center around God's departure from and later return to Jerusalem. The story of the coming to life of the dry bones (Ezekiel 37:1-14), which takes place in a pastoral setting, is immediately preceded by these verses:

> This also I will let the house of Israel ask me to do for them: to increase their men like a flock. Like the flock for sacrifices, like the flock at Jerusalem during her appointed feasts, so shall the waste cities be filled with flocks of men. Then they will know that I am the Lord. (Ezekiel 36:37-38)

THE CITY AS SYMBOL OF THE END-TIME

The Bible promises an urban eschaton. The heavenly city of Hebrews and Revelation is not identical with the restored earthly Jerusalem which the prophets promised, but there is continuity between them. This continuity is in the message which pervades the Bible that God can and does transform and redeem the works of humankind. Out of all the possible pictures which could have been drawn of the end of time, an urban scene dominates. In describing Abraham's journey of faith, and the journey of all God's people, the writer of Hebrews says about the God-given vision of the faithful: ". . . they desire a better country, that is, a heavenly one. Therefore, God is not ashamed to be called their God, for he has prepared for them a city [11:16]." And John of Patmos envisions the climax of human history as the consummation of God's purpose, revealed once in the Exodus, of creating a people with whom to dwell forever. The image of the divine presence among humans is that of a New Jerusalem, City of Peace:

> Then I saw a new heaven and a new earth; for the first heaven and the first earth had vanished, and there was no longer any sea. I saw the holy city, new Jerusalem, coming down out of heaven from God, made ready like a bride adorned for her husband. I heard a loud voice proclaiming from the throne: "Now at last God has his dwelling among men! He will dwell among them and they shall be his people, and God himself will be with them. He will wipe every tear from their eyes; there shall be an end to death, and to mourning and crying and pain; for the old order has passed away!"
> Then he who sat on the throne said, "Behold! I am making all things new!" (Revelation 21:1-5, NEB)

THE CITY AS CENTER OF PLURALISM

Early and late in the history of Israel, its prophets understood Jerusalem as a city of significance for the life of all human beings, not only the Jewish people. Prophets and psalmists speak of Jerusalem as a place of pilgrimage where "all the nations" and "many peoples" will acknowledge the lordship of Yahweh (Isaiah 2:2). After the exile of 586 B.C., Jerusalem becomes the city to which faithful Jews return on days of "high" worship; but they come back bearing the marks of their foreign, exilic cultures. Thus is set the stage for the emergence of a pluralistic urban ethos whose members, if they are to affirm a community with one another, must do so on the basis of beliefs and laws that transcend local cultures. Post-exilic Jerusalem is thus the anticipation of a world human community as well as a center from which the word of the Lord goes forth.

This vision is the historical-cultural background of the first chapters

of the Book of Acts, where we read about the urban beginning of the
Christian church with Jewish pilgrims from many cities of the surrounding
world. The startling claim about the "descent of the Holy Spirit" upon
the new church is not that its members speak in strange, spiritual "tongues."
Rather, the miracle is that "we hear them telling in our own tongues the
mighty works of God [Acts 2:11]." Here the great work of God's Spirit is
to enable people of radically diverse human cultures to affirm each other
across those cultural barriers. There is a unity available now for the diverse;
there is a possibility that all people might now dwell together in one city.
This is the ultimate vision of the Book of Revelation, but its historical
anticipation is first in Israel and then in the church of Jesus Christ. Little
groups of Christians scattered around in the cities of the Roman empire
were, in this sense, anticipators of the "better city" envisioned in the book
of Hebrews. This city was better because of its hospitality to all the races
of humankind.

THE CITY AS EXPRESSION OF HUMAN RESPONSIBILITY

The prophets of Israel were unanimous in claiming that we cannot
blame our social and economic ills on fate or demonic powers. We are
responsible for the things we have manufactured, for the kinds of cities
we sustain, for the justice and injustice we foster, and for the ruining of
our own future.

This responsible role of humanity has strong support in the whole
biblical tradition. Human responsibility is set within the context of divine
creation. Humans are partners in the sustaining of what God has created
in its change and development for good. Helen A. Kenick has portrayed
this understanding of "humanness" in a summary of the first two chapters
of Genesis.

She points out that the biblical author puts persons in the following
web of relationships and responsibilities:

1) The mutual relationship between Creator and creature. The Creator shares life with human beings, and gives them the responsibility
of being the divine representative in the continuing stewardship of
creation.
2) The mutual relation between human beings and the world of
nature. While humans draw sustenance from the natural world, they
are also responsible for preserving it.
3) The mutual relationship between human beings who are co-
creators and co-responsible for the nurturing of life.

In these terms, to be human is not to stand alone, but to be in relation to God, world, and persons. It is also to be a center of responsible power in living out one's stewardship.

The task of caring for God's creation is not for individuals. "Male and female he created them. And God blessed them, and God said to them, 'Be fruitful and multiply, and fill the earth and subdue it' [Genesis 1:27-28]." Caring for the world is a shared task by divine intention, not a static preserving of existing structures. Respectful of these, this stewardship means engaging in the achievement of God's purpose for the world. The Bible has a number of names for this purpose; one is the word which we ordinarily translate by the English word "peace." To the meaning of this concept in its biblical context we now turn, for we believe that it is a comprehensive key to the biblical vision of the human city.

SHALOM AND THE CITY

The thought-world of Israel and the Hebrew language itself render difficult the attempts of a rationalistic, specialized culture like our own to match one word with one fact in external reality. The ancient Hebrew, like many historic traditions, did not separate reality into discrete little packages of facts. The world, to that culture, was like woven cloth; each strand connected with the others, each subject stretched and shaped by the other. It is thus with the Old Testament words for the world being envisioned.

One illustration is the Hebrew word for peace with its kinship to words like righteousness, justice, love, and blessing. Again, rationalistic moderns are likely to be impatient with the apparently clumsy match between description and thing described here. But faithful Bible readers know that there is a different sort of scientific precision at work here. The greatness and goodness of God in human history are much too great and good to be described with precision by our language. Who are we to describe exactly the One who is "above all that we ask or think"? Why should not our words more or less stumble over each other as we seek to describe the indescribable? Indeed, the most weighty, comprehensive words of the Bible need the help of historical event and the interpretations of other words to give them context, specificity, and illuminating power. Among these weighty words is the Hebrew, *Shalom*, a word that occurs so frequently in connection with the good of human society (and the good of human cities in particular), that we are inclined to see in it a strong biblical tag for the concrete purpose of God for this world. It is the word that we shall use in this book to connote the amazing, complex nature of God's will for human society. As Helen Kenik puts it:

> God's will is for *shalom* in society: God intends that life flourish and that all obstacles to life be removed. Hence the primary motivation for judgment can be expressed as *justice*; God's concern is for the poor, the captives, the blind, the stranger—all those who become the objects of abuse.

She adds that:

> Judgment finds its object in the concrete needs within society. Its purpose is to assure that society experience the peace and whole-ness intended with creation.[13]

Our biblical heritage is distorted by casting these imperatives of hu-maneness, life, and justice as rules to be laid upon a dynamic, creative process of society. Rather, they project human community in an image of sharing, mutuality, preservation of life and care for all of God's creatures, especially the least. The justice of God is the power to bestow life on all creatures. In this context, the proclamation of the Kingdom of God in the ministry and person of Jesus the Christ can be seen as continuous with the summoning of the creatures to partnership. It is the power of self-giving love that transforms hostilities into *shalom*, the dead into life, the despairing into hope.

That the mission of the church is to seek the *shalom* of the city is clearly brought out in two texts in the Bible. Of particular significance for understanding the inter-relationship between *shalom* and the city is Jere-miah 29:7: "Seek the welfare (*shalom*) of the city where I have sent you into exile and pray to the Lord on its behalf, for in its welfare (*shalom*) you will find your welfare."

The admonition from the prophet must have been startling for the Israelites who were living in exile. For a people who basically understood God as one who acts in history, the exile was a moment of revelation second in importance only to the Exodus. It told them something new about their Lord. "The suggestion that Yahweh was interested in the welfare of Babylon was contrary to all they had known of him. . . . In contributing to the good of that state the exiles would further his purposes."[14] Their God was not only the God of Israel, but a universal Lord, concerned for the welfare of all.

But as a moment of revelation, it also told them that they are, by divine intention, to be engaged in the work of the *shalom* of the city. They are not to form a community apart, a safe harbor away from the blandishments of a pagan city. Their mission is to infuse the city with the promises of *shalom*.

Jeremiah 29:7, however, does not apply exclusively to Babylon. "City" in this verse must be taken, according to John Bright,[15] to refer to whichever city they find themselves in. Literally, the verse reads: "In its welfare (*shalom*) shall be your welfare (*shalom*)." This suggests that the relationship between the *shalom* of the city and that of its urban inhabitants is intrinsic, not extrinsic. Their welfare depends upon the welfare of the city. To seek the first without seeking the second is unthinkable. In working for the welfare of the city they are working for their own *shalom* and furthering the purposes of God.

The relationship between *shalom* and the city bears the same weight in Luke 19:41-42: "And when he drew near and saw the city he wept over it, saying, 'Would that even today you knew the things that make for peace! But now they are hid from your eyes.' " This verse is generally interpreted as a condemnation of Jerusalem for its rejection of Jesus' messiahship. But Jesus mourns over the Jerusalem of his day because it did not know and accept the things that made for *shalom*, which were concretely embodied in his mission, in love of neighbor, the poor, and the oppressed.

The scriptures abound with references about *shalom* and the city. In Genesis 29, Abimalech visits Isaac in Beersheba, and they share *shalom*. A Levite is offered *shalom* in Gebeah (Judges 19), as is Samuel in Bethlehem (1 Samuel 16). The backdrop for the discussion of the New Jerusalem in the Book of Revelation is *shalom*.[16] In each case, *shalom* is associated with the sharing of a banquet or someone's home. Though it is often translated as "peace," *shalom* does not mean peace of mind or of soul. According to Gerhard von Rad,

> There is no specific text in which it (*shalom*) denotes the specifically spiritual attitude of inward peace. There are, indeed, more passages in which it is used of groups rather than individuals . . . In its most common use, it is an emphatically *social concept*.[17]

Perhaps *shalom* is best translated as social or communal well-being. This also suggests that God creates, sustains, and makes possible better qualities of life through the pursuit of common well-being. In this way, God's creative purposes bear fruit for all.

Shalom always is a corporate virtue, signifying good relations between persons, families, peoples. It conveys abundance and success in human life such as material prosperity, bodily health, happiness, and the use of resources for positive well-being.

It also has strong ecological resonances, referring to well-being between persons and their environment. This is particularly clear in Ezekiel 34:25-29:

> I will make with them a covenant of peace and banish wild beasts from the land, so that they may dwell securely in the wilderness and sleep in the woods. And I will make them and the places round about my hill a blessing; and I will send down the showers in their season; they shall be showers of blessing. And the trees of the field shall yield their fruit, and the earth shall yield its increase, and they shall be secure in their land; and they shall know that I am the Lord, when I break the bars of their yoke, and deliver them from the hand of those who enslaved them. They shall no more be a prey to the nations, nor shall the beasts of the land devour them; they shall dwell securely, and none shall make them afraid. And I will provide for them prosperous plantations so that they shall no more be consumed with hunger in the land, and no longer suffer the reproach of the nations.

It is wrong to think of *shalom* as merely the absence of conflict, the opposite of war. *Shalom* is the harmony and wholeness which flows from the establishment of proper relationships between God, persons, and the world. As such it assumes a just distribution of material goods.

In the New Testament, the content and good of all Christian preaching is *shalom* (Ephesians 6:15), and the legacy Jesus leaves us is *shalom*: "Peace I leave with you; my peace I give to you [John 14:27]." Its decisive aspect is Jesus Christ himself: He is our *shalom* (Ephesians 2:14).

The Jesus referred to in this verse is not the individual man, Jesus of Nazareth, but Jesus as the manifestation and anticipation of the new humanity.[18] The risen Jesus is bringing a new human community into being. By the power of the Spirit, God is gathering together all alien groups into a new unity with Jesus Christ himself:

> And he came and preached peace to you who were far off and peace to those who were near; for through him we both have access in one Spirit to the Father. So then you are no longer strangers and sojourners, but you are fellow citizens with the saints and members of the household of God, built upon the foundation of the apostles and prophets, Christ Jesus himself being the chief cornerstone. (Ephesians 2:17-20)

The dynamism of *shalom* also has eschatological dimensions. Never to be fully realized in the present, its fulfillment lies at the end of history. As God's promise for us, it reveals what our true potential and that of the world is and has always been. It is a divine power enabling us to envision the present and to move the present towards its future realization.

The destiny of the world is an absolute future of peace, *shalom*. Those who actively anticipate it already have a foretaste of its fulfillment. But the path to *shalom* remains subject to the law of the cross. Where human community is fractured, where person is set against person, where the well-being of some is denied for the sake of the well-being of others, *shalom* is not present. Between this time of fractured human relations and the ultimate *shalom* of God's future, Christians follow their Lord along the way of the cross. And many a shared step on this way will be that anticipation of *shalom* which bears the name of justice.

From the writings of Amos to those of Paul, justice is a quality of God akin to graciousness. It is gratuitous saving power, a divine will to favor human beings apart from any merit of their own, to remain faithful to us despite our weakness and infidelity. As eschatological promise, *shalom* is ultimately a sharing of the justice of God in the New Jerusalem of the end-times.

The Bible is unequivocal about the place of justice in the life of Christians. Their mission is to do the works of justice. The biblical writers are concrete and insistent concerning this.

> God has taken his place in the divine council; in the midst of the gods he holds judgment: "How long will you judge unjustly and show partiality to the wicked? Give justice to the weak and the fatherless; maintain the right of the afflicted and the destitute. Rescue the weak and the needy; deliver them from the hand of the wicked." (Psalm 82:1-4)

> Woe to those who decree iniquitous decrees, and the writers who keep writing oppression, to turn aside the needy from justice and to rob the poor of my people of their right, that widows may be their spoil, and that they may make the fatherless their prey! (Isaiah 10:1-2)

> Thus says the Lord: Do justice and righteousness, and deliver from the hand of the oppressor him who has been robbed. And do no wrong or violence to the alien, the fatherless, and the widow, nor shed innocent blood in this place. (Jeremiah 22:3)

The litany of demands for social justice in Luke's gospel are direct, even bald and jarring. At the beginning of his mission, Jesus' forerunner John the Baptist declares: "He who has two coats, let him share with him who has none; and he who has food, let him do likewise [Luke 3:11]." To tax collectors who asked what they must do, John said "Collect no more than is appointed you [Luke 3:13]." Jesus duplicates such themes with hardly a variation. He contrasts the blessing that God pours upon the poor with

the following woes that will befall the rich in their enjoyment of the fruits
of injustice:

> "But woe to you that are rich, for you have received your con-
> solation. Woe to you that are full now, for you shall hunger.
> Woe to you that laugh now, for you shall mourn and weep."
> (Luke 6:24-25)

And, concerning the Pharisees, with their legalistic definitions of justice,
he says:

> "But woe to you Pharisees! for you tithe mint and rue and every
> herb, and neglect justice and the love of God; these you ought
> to have done, without neglecting the others." (Luke 11:42)

Modern thinking, however, tends to distort the biblical teaching on
justice. We read it individualistically or juridically. Fortunately, the excessive individualism of the late-nineteenth and early-twentieth century is
being corrected with our experience of interdependence, the realization
that the earth is a global community ecologically comparable to an or-
ganism. Such a small thing as tracings of air pollution frozen in the arctic
polar cap has reminded us that our lives are inalterably, for good or ill,
bound up with each other. For example, E. R. Achtemeier[19] has pointed
out that justice

> is not behavior in accordance with an ethical, legal, psychological
> norm. It is not conduct which is dictated by either human or
> divine nature, no matter how undefiled. It is not an action ap-
> propriate to the attainment of a specific goal. It is not an impartial
> ministry to one's fellow men. It is not equivalent to giving every
> man his just due. Rather, righteousness [justice] is in the [Old
> Testament] the fulfillment of the demands of a relationship,
> whether . . . with men or with God.

In the Israelitic world, to live is to be part of the covenanted community. It is to be united with others in a context of family, tribe, nation,
or covenant. This being-in-relationship by being-in-community gives the
Israelite a "right" to a share in community. Justice makes for the peace,
harmony, and well-being of the people by establishing the proper relationship among them. It creates the conditions that allow *shalom* to blos-
som. Unjust acts tear apart the community and prevent *shalom* from
occurring.

Two other aspects of justice, besides its communal nature, are peculiar
to the Bible: the bias for the poor and powerless and the link between the
doing of justice and knowing God.

The Bible is concerned with justice for all, but it has a particular concern for the poor and powerless. The source of this bias is the very nature of God himself, who characteristically manifests justice to the poor and the oppressed. This emphasis is present in all biblical traditions. It is most prominent in that classical moment of revelation, the Exodus:

> Then the Lord said, "I have seen the affliction of my people who are in Egypt, and have heard their cry because of their taskmasters; I know their sufferings, and I have come down to deliver them out of the hand of the Egyptians, and to bring them up out of that land to a good and broad land, a land flowing with milk and honey, to the place of the Canaanites, the Hittites, the Amorites, the Perizzites, the Hivites, and the Jebusites." (Exodus 3:7-8)

In the New Testament, Jesus preaches salvation to the outcasts—the poor and the powerless. In fulfilling the law and the prophets, he subordinates the established laws (ecclesiastical and secular) to the overriding rule of love for God and neighbor. Love for the poor neighbor in his teachings is the test of genuine love. By his words, actions, and associations, Jesus makes the forsaken and despised of society unmistakably central elements in the kingdom of God. From the first glimmers of that kingdom in a poor woman named Mary to the victory of her son over his death in his resurrection, God is "putting down the mighty from their thrones" and "exalting those of low degree" (Luke 1:52).

One meaning of the resurrection, from this perspective, is the virtual abolition of distinctions made on the bases of power, wealth, status, and knowledge, and the establishment of a church which should incarnate the opposite values of powerlessness, humility, service, commonality, and equality. As William Coats comments, in the New Testament "the commitment to equality not only implied forsaking rank, status and wealth, and a mandate to share goods and property, but it also implied the establishment of human relationships on an intrinsic basis."[20]

Besides its bias for the poor and powerless, another distinctive biblical perspective on justice is the relationship between doing justice and knowing God. Jeremiah is quite clear about this:

> Do you think you are a king because you compete in cedar? Did not your father eat and drink and do justice and righteousness? Then it was well with him. He judged the cause of the poor and needy; then it was well. Is not this to know me? says the Lord. (Jeremiah 22:15-17)

The source for this understanding of justice is the experience of the justice of God, the Exodus. Yahweh is known and experienced in the doing of justice.

Matthew brings this out in his famous description of the last judgment, which has often been used to motivate Christian social action:

> Then they also will answer, "Lord, when did we see thee hungry or thirsty or a stranger or naked or sick or in prison, and did not minister to thee?" Then he will answer them, "Truly, I say to you, as you did it not to one of the least of these, you did it not to me." And they will go away into eternal punishment, but the righteous into eternal life. (Matthew 25:44-46)

The Son of Man remained hidden from those who did not do justice. This is not to say that God simply withholds justice from us until we do justice to our neighbor. Jesus' parable of the unforgiving servant (Matthew 18:23-35) suggests that God's justice has already been poured out to us in superabundance. Our little acts of justice will never truly equal his, but it is clear that we experience God and reflect his justice when we do justice. Not to do so is to remove ourselves from the sphere of the divine order and to subject ourselves to separation from God, the wrath of God. Even worship is empty without justice, a claim that both Amos and Jesus make in common:

> I hate, I despise your feasts, and I take no delight in your solemn assemblies. Even though you offer me your burnt offerings and cereal offerings, I will not accept them, and the peace offerings of your fatted beasts I will not look upon. Take away from me the noise of your songs; to the melody of your harps I will not listen. But let justice roll down like waters, and righteousness like an everflowing stream. (Amos 5:21-24)

> So if you are offering your gift at the altar, and there remember that your brother has something against you, leave your gift there before the altar and go; first be reconciled to your brother, and then come and offer your gift. (Matthew 5:23-24)

In *A Theological Word Book of the Bible*,[21] Alan Richardson has written under the entry "city":

> The equivocal attitude of the Bible towards the culminating point of human social organization, the city, constitutes a good example of the biblical dialectical point of view. On the one hand, a city may be a lovely and noble place: the earthly Jerusalem is to be God's dwelling place. . . . On the other hand, cities may become the habitation of all that is vile, oppressive and horrible in human life. . . .

The Bible is equivocal in its attitude toward the city. The biblical images contain a realistic assessment of what the city is and what it is supposed to be. Yet the equivocal attitude does not apply to God's ultimate purpose for the city nor to our mandate about the city as the people of God. Throughout the biblical narrative God's love for the city is never in doubt. In judgment, always tempered with a vision of redemption, God's love is present. God holds out for us and demands from us a city of justice and righteousness.

If the Christian community is to be that community of hope which shows forth the end-times in the present, we cannot sit back in judgment or apathy toward the city. The biblical message is clear: God is at work in the city redeeming his creation. If those of us who see ourselves as God's people are to be part of that new creation, then we must join in that process.

NOTES

[1] The Washington Metropolitan area covers an area of 2,812 square miles. It includes the District of Columbia, and the following counties: Montgomery, Prince George's, Arlington, Alexandria, Fairfax, Prince William, Loudon. It has a total of 1,052,100 households and a median income of $19,800. It has a population of 3.2 million people. Of these, 70% are white and 26.8% black. The District of Columbia has an area of 65 square miles, and a population of 635,185: 26.7% are white, 70.6% black.

[2] By 1979, 8% of all rental units had been sold or marketed as condominiums. In 1970, there were 188,558 rental units in the District. In 1977, this had declined to 174,900.

[3] Donald W. Shriver and Karl A. Ostrom, *Is There Hope for the City?* (Philadelphia: Westminster Press, 1977), p. 21.

[4] Ibid., p. 23.

[5] *The Meaning of the City* (Grand Rapids, MI: Eerdmans, 1970), pp 7–8.

[6] Ibid., pp. 22, 24–25, 41, 50, 51, 55, 60–61, 83, 113, 125 and 168.

[7] Ibid., p. 171.

[8] *The Secular City* (New York: Macmillan, 1965) pp. 40, 47.

[9] Pages 56–58.

[10] Page 116.

[11]Page 123.

[12]Bernhard Anderson, "The Babel Story: Paradigm of Human Unity and Diversity," in Andrew M. Greeley and Gregory Baum, *Ethnicity* (New York: Seabury Press, 1977), pp. 66–67.

[13]Helen A. Kenik, "Towards a Biblical Basis for Creation Theology," in *Western Spirituality*, edited by Matthew Fox (Notre Dame: Fides/Claretian Press, 1979), pp. 37–38.

[14]Charles F. Whitley, *The Exilic Age* (Philadelphia: Westminster Press, 1957), p. 53.

[15]John Bright, *Jeremiah* (Garden City, NY: Doubleday, 1965), p. 21.

[16]J. Teran-Duarte, "Peace," in *Sacramentum Mundi*, vol. 4, edited by Karl Rahner (New York: Herder and Herder, 1968), p. 308.

[17]"*Eirene*," in *Theological Wordbook of the New Testament*, vol. 2, edited by G. Kittel and G. Freidrich (Grand Rapids, MI: Eerdmans, 1964), p. 406. Italics added.

[18]John Macquarrie, *The Concept of Peace* (New York: Harper & Row, 1973), pp. 20–21.

[19]"Righteousness in the Old Testament," *Interpreter's Dictionary of the Bible* (New York: Abingdon Press, 1962), vol. IV., p. 80.

[20]Coats, *God in Public: Political Theology Beyond Niebuhr* (Grand Rapids, MI: Eerdmans Publishing Co., 1974), p. 51.

[21]Alan Richardson, *A Theological Word Book of the Bible* (London: SCM Press, 1950), p. 49.

2.

A World of Cities:

Toward What Future?

IF THE past we celebrate pre-enacts the future we hope for, the present we analyze is a similar pre-enactment. In this chapter, we offer a general analysis of human distress and promise in the cities of the contemporary world. Like our reading of the "urban vision" of the Bible, our understanding of the contemporary empirical situation of the world's cities has been profoundly conditioned by our values, our faith, and our hopes for the future of human life on this planet. Our focus on what may be wrong with our cities reflects our definition of what would be right for them.

We take as partners in the task of understanding and acting as responsible citizens of cities, the social scientists, historians, and other observers of the contemporary world whose viewpoints have enriched, complicated, and sobered our own. We acknowledge our need for similar help from all other human beings who compose the great public of cities, nations, and the world.

One purpose of the analysis below is to prepare us to look at the immediate past of urban policy in the United States in the context of urban life throughout the world. As the first chapter above sought to overcome the snobbery of ignoring human wisdom from the ancient past, so here we seek to avoid the snobbery of American localism. Urban crisis and promise in the United States is distinctive but not unique.

We have divided this analysis into two parts: a survey of certain general conditions that affect cities throughout the world, and a survey of some major alternative scenarios that observers propose as possible for the urban future of the world. Here we wish to indicate how far away our cities are from *shalom* and also to demonstrate, using the resources of social science, that social well-being is a realistic possibility.

GLOBAL CITIES

We have heard often that the cities of Europe are different from the cities of America, and therefore belie comparison. This is becoming less true. Similar urban problems are appearing in one country after another, particularly, though not exclusively, in cities of the West. This was underscored in the congressional hearings "Successes Abroad: What Foreign Cities Can Teach American Cities." Much was said about the benefits of public policies friendly to cities, but the point was made over and over again that European cities are a lot closer to our situation than is generally presumed and are displaying tendencies long familiar in the United States. The Director of General Planning for Copenhagen admitted that "most fundamental problems in Copenhagen are of the same nature as the problems in American cities" and went so far as to say that American government reports he had seen on "urban growth management . . . might just as well be read as a description of the situation in Denmark."[1]

One would expect the picture in the developing countries of Latin America, Africa, and Asia to be markedly different, and in at least one aspect they are. The rate of urbanization is occurring three or four times as fast as the rate in industrialized countries. The increase in urban population in these areas is expected to exceed one billion people by the year 2000. Conservative estimates put the population of Mexico City at about 30 million by the end of this century. In each year of the mid-1970s, Sao Paulo grew by over a half-million people while Jakarta and Seoul grew by over a quarter million.[2] Yet the problems these cities face are similar to those of many cities of the industrialized countries: large concentrations of the poor, high levels of unemployment, congestion and pollution, displacement, and inadequate housing.

One needs to take heed not to blur the important cultural, economic, and policy differences among these cities. European public policy has been more supportive of its urban forms and functions than American policies which to date have abetted urban sprawl and the forces of decentralization. Many Asian and European cities have longer histories than American cities and are vital centers of culture and hearthstones of the national spirit. For how long has Paris been identified in the mind of the French with France? When Henri IV became a Catholic in order to become King of France, he explained it this way: "Paris is worth a mass." Where is the Italian peasant who does not often repeat the proverb: "See Naples, and then die." What animating spirit caused the resurrection of Delhi so many times from its ashes? These attitudes harbor the same sense of pride and urban spirit that are contained in the words of the Psalmist: "By the waters of Babylon, there we sat and wept, when we remembered Zion [137:1]."

These aspirations need to be compared to statements which refer to San Francisco as Sodom and Gomorrah and New York as a New Babylon, reflecting an anti-urban bias in America that contradicts the reality of the centrality of cities in American life.

There are differences, but economic, political, social, and technological realities in a shrinking world are creating global urban problems that are breaking through cultural and social variations. The characteristic problems of urban areas are becoming more and more similar. The differences, however, do matter. Solutions will vary. What makes sense on the sidewalks of Chicago may not find a heeding ear on the streets of Warsaw. Culture differentiates. What will be a priority for one group may not be for another.

The policy answers to this international phenomenon of problematic urban growth have not yet been found. Perhaps the reason lies in an unwillingness to take medicine strong enough to cure such a debilitating disease. At any rate, we must be impressed with the strength and endurance of the malady as one characteristic of the world of cities.

What has been variously called the pathology of cities, the taxonomy of inner city problems, or urban crisis conditions constitutes another characteristic of urban reality. In the industrialized world, where the urban population as a percentage of total population reached 74.4 percent in 1975 and is expected to be 83.6 percent by the year 2000, and where the problems of the cities are the problems of the society as a whole, a description of the pathology or crises of cities must begin with the inner or central city precincts for it is here that many of these problems are most evident.

A detailed discussion of these signs of distress need not detain us, for while urban specialists may disagree on underlying causes and appropriate solutions, there is a general consensus about what is happening in the United States and many other large urban centers. We find loss of population, mismatch of jobs and skills, private disinvestment on the one hand coupled with displacement of the poor through reinvestment on the other, environmental deterioration, continued decline in public and private services, facilities, and infrastructure, fiscal crises, racial strife, and increasing concentrations of the poor.

The problem of jobs is particularly acute. In the industrial countries, the situation is less one of an absolute shortage of jobs than a shift in the manufacturing and industrial sectors of the economy away from the large central cities leaving behind unskilled and semi-skilled work forces unable to pursue their employment. An urban profile of Great Britain points out that "for professional and skilled workers, a whole conurbation, or sector of London, may be a viable labour market; but for unskilled workers, the labour area will be more confined to the immediate locality."[3] In West Germany between 1970 and 1975, Hamburg, Stuttgart, Frankfurt, Munich, and West Berlin lost between ten and twenty-three percent of their industrial jobs.[4]. During the same period in the United States the exodus from frostbelt to sunbelt took on significance with eighty-six percent of the country's new jobs being produced in the south and west and a net loss of employment opportunities in the northeast. The population side of the equation shows a similar trend.[5]

It is not the exodus of industries that is causing the unemployment problems of the developing countries, but the stark increase in the population. Economic development cannot keep pace with the rapidly growing numbers of unskilled workers. Urban poverty is principally associated with households in which the primary wage earners receive low pay and have high numbers of persons dependent on them for sustenance.[6]

If the jobs and population picture offers little encouragement, at least in the short run, those activities which fall in the category of disinvestment and reinvestment are more difficult to interpret. Default by the private sector in its failure to invest in the inner city has traditionally and justifiably been cited as a main cause of the shrinking tax base and group need for services. There is an opposite trend, more pronounced in the United States but present in Europe as well:

> There are now some hopeful signs which the outside world—and even many Americans—have yet to appreciate fully. Included are such phenomena as massive center city rebuilding, middle-class reclamation of a significant number of rundown inner-city neighborhoods, rekindled interest of big developers in downtown sites, and the growth of vibrant neighborhood citizen activism.[7]

This trend will be put to the test by the Reagan Administration's urban enterprise zones. It remains to be seen whether this reinvestment which brings with it an increased tax base will offset the more established patterns of recurring fiscal crises as cities seek to deal with the contradictory needs of balanced budgets and increased expenditures to upgrade their deteriorating infrastructures; of reduced payrolls and increased programs for a declining but more dependent population; and higher taxes from the new middle class, and the need for greater amenities to attract and retain this recent influx.

Perhaps more seriously, what has been labelled "collective depriva-tion" or "the gap between the quality and quantity of opportunities provided by the inner city environment and the needs of all those people sharing that environment, irrespective of their personal circumstances" is the prob-lem of such magnitude that it will take more than the current rate and type of reinvestment to resolve it.[8] There is a basic contradiction in the flow of persons and wealth within urban areas. Industry and wealthy tax-payers are moving to the suburbs, costly problems are being paid for at the urban core by municipalities with diminishing revenues.

An even more important question than whether or not reinvestment will play a significant role in the urban crisis is the negative impact it may have. And unfortunately in this case, the jury is in, at least for the time being. Reinvestment, for example, has offered little benefit to the urban poor who lack sufficient training or skills for the new types of employment created by modern technology. If anything, this downtown development has served to increase the mismatch between jobs and skills.

Another negative result of increased interest in the city is that it has exacerbated the housing problem for the poor who are being displaced by middle class reclamation efforts. Even in countries such as West Germany and Great Britain where there is no longer the shortage of housing that exists in the United States, the trend is toward a decrease in decent, affordable rental housing in the inner city. The poor have been twice victimized, by redlining and gentrification, and even seemingly helpful measures such as rent control have resulted in the increased abandonment and deterioration of the housing stock. Thus, new strategies are needed to ameliorate the conditions of urban centers without detriment to the poor and their support communities.

In the developing countries, housing problems are further exacerbated by limited municipal fiscal resources and institutional barriers. The rapid urban population growth puts great stress not only on the housing stock but also on the infrastructure—roads, sewerage disposal, water supply, hospitals, schools, fire and police protection. The urban purse cannot meet the demand for new construction in these necessary areas. As a result, there have been deleterious effects on health care and the environment. The incidences of infant mortality, tuberculosis, malnutrition and anemia have increased in Calcutta, Madras, Kingston, and Sao Paulo. The 1970s witnessed resurgences of malaria, bubonic plague, and meningitis. The urban poor are caught in a vicious circle. Low incomes prevent them from obtaining better education, nutrition, and health care. The ignorance and disease that result reduce their productivity and keep their incomes low.

The problems of the poor are compounded when the racial factor is introduced:

> The fact has to be recognized that where poverty wears a differently colored face or practices a very different culture, city segregation, injustice, and environmental degradation become infinitely more intractable.[9]

Whereas racial issues have traditionally been seen as an American problem, they are now a major factor in many other cities as well. France with its *Bidonvilles*, West Germany and its guestsworkers and Great Britain's new commonwealth immigrants illustrate that racism is a global, not a regional problem.

The fact that these ethnic minorities tend to be crowded into the inner cities only serves to compound the problem and increase the likelihood that what in West Germany has been called a "social time bomb" will explode. Despite certain historical events, such as a virtual halt of the black migration from the rural south to the urban north in the United States and controls put on the influx of guestworkers into Common Market countries and New Commonwealth immigrants into Great Britain, the demographic picture does not offer an easy way out of the dilemma. In the United States, for example, the Hispanic population will become the largest minority group during the 1980s. In the Federal Republic of Germany, the guestworker has become a structural constant in the population with the birth of the sons and daughters of the original migrants. And in Great Britain there have been forecasts of high unemployment among New Commonwealth residents lasting for two or three generations amidst a growing sense that race is becoming a major source of division in a country that was once held up as an example of urbane tolerance and harmony in racial matters.

Whatever one may think of the causes of the above brief and necessarily incomplete description of the pathology of cities, the taxonomy of urban problems, or the severity of the issues, there must be universal agreement that nobody planned it that way. What we are dealing with is the unintended city or patterns of uncontrolled urbanization left to haphazard chance and random change.

The future of urban reality centers in those issues related to governmental institutions responsible for management, administration, and planning. These institutions have not been up to the task of building and presiding over intentional cities.

> Our first impression must surely be the degree to which the industrial city appears to have been not so much planned for human purposes as simply beaten into some sort of shape by repeated strokes from gigantic hammers—the hammers of technology and applied power, the overwhelming drive of national self-interest, the single-minded pursuit of economic gain.[10]

Given the current world economic situation with questions of energy supply, inflation, and limits to growth, cities can hardly expect to meet their problems with great new influxes of public or private money.

Race relations excepted, the most serious challenge of inner cities in the next years may be the better management of the resources available to them. This agenda requires the creation of "some municipal order, some principles of cooperation, some sense of direction, justice, and environmental control out of what is all too often one big muddle of overlapping, competing and even hostile authorities."[11] Even in the developing countries, the constraints lie not in the limits on the demand side, but in inadequate response on the supply side.[12]

The United States presents a particularly disturbing picture with more than 22,000 independent local governments in its 288 standard metropolitan statistical areas (SMSAs).[13] By contrast, European metropolitan areas are models of an orderly governmental process in which local government associations play a role in the national policy-making process. In the United States, for example, the National League of Cities and the U.S. Conference of Mayors are important but still unofficial participants in the urban policy process. In West Germany and Great Britain, on the other hand, consultation with analogous organizations is formally integrated into the national governmental machinery.

Despite this difference of approach on the two sides of the Atlantic, similar problems exist in managing change and development in large metropolitan areas. What Barbara Ward calls a free-for-all in urban land lies behind many of the problems. "In mixed economies, distortions of price in the private urban land market have continued to determine much of the cities' location and use."[14] Even in Europe where planning is much more of an accepted fact of life than it is in the United States, the price of land in the city is a crucial factor in the location of business and industry, the construction of housing, the diminishing presence of parks, and the like. The exodus to the suburbs underscores the higher price for land in the city. It also underscores the inability of many large cities to annex suburban jurisdictions. For some cities, like Singapore, the only way of adding to the urban land area is through land reclamation. In others, it is extremely difficult to assemble large enough tracts of land for the purposes of urban development because of zones, regulations, land transfer taxes and other institutional barriers.[15] This prevents them from gaining control over the surrounding land and over those who make their living off the urban core.

To single out problems of land use is, of course, not to limit questions of management and planning to the physical dimension, but only to emphasize that land remains a fundamental component in human settlements. Indeed, planners are gradually recognizing that there has been insufficient interaction of economic, social, cultural, and physical development. Too much stress has been put on a physical approach. Such a narrow base for revitalization is indicative of poor planning and management.

The subject of planning and planners as it relates to overall issues of management administration has another dimension to it as well: the lack of democratic processes in the attempts by urban professionals at social reconstruction. Their hegemony has been broken by the rise of citizen participation and neighborhood activities in the United States and Western Europe.

It is difficult to find anyone against citizen involvement in principle. It is a basic assumption of democratic polity. However, in its "Declaration of Principles," the 1976 United Nations Habitat Conference in Vancouver went beyond mere encouragement of participation by all people in the planning, building and management of their human settlements. Recognizing what the Bible has long taught, it stated that "all persons have the right and the duty to participate, individually and collectively in the elaboration and implementation of policies and programmes of their human settlements."[16]

The issue is not simply the principle of citizen participation, nor is it that of planning as a constructive approach to urbanization. Rather, the tension between citizen groups on the one hand and the governmental bureaucratic structure on the other revolves around "ways in which citizen interests and public performance can be balanced in more effective planning, in the search for justice and in a better environment."[17]

The United States has retreated from the days of the 1960s when the Office of Economic Opportunity (OEO) and even the Model Cities Program were instrumental in creating an adversary relationship between City Hall and neighborhood citizen groups. With the dismantling of OEO and the incorporation of Model Cities into the Community Development Block Grant program, the amount of direct funding to neighborhood groups has become insignificant in terms of total federal money flowing into urban areas. Nevertheless, citizen participation still remains a strong and viable force.

Although citizen participation may not be as widespread in Europe nor operate at the same overall level of intensity as it does in the United States, the differences appear to be narrowing rather than growing wider. For example, West Germany and Great Britain have had legislation since 1971 mandating citizen involvement in key aspects of urban planning and development. Germany has seen the nationwide growth of the Federal Union of Citizen Action Groups in a pattern of development similar to that in the United States where single-purpose groups take on multiple causes and separate organizations join together or form coalitions to work for common goals. Although the prevailing attitude in the German bureaucracy is still that citizens are unqualified to play a substantial role in the planning process, the very fact that consultation is now regarded as a necessary evil indicates the extent to which citizen participation has become a fact of life and an ongoing source of tension in the developed urban world.

The need for citizens' participation in the development of their own social order is most intense "in developing countries where, if people are not allowed and encouraged to help themselves and each other—and indeed respected for doing so—the tasks of the next twenty-five years will, quite simply, surpass the capacity of any organized political system."[18]

Citizen participation has its ambiguities as well as the tenuous foothold it has gained in the fast-changing urban political process. As stated earlier, the issue is not the principle but the practice of citizen participation. While citizen participation underscores the right of people to a share in the planning of their future, it is laced with the hazards of short-term thinking in the midst of cities that are deteriorating for want of long-term planning. These hazards are only accentuated by the increasing complexity of urban planning due to the technocratizing of knowledge. The information explosion raises the prospect of the destruction of democracy through sophistication of the knowledge required for decision-making.

These ambiguities are not to be taken lightly. They go to the heart of what is perhaps most crucial to the future of cities: a sense of community in urban societies. There is also a limit to which human beings, whether or not they are materially well-off, can be subjected to feelings of dependency, powerlessness, and fragmentation in their personal and civic lives without society as a whole becoming imperiled. That such feelings run deep in totalitarian societies is taken as a given from the perspective of the free world. That this same malaise exists in the urban centers of the United States and Western Europe is generally conceded by sociologists, but is all too often given short shrift by policy analysts intent on technical solutions to urban problems.

Questions of the quality of life move us from objective to subjective conditions of urban life, and from the central core to the metropolis. This is not to say that concerns about a sense of community and the quality of spiritual life are not felt by those who inhabit the ghettos of the world's cities. If anything, these concerns are compounded by the lack of material well-being. Rather, it is to observe that in the midst of wealth and increased consumption there is a general malaise, an almost universal feeling of alienation and powerlessness toward the huge size and complexities of the society we live in. If in the inner city there has developed a feeling of a lack of personal control, many of the remote employers and local authorities also feel themselves increasingly dominated by scientific, technological and economic interests. In effect, we may be witnessing a movement toward an urban-industrial world in which the citizenry is developing a sense of learned dependency on a world over which they feel little or no control.

To refer to the concept of community is to run the risk of becoming obscure. But if we adopt the premise that "a group of people make up a community insofar as they join together in valuing something," then there is strong evidence to suggest that "by contrast with earlier forms of human settlement the modern city lacks community."[19] An idea which can further pull us back from the edge of obscurity, is that of the interactive system. For as Haworth points out:

> The great mistake we make in thinking about community is that we subjectivize it. . . . The city has a definite structure. It is compounded of relatively fixed institutional elements that appear to be largely responsible for setting the direction and quality of the life led by the inhabitants. Community is something which, if it happens at all, happens in this institutional structure.[20]

As was the case with the principle of participation, one could find little disagreement among observers of the modern urban scene that there is a profound and deepening skepticism about the efficacy of almost every level and kind of institution in society. Reactions to this development, understandings of the causes, and prescriptions for the societal patient may vary according to political and even religious persuasion, but that institutions, and the quality of life and sense of community they represent, are in trouble is not in serious dispute. Citizen participation may be a permanent fixture on the urban scene, but so, too, may be its ineffectiveness if we continue to witness the weakening of those institutions and communal systems that create a sense of urban togetherness.

Americans have peculiar attitudes towards cities. They are more apt to approve government backing of a failing corporation like Chrysler than a city like Cleveland. Just a few years ago, during New York's fiscal crisis, and before the federal government's arm was twisted by reasons of political self-interest, the New York *Daily News* printed this headline: (President) "Ford to New York: Drop Dead." The headline reflects America's anachronistic anti-urban bias. It also reflects the failure to perceive that in the modern world, urban problems are national problems.

There is a direct cause/effect relationship between public policy and urban problems. The familiar list of inner-city problems symbolizes serious shortcomings in their national societies. National policies have encouraged suburbanization and the decentralization of economic activity. They have favored development in certain regions to the detriment of others. They have withheld control from land prices, putting the cost of land out of the reach of cities needing it for public purposes. The inability of national governments to deal with inflation has had disastrous consequences for urban areas through the rise in interest rates and the escalating costs of municipal services.

The United States has failed to take account at the national policy level of the tremendous drain of resources from the frostbelt to the sunbelt, but regional imbalances have exhibited a certain intractability in Western Europe as well. Great Britain has had a policy in place since the 1940s attempting to reduce disparities by channeling investment to "assisted regions" in the older industrial sections of Scotland, Wales, and northern England, yet "these policies for controlling the location of new investment may have harmed the inner areas of cities such as London and Birmingham, outside the assisted regions."[21]

In highly-centralized France, the problem is to move the attention of investors away from Paris toward the west and southwest, while in Italy the obvious partiality towards the development of the north to the corrosive neglect of the south has been cited again and again in its technical and artistic literature.

There is yet one more area of concern as we examine this national characteristic of urban problems: the rural migration to cities. The United States, with its lack of a coherent national welfare policy, has in effect encouraged an influx of the rural poor to places like New York City. Yet, in Western Europe, where the welfare state is much more firmly en-trenched, the story is not much different. In the developing countries, migration is second to natural population growth as the major source of population increase in the cities.

But an urban analysis cannot stop at the traditional boundaries of the nation-state. While the primary decisions about our cities rest squarely on the shoulders of local and national governments, those same cities are part of the larger web of international forces which determine global existence. This contributes to the problem cities and nations have in gaining control over their problems. One observer of the urban scene says:

> Neither the urban explosion, central area decay and suburban sprawl, congestion, pollution, nor any of the urban social prob-lems . . . can find its causes or its cures in the city. Their origins are not local, or any longer territorially defined. These are societal problems, observable on a national and international scale, that are localized in cities. They are not peculiar to cities or susceptible to correction by cities or city dwellers acting on their own.[22]

The multinational corporations have moved urban problems into an international context, forcing cities to think in global terms when they contemplate issues of employment and investment. Capital is organizing itself on an international level, under the control of highly centralized corporate structures with global networks. Urban centers are often, quite literally, at the mercy not only of multinational corporations but seemingly even more impersonal forces such as anonymous private foreign investors, world-wide inflationary pressures, money market fluctuations, and the like.

Although the Habitat conference declared that "every state has the sovereign right to rule and exercise effective control over foreign invest-ment . . . within its national jurisdiction, which affect directly or indi-rectly the human settlements programmes,"[23] this is more wish than reality anywhere on the globe.

Another new and perplexing problem is environmental deterioration. Here, too, the problems of cities merge into the problems of global society. Issues of limits to growth, environmental quality, and the pluses and minuses of various forms of energy are not confined to urban centers, but the city is peculiarly victimized by the failure of all levels of government to come to grips with our fundamental dependence upon the earth.

WHICH WAY URBAN HUMANITY?

American cities need a vision that contains just economic and social structures, the biblical vision of *shalom*. Considering the centrality of cities to human life as we know it, little thought has been given to envisioning the future of our cities. Each of the disciplinary areas essential to an adequate consideration of urban futures reveals a serious void. Urban studies tends to be crisis-oriented, technocratic and bureaucratic, hardly possessed of vision. Future studies barely focus on the city as a whole. Theology and social ethics have often neglected the theological and ethical foundations of community and the positive hopes of urban dwelling.

The importance of a guiding vision of the future cannot be underestimated. We can shape our future, or we can stumble into it.

For Christians, the issue resolves into two possibilities: plan or perish. Planning in this case means developing a hard vision of the future, the essence of which is justice for the poor. The vision of a just future takes planning because the history of economic activity has demonstrated that an uncorrected market does not help the poor. Barbara Ward has said about the bias of the free market:

> It is a mechanism for satisfying the demands of those who command resources and can enter the market as purchasers. Those who lack the income stay out. It is also a system of power in which decisions about the distribution of wealth are made by those with enough clout to command a bargain. [24]

In either case the poor, those without income or power, are marginalized and forced to be dependent on those with wealth and control. Public policy and centers of power influence the distribution of justice and peace. Doing the work of justice is the essential mission of the Christian. God is known in the doing of justice. [25]

Willis Harman offers this summary of the major assumptions of our social system:

- The development and application of the scientific method;
- The wedding of science to technological advance;
- Industrialization through the organization and division of labor;
- The replacement of human labor by machines;
- Acquisitive materialism as a dominant value; the work ethic; an economic image of man;
- Belief in unlimited material progress and in technological and economic growth;
- Manipulative rationality as a dominant theme; a search for control over nature; a positivistic theory of knowledge;
- Pragmatic values held by the individual; individual determination of what is good; individual responsibility for his own destiny;
- Freedom and equality as fundamental rights;

- Society viewed as an aggregate of individuals pursuing their own interests.

Industrial societies, both capitalist and socialist, have been extraordinarily successful at achieving materialist goals. Material standards of living are higher than ever before. Better nutrition, universal education, longer lives, efficient production systems, and widespread affluence are hallmarks of the industrial state. But there are certain problems of modern industrial society—many of which have been listed earlier.

A world forecast was prepared in 1975 by the Center for the Study of Social Policy at Stanford Research Institute. Each of its scenarios considers the interaction of such variables as climate, food and energy supply, the life style of the individual, the economy, the state of science and industry, ecological values and social systems.[26]

Scenario 1—Bingo! There would be abundant energy, widespread prosperity, highly responsible business leadership, worldwide environmental cooperation, and a scientific community able to contend with most of the earth's technical problems. Even nature would act kindly, providing favorable climate and plenty of food. This material success would have the effect of reinforcing existing social values in the West and bringing about their further acceptance elsewhere.

In this case the process of urbanization would continue unabated. Rural populations would decline even further in the West and throughout the world. Vast investments in housing, sewage systems, and other public utilities and the expansion of health, fire and police, and social welfare systems would resolve the physical problems of the urban environment. Characteristic of the urbanization process could be the development of numerous satellite cities which could repeat on a lesser scale the apartment-style of living that would replace the single-home suburb.

Scenario 2—Renaissance: A long recession could lead to a subsequent curbing of economic growth. Development of a new energy technology in the nick of time could then lead to rapid growth. A chastened America, now cognizant that it lives on a finite earth not able to stand rapid growth and waste, could create a nonwasteful, nonpolluting country with a purposeful goal of slow growth.

In this case, urbanization would continue, but better-planned satellite cities of manageable size would replace the sprawling conurbations of previous years. The apartment house more and more would replace the detached single family house as the usual dwelling, but parks, municipal gardens, community workshops, would become adequate substitutes for home workshops and gardens.

In a "bust" economy, in which doomsday forecasts of ecological disaster became a reality, these are the possible scenarios:

Scenario 3—Modest Expectations: A decline in energy supply, worsening climate and food shortages combine to create a major depression. Accommodations could be made and our social and economic institutions could be characterized by an adaptation to temperate, resource-conserving behavior. A major factor in making all of this work would be the growth of a sizable minority of frugal people intensely concerned for conservation, backyard gardening, and other technologies of scarcity. Expectations would no longer be so high.

The depression would have this meaning for the cities: Power outages and shortages of raw materials, squatting in abandoned buildings, begging, pilfering, and ultimately accepting the barest conditions of survival as enough. There might be modest productive activities, community services, repair and maintenance programs, to supplement or replace what the traditional government or economic institutions could no longer deliver with regularity.

Scenario 4—Brave New World: Despite energy shortages, bad climate, and an eroding living standard, the established order of big business, big agriculture, and big government could retain its power and control, creating a system that is more authoritarian and highly regulated.

Here the situation desperately approaches Huxley's pernicious utopia in Brave New World. Cities remain big and get bigger, depending on increasingly complex science and technology. A welfare state encourages a permissive, consumerist ethic. This, along with a decrease in private homes and automobile ownership, increases homogeneity in life style throughout the developed societies of the world. Everything is controlled by a scientific oligarchy and modernization moves ahead apace, with little participation by its citizens.

Scenario 5—The Return of Frugality. Generally, things go from bad to worse. Seemingly unending bad climate and recession lead to a withering of the Western industrial states and the grudging acceptance of a starkly frugal life style. The dominant worldwide mood is pessimism. There is a rapid turn to decentralization, to developing alternative economies based on "small is beautiful," and policies of caring for our own. People will live in islands of relative prosperity in favored regions, or in an Appalachia-like poverty culture.

Beyond these "boom" or "bust" economies, transformation—the creation of new social orders based on new societal assumptions—is possible. A possible scenario follows:

Scenario 6—American society comes very close to collapsing but survives, creating a new social order in which the frugal become the major force in the society. High growth and ever-rising affluence had expended resources rapidly, but two major events shatter the dream: we run out of energy and the climate deteriorates markedly. However, with the large scale adoption of frugal values and practices and a few good food years, the general outlook gets hopeful.

To meet the crisis, Western governments of national unity are formed to impose systems of controls on energy use and other forms of consumption and to organize massive programs for the development of new energy technologies. Awareness of the size of the problem induces them increasingly to pool their resources and internationalize their programs.

What would this mean for cities? In effect, a parallel system of self-governing, self-regulating communities concerned with both economic survival and personal growth would expand alongside the faltering but still functioning structure of corporate manufacturing and service. Gradually a post-industrial, low growth, diversified, and decentralized world system would take shape. The old system is defunct. The post-industrial system committed to low-technology, small-is-beautiful, humane and self-fulfilling goals and a spaceship Earth philosophy would emerge.

The key factor in this future is the rapid shift in the values of the average American, who quickly realizes that he or she must temper the urge to be affluent with the realities of limited resources. The average American becomes a frugal person who fully understands the need for such national policies as zero energy growth for the foreseeable future.

Some key characteristics of this new society: (a) resilience—people realize that there would not be a return to the wide-open economic growth of the heyday of industrialization; (b) subordination of perceived national interests to world interests; (c) de-emphasis of mastery over nature and private property rights; (d) the growth of individual or communal self-reliant enterprise; (e) the renewed importance of the relatively self-sufficient small town and city; (f) experimentation with a variety of basic social forms, with the extended biological family tending to predominate.

These scenarios are woefully inadequate to the constructive task. They serve less as guides than as threats. They are threats to the pessimistic who take the "bust" scenarios as fate. They are threats to the optimists who sense that the perpetual boom economy can never really occur on a limited planet.

There is a position for the realist with hope, who senses the possibility of a transformed future on the basis of almost Franciscan sensitivity to our human and natural resources. These might be called the meliorists. They have a radical vision with adaptive incremental strategies. Willis Harman has proposed the main components of their platform:

Construct a guiding vision of a workable future society, built around a new social paradigm; foster a period of experimentation and tolerance for diverse alternatives both in life-styles and social institutions; encourage a politics of morality in government and a heightened sense of public responsibility in the private sector; promote systematic exploration of and foster education regarding the inner life; accept the necessity of social planning for the transition period while safeguarding against longer-term losses of freedom.

As particular illustrations of his adaptive strategies Harman strongly affirms the importance of: *Anticipatory Democracy*, i.e., widespread citizen participation in designing the future; *Appropriate Scale*—institutional mechanisms for achieving the necessary regulation of political, social, and economic affairs at the lowest practicable level, which may be the local community for human-welfare issues and the planetary level for oceanic pollution; *Appropriate Technology*, that is, small, decentralized, resource-conserving, environmentally benign, person-enhancing and under the control of the user; *Networking*; *New Synergistic System Incentives*—so that behavior which will presumably benefit society in the long run is fostered instead of frustrated.

This chapter has sketched a larger perspective within which to view the American city. A global and futuristic view of the city has demonstrated that there are problems, but there is also promise. Cities can become what they perhaps once were, but surely can be: extended neighborhoods in which humans can find themselves at home. They can be concentrations of economic and social activity at the service of those who dwell within, rather than lifeless Goliaths which threaten the existence of those who have built them.

The content of our vision of the cities should be inspired by the biblical vision of *shalom*. It would mean, among other things, a fair distribution of resources, an end to concentrations of wealth, the affirmation of the value of the individual person, the recognition of fundamental human rights, the acceptance of cultural diversity, a rehabilitated environment, the beating of weapons into plowshares, the participation of all persons in the planning of their own future, improved quality of life, social well-being.

The task of developing and joining the vision of such a good and just city with the reality of the present urban situation is a difficult one, but it is not impossible. The following chapters offer suggestions for applying the vision of *shalom* to American urban policy.

NOTES

[1]U.S. Congress, House Committee on Banking, Finance and Urban Affairs, *Successes Abroad: What Foreign Cities Can Teach American Cities, Hearings before the Subcommittee on the City.* 95th Congress, 1st session, 1977, p. 258.

[2]See *World Development Report, 1974.* Washington, D.C.: World Bank, 1979, p. 73.

[3]H.W.E. Davies, *An Urban Policy Profile of Great Britain* (Columbus, Ohio: The Academy for Contemporary Problems, n.d.), p. 15.

[4]See Sigmund Grede, Werner Heinz, and Peter Rothammer, *Urban Policy Profile for the Federal Republic of Germany,* trans. Carolyn Herde (Washington, D.C.: The Academy for Contemporary Problems, 1979), p. 55.

[5]President's Urban Regional Policy Group, *A New Partnership to Conserve American Cities,* March 1978, pp. 1–15.

[6]Johannes F. Linn, *Policies for Efficient and Equitable Growth of Cities in Developing Countries* (Washington, D.C.: World Bank, 1979), p. 60.

[7]Neal R. Peirce and Jerry Hagstrom, *Traditional Cities Exchange: Three Nations Seek to "Save" Their Inner Cities* (Washington, D.C.: The Academy for Contemporary Problems, October 1978), pp. 2–3.

[8]Davies, *Urban Policy Profile of Great Britain,* p. 7.

[9]Barbara Ward, *The Home of Man* (New York: W.W. Norton and Co., 1976), p. 51.

[10]Ibid., p. 29.

[11]Ibid., p. 234.

[12]Linn, *Policies for . . . Growth of Cities,* pp. 220–231.

[13]By government definition, an SMSA is a county or group of counties socially

and economically integrated with a central city of 50,000 persons. It is usually named for its central city.

[14]Ward, *Home of Man*, p. 179.

[15]Linn, *Policies for . . . Growth of Cities*, pp. 220–21.

[16]United Nations, *Report of Habitat: United Nations Conference on Human Settlements*, Vancouver, May 31–June 11, 1976 (A/CONF. 70/15), pp. 4–5.

[17]Ward, *Home of Man*, p. 246.

[18]Ibid.

[19]Lawrence Haworth, *The Good City* (Bloomington: Indiana University Press, 1963), p. 148.

[20]Ibid., p. 25.

[21]Davies, *Urban Policy Profile of Great Britain*, p. 20.

[22]Thomas J. Blair, *The International Urban Crisis* (New York: Hill and Wang, 1974), p. 165.

[23]United Nations, *Report of Habitat.* p. 6.

[24]Ward, *Home of Man*, pp. 263–64.

[25]Material in this section is based on: Willis W. Harman, *An Incomplete Guide to the Future. The Portable Stanford* (San Francisco: San Francisco Book Company, 1976), 161pp.; Willis W. Harman, "The Coming Transformation," *The Futurist*, Part I, February 1977, pp. 4–12; Part II, April 1977, pp. 106–12; Thomas E. Jones, Class Notes and Chapter on "Thought of Willis Harman," in Jones' *Options for the Future*, manuscript and course at School for Social Research, 1978.

[26]Stanford Research Institute, Center for the Study of Social Policy. *Alternative Futures for Environmental Policy Planning: 1975–2000*. Washington, D.C. 20460: Environmental Protection Agency, Office of Pesticides Program, 1975. The scenarios represent modifications of some of their projections.

3.

The Carter Urban Policy

LEWIS MUMFORD begins his magisterial study of *The City in History* with these questions: What is the city? What processes does it further? What functions does it perform? What purposes does it fulfill? He concludes that the city's mission is

> to put the highest concerns of man at the center of all his activities: to unite the scattered fragments of the human personality, turning artificially dismembered men . . . into complete human beings, repairing the damage that has been done by vocational separation, by social segregation, by the over-cultivation of a favored function, by tribalisms and nationalisms, by the absence of organic partnerships and ideal purposes.[1]

Mumford's is a good vision of the city. It is reflected in tensions within American urban policy.

In this chapter and the next we will examine the urban policies of Jimmy Carter and Ronald Reagan. Their policies will be scrutinized principally for the assumptions that inform them. Those assumptions are the structural elements of their vision of the city, giving shape to their policy. At bottom, they seem to say that the business of cities is business. This is, we believe, a truncated vision, not sufficient to "unite the scattered fragments of the human personality," one that belies the social, historical, cultural, intellectual, and religious functions of cities. It falls short of the larger vision elaborated in the biblical concept of *shalom*.

THE BELATED URBAN CONCERN OF GOVERNMENT:
1892–1980

The role of government in American urban affairs has been remarkably similar to the role of the churches, except the churches were on the scene first. It was not until the 1920s that the federal government took any effective action towards dealing with urban problems. Federal intervention increased rapidly over the middle decades of the century, often with good effect, sometimes at cross purposes.

One striking pattern of federal views on urban problems was the fanning out of its perspectives. In 1892, Congress passed a resolution authorizing an investigation of the slums of cities containing 200,000 inhabitants or more. The report, which includes no conclusions or recommendations, was a statistical representation of the characteristics of the slums and their residents.

During the 1920s, the Division of Building and Housing in the National Bureau of Standards published a series of model building codes, zoning ordinances, and city planning enabling acts. These were adopted by many states and local communities. Even in 1980, housing in inner city neighborhoods can be clearly divided between "old code" and "new code" building by the location of their windows and plumbing.

Federal urban activity began to pick up in the 1930s. In 1933, a federal government program was established for slum clearance and the rehabilitation and construction of housing under the direction of the Housing Division of the Public Works Administration. The target of action here was expanded from the slum to the "blighted area"—obsolete industrial, commercial, and residential facilities.

This program was succeeded by the Housing Act of 1937 which established the low-rent public housing program in which every community eradicating a slum dwelling had to provide one that was decent, safe and sanitary. This program recognized that slums and blighted areas involved forces at work in the metropolitan area as a whole.

This basically sound piece of public policy was weakened over the years. In 1949, it was watered down to allow a five-year delay between construction and clearance. This new provision meant that substandard units could remain in use. Public housing was no longer a tool for eliminating unsafe or unsanitary conditions. The provisions of 1949 attacked the very notion of slum clearance at which the original 1933 legislation was directed.

The Housing Act of 1949, however, was a milestone of federal urban redevelopment action. It authorized private investment to rebuild blighted areas and the production of 810,000 low-rent public housing units to be built over a six-year period. Also beginning with this act was an emphasis on the development of community-wide and city-wide plans for redevelopment.

The Housing Act of 1949 was revised in 1954 to include the recommendations of President Dwight Eisenhower's Advisory Committee on Housing Policies and Programs. A key recommendation of the committee was to assist communities in rehabilitation and conservation, clearance and redevelopment. The Housing Act of 1954 substituted "urban renewal" for "urban redevelopment" and made rehabilitation projects eligible for federal support for the first time.

The General Neighborhood Renewal Plan (GNRP) was enacted in 1956, to coordinate physical planning of urban renewal areas and areas adjacent to them. In 1959, the Community Renewal Plan (CRP) required a city to set out citywide needs in order to facilitate coordination and assist in determining priorities.

The Housing Act of 1960 was another milestone. It provided for 2 billion dollars in new capital grant funds for urban renewal, and an additional 55 million dollars for urban planning. It contained a number of other liberating features, including the creation of job opportunities, the provision of urban mass transportation, the revitalizing of the economic and tax base of the city. In short, the legislation over the years moved from one narrowly conceived in terms of slum clearance to one that recognized the healthy city as a system in which housing was a vital factor along with these others.

In 1966, President Lyndon Johnson called for the enactment of a "Demonstration Cities Program" which eventually was called "Model Cities." The original act provided for a three-year, 1.2 billion dollar demonstration-cities plan to pull together the vast array of existing federal grant programs and supply additional money for the provision of the social services required to supplement physical development. Model City funds were used to plan and carry out a large variety of activities in these areas: housing, health, education, job development, commercial development, crime prevention, recreation, citizen participation, transportation, and program administration.

However, when captains of city political establishments felt increasingly annoyed by pressures from citizen activists and when the Nixon administration made clear its own antipathy to the Model Cities concept the program was consolidated with Urban Renewal, Neighborhood Development Grants, and several other programs.

Though it is in current operation, the General Revenue Sharing Program, originated in 1972, was soundly battered after the elections of 1980. Funding was initially withdrawn, then slowly restored to its current level, well below what the cities have come to depend on. Revenue sharing provides general-purpose funds to state and local governments, as well as anti-recession aid. The anti-recession (also called countercyclical) funds become available when the national unemployment rate is six percent or higher. Other elements—the Gross National Product—are factored into this allocation formula.

In housing, government aid and intervention is currently in the form of financing assistance, rather than direct aid. The Federal National Mortgage Association (FNMA) and the Government National Mortgage Association (GNMA) put up guarantees for mortgages. Sections 235 and 236 of the Housing Act provide interest-rate subsidies for moderate and low-income housing. Section 8 of the Housing Act pays a rental supplement for low and moderate income families directly to the landlord. These last three programs are being severely curtailed by the Reagan Administration.

THE CARTER NATIONAL URBAN POLICY: A CASE STUDY

In redeeming a campaign pledge to the nation's mayors, President Jimmy Carter announced, on March 27, 1978, a national urban policy, "A New Partnership to Conserve America's Communities." In brief, the policy rested on these principles: (1) A national urban policy must reflect the diversity of American cities and their problems. (2) The federal government must lead and play a central role in urban policy: urban problems are national problems; the health of cities is necessary to the health of the body politic; the nature of interdependencies in the federal system has become increasingly apparent. (3) A national urban policy must reflect a set of federal commitments and priorities in income and service strategies, while requiring state and local government participation in every phase. (4) A policy should reflect the need to strengthen sub-state and metropolitan institutions, while emphasizing the important roles of neighborhood and voluntary associations in city-building. (5) Public sector–private sector partnership is necessary.

From these principles, ten major policy elements emerged. The first four were directed at institutions to strengthen their capacity to deal with problems:

1. Improvement in coordination and effectiveness of existing federal urban programs.
2. Federal encouragement of states to develop their own urban strategies.
3. Federal sponsorship of improved city planning, and local management capacity-building.

4. Federal support of revitalization efforts of neighborhood organizations and voluntary associations.

The next two elements were "people-oriented":

5. Continuance of federal efforts to eliminate discrimination and
   racism in urban life.
6. Federal help for business and job opportunity expansion for the
   urban poor and minorities.

The final four were primarily "place-oriented":

7. Offer of strong federal incentives for businesses and industries
   to locate, remain, or expand in economically-troubled central
   cities.
8. Federal aid to distressed cities with critical short-term fiscal problems.
9. Federal improvement and expansion of the range of social and
   housing services to households in central cities.
10. Federal help for cities to develop efficient land settlement pat-
    terns, discourage sprawl, encourage energy-efficient and envi-
    ronmentally-sound land use in urban areas.

Originally, these objectives were to be achieved through thirty-eight
new urban programs and over one hundred recommended changes (mostly
administrative) in existing federal programs. A total of 8.3 billion dollars
in the 1979 budget authority, and 11.3 billion dollars for fiscal year (FY)
1980 was recommended. Actual congressional performance in authori-
zation and appropriation did not approach the FY 1979 recommendation;
FY 1980 budget was substantially altered, and achieved little.

The history of this urban policy-making process is politically instructive. The President established an Urban and Regional Policy Group in
April, 1977. The URPG promptly divided into a number of inter-agency
task forces to carry out its work. It labored in several significant contexts.
The White House Conference on Balanced Growth and Economic Development in February 1978 provided some parallel analytical work, as
did the HUD staff working on the first Presidential National Urban Policy
Report. URPG also carried out its work against the background of active
Executive Reorganization Task Forces located in the Office of Management and Budget (OMB). Participants in URPG were quite aware of the
potential programmatic and organizational implications of this background. The process was remarkably open, with a set of public hearings
across the nation, and extensive consultation with a large variety of interest

groups and associations. A political challenge from Vernon Jordan of the National Urban League in August, 1977 gave added impetus to the job. The major substantive issues debated during the URPG process were:

1. Was the policy to emphasize the problems of people or the problems of places? A "peoples" approach would look for solutions in terms of income strategies and subsidies for the poor. Community and economic development, and central city revitalization would result from a "place" emphasis.
2. Should the policy seek to define urban problems narrowly or broadly? A "distressed cities" policy or one directed to all urban areas? Central cities only or metropolitan areas? Targeted programs or formula programs for all cities?
3. Should problems be addressed by government alone, or should they involve the private sector?
4. Are urban problems the burden of the federal government, or is it intergovernmental, involving the states and other local jurisdictions?
5. Should responses be long-term or short-term? Should they only ameliorate or address basic causes?
6. Which agencies should be involved and how should they operate—comprehensively or programmatically?

As the policy resolved these issues, it tended to resolve them on the broader, longer range, more inclusive side. Hence, "partnership" between governments, corporations, and voluntary agencies.

A large number of legislative and administrative programmatic activities flowed from the policy elements in the first year. Many actions in the executive branch were taken to improve federal coordination and effectiveness of urban aid, all the way from simplifying a number of planning and grant requirements for localities to the signing (August, 1978) and initial implementation of four major Presidential Executive Orders:

1. Establishment of a White House Interagency Coordinating Council to deal with interagency urban program turf battles.
2. Requirement of Urban and Community Impact Analysis (UCIA) for all significant new program initiatives for all executive agencies.
3. Requiring federal governmental procurement of materials and supplies from businesses and firms located in cities, as first priority consistent with agency mission.
4. Requiring federal facility site locations in cities, as first priority consistent with agency mission.

The Council met regularly. The Urban and Community Impact
Analysis was required of all agencies for the first time during preparation
of the FY 1980 budget. Lester Salamon of OMB reported to a conference
on Urban and Community Impact Analysis (Washington, February 8,
1979) that, for the first round, twenty-five UCIA's were received from
agencies by OMB. This has meant the addition of an urban dimension
of thinking for the OMB budget examiners.

Congress had a mixed record on the major pieces of national urban
policy submitted to it in 1978. Among the items in the urban package
which passed were: larger urban mass transit aid, a consumer cooperative
bank bill, business investment tax credit (extended to cover rehabilitation
in cities as well as new construction), urban parks, central city health
clinics, neighborhood self-help program, housing rehabilitation.

Among the major items which Congress failed to pass were: renewal
of anti-recession fiscal assistance (or the Administration's proposed supplemental fiscal assistance alternative), "soft" public works, the national
development bank, the state incentive grants for urban strategies, the urban
volunteer corps, and the livable cities program. In addition, Congress
substantially reduced Comprehensive Employment and Training Act (CETA)
appropriations.

In summary, the larger budget items failed to pass, and the major
programs proposed under several distinct elements of the urban policy were
not approved by Congress. The first year performance was mixed. The
second year's record was subdued. The Carter Urban Policy, for all intents
and purposes, was shattered on the craggy shoals of administrative ineptitude in legislative liaison, congressional self-interest, and the pernicious
anti-urban sentiment among many policy makers.

The progress made after April 1979 was even less impressive. Many
of the legislative proposals that were not enacted in the first year were
withdrawn, but their substance was incorporated, where possible, into
existing programs.

Since its first year, many events overshadowed the National Urban
Policy. Undoubtedly, an approaching presidential election had a considerable effect on events, because opponents of the administration often help
to define the issues. The major issues were inflation and recession do-
mestically, and demand for increased military expenditures on the international front.

In order to address inflation, a recession was induced through Federal
Reserve policy governing interest rates and the supply of money. It was
very slow in coming, so inflation soared much higher and longer than

anticipated. The charge that government spending is the major cause of inflation was heard throughout Congress. Hence, budget balancing was soon in vogue.

In March 1980, President Carter announced his 13 billion dollar cutbacks in the FY '81 budget, as his attempt to balance the federal budget. Those cuts had enormous implications for the programs covered under the National Urban Policy. For example, they led to the postponement of welfare reform, reductions in grants for mental health programs and treatment for alcohol abuse, cutbacks in loans to small businesses and home rehabilitation, major cutbacks in revenue sharing for states and cities plus reduction in grants for economic development, parks, pollution control, highway building, mass transit, public service jobs, and law enforcement.

At the same time, international events such as the taking of the hostages in Iran and the Soviet invasion into Afghanistan generated a strong "pro-defense" posture throughout the nation, and especially in Congress. The question was no longer whether military expenditures would be increased, the question was by how much? The dual desires to balance the budget and yet increase defense expenditures did not bode well for the programs under the new National Urban Policy. Nevertheless, the federal government's involvement in urban affairs continued. The older programs through HUD continued—community development block grants and housing. Other programs such as social services (Title XX), and Economic Development Assistance grants remained large.

Of the new programs in the Carter urban program, one of the most interesting was UDAG—Urban Development Action grants, which are attempts to use public funds to secure private capital. Carter referred to the UDAG as the "centerpiece" of the National Urban Policy. By November, 1979, 841 million dollars of UDAG funds were given that leveraged 5.1 billion dollars in private investment. There have been a host of examples. In Kansas City, Missouri a 2.9 million dollar grant was used to trigger the construction of a 13 million dollar downtown hotel, thus contributing to downtown revitalization. In Buffalo, New York, a 4 million dollar grant helped to put a 17 million dollar hotel on a lake-front site that was cleared for urban renewal seventeen years ago. In Lowell, Massachusetts a 5 million dollar grant was used to attract new industry. Wang Laboratories, Inc., a growing computer firm, is building a 33 million dollar headquarters rather than moving out of the city. As Wang repays the twenty-five year, 4 percent loan, the money will be recycled—80 percent to attract new industry, and 20 percent for housing and neigh-

borhood improvement loans. By October 1980, grants under UDAG to-
taled around 1.5 billion dollars, leveraging around 8 to 9 billion dollars
of private funding.

The UDAG "centerpiece" has not been without its critics. Some
question whether those who are most victimized by the urban environment
are really helped by UDAG. The record is mixed. Downtown revitalization
usually does not have direct effects on helping the urban poor, but the
effects of "trickle-down" vary from area to area. Where the revitalization
stimulates the wider business climate resulting in many additional employment opportunities, UDAG can be applauded. But this is not always
the result. Some critics contend that UDAG is usually using government
funds for projects that would have occurred anyway. Hence, it serves as a
subsidy to the private investor. There are instances, however, where the
project could not have occurred without UDAG, such as the Kansas City
hotel. Furthermore, the constraints that are often imposed upon the project
in order to make it more compatible with the surrounding community
often could not be accepted without UDAG. In other words, the presence
of UDAG allows planning flexibility and development that is more responsive to community concerns.

ASSUMPTIONS UNDERLYING THE CARTER URBAN POLICY

It is customary in America to blame the victims of unemployment,
inadequate schooling, dilapidated housing, and deficient health care. Even
the unemployed men and women of the Great Depression refused to blame
the American economic system for their sufferings, finding somehow a
fault in themselves for these systemic evils. The same thing happens today
as the cities go through financial and political crises. However, the evidence
indicates that the ills of the cities and the suffering of many urban residents
result from systemic problems in our communal life, economic organization, and political system.

On the face of it, the Carter Urban Policy Proposals seemed to confront some of the basic problems of the cities, attempting to allocate
resources in order to meet their major ills. However, there was a basic
contradiction between the policy's analysis of urban ills and the medicine
prescribed. The ills were diagnosed on a structural level, indicating the
economic, social, and political deformities which are crippling urban communities. The prescriptions were largely business as usual. This failure to
deal with the systemic problems of the urban communities only comes

fully to light as we consider some of the basic assumptions undergirding the policy proposals.

Its assumptions reveal both how the society perceives itself, and the reasons for its proposed solutions and plans of action. Assumptions influence how society will respond to complex issues.

It is in a society's foundational documents—a constitution, for example—and policy and legal statements, that its assumptions are apt to be clustered. A case can be made for seeking those fundamental principles through an examination of the Carter Urban Policy. It is, in the first place, the first statement of a coherent federal urban policy in American history. Secondly, it is the result of an open process of consultation with urban experts and residents throughout the nation, a basic reflection of the long history of urban policy in America.

While the Carter statement is one grand step for the articulation of a coherent urban policy, it is one small step for the cities. The assumptions of the statement are basically economic; it views the city as a coordinated system of buyers and sellers, resource providers and service/goods users.

There are, however, some appropriate assumptions in the urban policy statement. In view of the biblical analysis and articulation of standards of justice in the preceding chapters, it is easy to agree that the city is important to the health and vitality of the nation, that the federal government must play a role as an advocate of the poor.

Two other assumptions are appropriate for different reasons. The first, that the city is important as a conserver of energy, is true when understood according to the law of large numbers. Supplying energy and basic services to great concentrations of people produces smaller amounts of wastage in precious resources. Cities in America, on the other hand, are hamstrung by their inability to do long-term planning due to their dependency on the largesse of state and federal governments for much of their fiscal life. The oscillations in the tides of CETA funding and revenue-sharing in an era of budget-balancing and presidential elections demonstrate the problem. Opportunistic, short-term planning leaves long-term problems intact.

Another appropriate assumption of the Carter policy on cities is that the federal government has played a major role in creating urban distress. But focus is necessary here, or this assumption could become fuel for new anti-urbanism.

Certain government policies have indeed created an urban doughnut: central city decay, surrounded by rings of suburban prosperity funded by mortgage insurance and serviced by super highways. A frequent example is tax policy which has favored new construction over revitalization. The chaotic multitude of domestic programs developed over the years of urban policy-making have had a cumulative impact on the cities that was beneficial in many respects, particularly in the last two decades. Cities were being helped in many ways, often at cross-purposes. A coherent urban policy could untangle the knots, limit waste, and abet the efficient use of funds. Government can help solve the problems of cities.

The Carter urban policy makes some modest attempts at taking a comprehensive view of the city. It recognizes that America's cities exhibit a great diversity. It testifies that cities are centers of learning and culture as well as sources of jobs, communications, and commerce. It recommends a smattering of programs to preserve these historical functions of the city. But the bottom line is economics. The city is a market place.

Six dominant economic and political assumptions can be identified:

1. The primary problem for the city is wealth production.
2. The primary means to wealth production is technological development.
3. The best form of social organization for wealth production and technological development is the modern corporation.
4. The role of government is to put in place the infrastructure, maintain the working rules which protect the markets, limit negative neighborhood effects or unintended consequences, pay for research and development and the education of the work force.
5. Problems which remain after production adequacy has been achieved can be dealt with by increasingly professionalized and bureaucratized social service structures.
6. Any remaining problems require some combination of charity and government payments to enable individuals and families to have access to the minimum goods and services needed for survival.

The Carter urban statement for the most part leaves intact the existing structure of federal agencies and the set of relations between these agencies and state and municipal governments. The consequence is that problems are defined and taken up categorically or in clusters which reflect the interests of particular constituencies. It should be a matter of concern that the nature of these constituencies is changing. Historically, the organized constituencies for federal urban programs have been the industrial and craft unions. These have been supplemented or replaced by organizations of municipal employees, teachers, and health care specialists—constituencies that are providers of services rather than goods.

With existing structures intact, the primary access of federal policy to the problems of poverty and unemployment remains direct family income maintenance programs or subsidized goods and services. Dependency is therefore taken as a given.

The consequences of these assumptions are clear:

1. Federal programs tend to be built around problem definitions and remedial action rather than development potentials.
2. The primary federal response in terms of resources committed is transfer payments or income maintenance.
3. The next major response is increased funding of service professionals who respond to "deficiency markets" which are invested into professional-client relations. The assumption is maintained that the "problem" is in the hands of the professional, and the governmental function is to fund the professional.
4. The problems in access to goods in the city are viewed as problems in income adequacy rather than as problems of the nature of tools or technologies which produce the goods. Goods, such as food or housing, are considered as separate elements rather than as part of a set.

It is clear that in the Carter urban policy, the city is accepted as an economic entity characterized by service domination and dependency. It further assumes that the present urban polity is the correct one and therefore little attention is given to more basic units of community—neighborhoods, ethnic groups, religious groups, family, workplace, communication systems—and how they relate to the whole. Where it does approach this idea, it suggests that partnership among groups differing in power and values is possible without any fundamental changes in the way our system operates. Thus there is no suggestion that legislative changes are necessary to enable the public or voluntary sectors to deal more effectively with the power of large corporations.

Overall, the Carter policy reads as follows: the city is an economic entity, a market, characterized by service domination and dependency. In the market, different interest groups collaborate as partners to achieve the well-being of all. The role of each group is that of buyer (user of goods and services) or seller (provider of goods and services). The motivation of each group is assumed to be self-interest. This principle, however, effectively atomizes the society and makes little provision for those who are unable to take care of themselves. Actual experience with the interplay of these forces or interests has shown that those most in need are not helped.

At bottom, the Carter and, as we shall see, Reagan policies are the same. They give priority to the workings of the open market. There are, however, sufficient differences to allow a preferential judgement to be made about the relative merits of each. These will be discussed at the end of the next chapter.

NOTES

[1]New York: Harcourt, Brace and World, 1961, p. 573.

4.

The Emerging Reagan Urban Policy

AS REQUIRED by law, President Reagan published an urban policy statement in July, 1982. It offered no new urban initiative, other than the often-promised enterprise zones. The document reduces the role of the federal government in urban revitalization to little more than gathering information and determining results.

It also clearly indicates that the central foundation of the Reagan urban policy is the president's economic policy. This suggests a direction for this chapter: to analyze the enterprise zone concept, and to review the impact of President Reagan's budget cuts on the cities.

Enterprise zones will be examined because they are the Reagan Administration's primary, if not only, urban initiative. As sure as one can be about anything in politics, we will have enterprise zones sometime in the near future. The legislation is before Congress. A report by a special commission is on the President's desk. When the first zone will be opened is a moot question. It took Great Britain, where the idea originated, five years to start up. The pace will probably be quicker in this country. The zones reveal, in a fundamental way, what the Reagan urban policy means for the cities, and what the assumptions of that policy are.

If the President's urban policy is his economic policy, it is equally true to say that his economic policy is essentially his budget policy. His 1981 Program for Economic Recovery included the following: supply-side tax reductions, dramatic increases in military spending, and drastic cuts in outlays for domestic programs.

"What we have is an anti-urban policy," declared one staff member of a congressman who represents an inner city district. "His budget cuts have completely devastated the cities. The enterprise zones—well, that's like trying to put out a fire with a water pistol."

"I would rather call it a non-policy," said someone on the staff of the

United States Conference of Mayors. "It's a complete indifference to the cities. Ronald Reagan is committed to a certain ideology which promises pie-in-the-sky in the future, while it keeps its fingers crossed things won't get too bad until then."

To test the impact of the budget cuts on the cities, the coping mechanisms of two cities will be examined—the Frostbelt's aging Milwaukee and the Sunbelt's burgeoning Tampa. Will they both survive? How?

Behind Ronald Reagan's action is his conservative commitment. Its primary postulate is this: the free market, in which individuals compete to maximize their own well-being, is the best hope for the woes that beset all levels of American society. This ideology will be examined because it is the formative matrix for the President's public policy decisions.

ENTERPRISE ZONES—THE ONLY GAME IN TOWN

Enterprise zones are Ronald Reagan's primary urban initiative. The structures of the zones are still indeterminate, but there are questions that need to be raised, particularly from the perspective of *shalom*.

President Reagan wedded himself to the enterprise zone concept during his presidential campaign. Criticized for being indifferent to the poor and probably racist, he responded by latching on to the enterprise zone idea advocated by fellow conservative Republican and confidant Congressman Jack Kemp of New York. The concept has been jostled about among partisans across a broad political spectrum since then, but it has yet to prove seaworthy. The President appointed a task force early in 1981 to scrutinize the idea more closely, while Congressman Kemp, along with politically liberal co-sponsor, Congressman Robert Garcia (Democrat-New York), also revised their version of the "Urban Jobs and Enterprise Zones Act."

The basic idea is to create a "climate of enterprise" within distressed areas—central cities for the most part—of America. The climate is expected to nurture growth within the blighted area and its environing municipality by increasing business investments and creating new jobs.

The zones will be designated areas of high unemployment and poverty. Local governments would be required to lower property taxes, improve public services and remove zoning and other regulations. The federal government would provide major tax incentives for job creation and business growth. Incentives probably will include reductions in social security payroll taxes on employees and employers, reductions in capital gains tax rates and business tax rates, accelerated depreciation on assets, a sub-minimum wage law for young workers.

The concept originated in Great Britain six years ago, inspired by the Free Trade Zones that dot the globe. Hong Kong is an often-cited model of these zones. It is a haven of free enterprise where income taxes are low and tariff barriers have been removed. The city-state has a booming economy, but it also enjoys an additional incentive that probably will not apply to the American and British versions—remarkably low labor wages.

It is only in the past year that the British zones have become operative. There will be little wisdom that we can gather from the experiment. They differ from their American counterparts in at least two respects, according to Stuart Butler, chief proponent of the concept in this country. In the first place, the British zones are to be activated on unused tracts of land, while the American equivalents will take shape in the blighted inner cities. A more important difference, however, is that the British zones are designed to attract large corporations, while in America the zones will be targeted at the creation of new types of small business.

This last stipulation is based on a study, often quoted in this context, by economist David Birch. He surveyed 5.6 million businesses over the 1970s and found that those generating new jobs tended to be small and young. Most had twenty employees or fewer and were less than five years old.

Puerto Rico offers one possible outcome of the urban enterprise zone strategy. "Operation Bootstrap" comprised a series of economic development programs begun by the government of Puerto Rico in the late 1940s. Providing a virtually complete exemption from taxes, its purpose was to attract businesses engaged in manufacturing, tourism, and exporting in order to create jobs for the unemployed and to raise taxes.

Why did businesses locate there? Was it the tax incentives or some other factor? In a report to the President in December, 1979, the Department of Commerce noted the chief inducement for business to locate there in the period from the 1940s to the 1960s was the low wages. Tax incentives were not essential at that time.

The study also found that these same businesses left Puerto Rico at the end of the tax exempt period in search of other havens of cheap labor. Edward Humberger does not have much to say about conditions in Puerto Rico that is positive or complimentary:

> After thirty years, it was evident that the free trade zone's economy was stagnant, needing yet another transfusion of industrial development at a still higher level of local development.

By now, seventy percent of the population was below the poverty line, and sixty percent were on Food Stamps. Inflation was up forty percent, and unemployment was up thirty-five percent. Fully twenty-five percent of the families earned less than $1,000 a year.[1]

The Puerto Rican experiences raise some red flags. There are three that are generally brought up in this context, and they have to do with 1) the cogency of tax incentives, 2) displacement of zone residents and 3) strains on municipal finances.

Tax incentives are of many types, but most have to do with property tax exemptions, tax exemptions on inventories and raw materials, corporate tax exemptions. Accelerated depreciation on business equipment and the physical plant also fall into this category.

There has been an ongoing debate over the attracting power of these exemptions. The *Economic Study of Puerto Rico*, referred to above, seems to indicate rather than attracting business, they enhance one that is already there. A survey of the Joint Economic Committee of Congress confirms this conclusion. It found that factors related to the cost of production were most important in the choice of location, followed by social amenities such as levels of crime, quality of schools and cultural attractions. Financial incentives were far down on the list. Other surveys have reinforced these findings.

But perhaps the tax incentives would be important to the small businesses the zone concept is designed to attract? That also appears not to be the case. What they need is start-up money and operating capital. It is only after three or four years that they have begun to generate enough revenue to pay taxes.

More attractive to business, according to the Joint Economic Committee survey, are the physical amenities connected to production. These include proximity to an adequate labor force and market, high quality roads, good sewer systems, adequate street lighting, police and fire protection, a benevolent public attitude towards business, access to raw materials. Most of these are elements that must be supplied by the local municipality, and therein lies a problem.

What are amenities for business are financial burdens for city governments. None of them come cheaply. The repair and up-dating of New York's infrastructure will cost 40 billion dollars over the next ten years. Where is such money to come from? Federal budget cuts have already put a great deal of stress on urban fiscal bases. Municipal funds are now being targeted on essential services. It will be years before the promised ripple effect on the whole urban economy moves out from its enterprise zone. The zones may turn out to be too expensive for the cities they are to save, the cure worse than the disease.

Some observers of the urban scene wonder if the real winners in the enterprise zone scramble would not be land developers and real estate speculators. The up-grading of the zone's infrastructure and the arrival of new commercial residents will cause land values to skyrocket. Rising property values will force the emigration of the zone's low-income and minority residents.

The process is called gertrification, and it has already been repeated in most of our major cities. Its victims are usually those on fixed incomes, who cannot meet the new property taxes or higher rents out of their income. A successful zone would displace the people who live there now, the very ones for whom the zone was created.

In the preceding chapter, the assumptions of the Carter Administration were deduced from the urban policy it promulgated. Here Ronald Reagan's enterprise zone concept will be examined instead of his urban policy statement. As an original urban initiative, the concept is a more apt subject for the kind of analysis employed in this book.

1) Trust the marketplace. This assumption should be no surprise. Reagan has been candid about his adherence to the ideology of conservative politics. The intent of the enterprise zone is to give free reign to the market, to the "invisible hand" that directs economic activity to the ultimate good of all peoples.

2) Taxes and government regulations are major deterrents to business. Reagan said he sought the presidency "to get the government off our backs." The enterprise zone is designed to prove the rectitude of this commitment. It will peel away as much of government regulation on the federal and local levels as is perceived to be a barrier to the free development of business.

3) Free enterprise will create jobs. The rejoinder to this claim is, "Of course, but for whom and to what effect?" The direct beneficiaries of the zone concept will be business enterprises; the indirect beneficiaries, the unemployed or low-income residents of the zones and nearby areas.

Is that sufficient? The work force of potential zone sites have generally low educational levels. There is no provision in the legislation, because it runs counter to conservative ideology, for job training or placement. There is also no incentive provided to hire zone residents.

Business development in the zones might create more jobs. It might even strengthen the economy of its city as a whole. But it seems unlikely to maximize jobs for present zone residents, or to offer skill training to them.

4) Tax reductions will be compensated for by tax revenues generated by new productivity. This assumption lies at the heart of the President's controversial "supply-side economics." Boiled down to its essentials, the theory proposes that high taxes discourage useful work and investment. It postulates, therefore, that reduced taxes will increase these. The newly-generated productivity in turn will direct new tax dollars to government coffers and decrease government outlays for unemployment compensation and related social service payments.

It is the economics of the Kennedy Administration that supply-side theorists turn to for validation. When that president announced his intention to ask Congress for a tax reduction, business investment spurted in anticipation of the cut. When the proposed reduction died an untimely death, investment activity stopped immediately. President Reagan has not fared as well with Wall Street. Increased investment has not been spurred by the tax program he engineered through Congress in 1981.

The inflationary climate accounts for the difference. Kennedy's reduction took place when the rate of inflation was 1.5 percent; Reagan's has to contend with the double digit inflation it is supposed to lower. His tax cut is not coming to tax payers as a bonus. High inflation is eating large chunks of it away, forcing them to use it to cover costs. When the inflation rate was only 1.5, they could use the tax bonus as venture capital.

Thinking about enterprise zones in the context of *shalom* raises troubling questions.

Can enterprise zones succeed if they are not an element of a coherent urban policy? Urban problems are structural and systemic. What we see are symptoms, the source of which cannot be solved by individual programmatic effects. Some government initiatives from the recent past—federal grants for urban renewal, model cities, the Great Society programs—were good, but not sufficient. The complexity of our urban economic and social problems is beyond the ministrating power of any single federal initiative. The federal government never had an effective, coherent urban policy to eradicate urban blight. The enterprise zone concept is not "the fluoride that will bring an end to urban decay." Urban professionals fear that the Reagan Administration is so mesmerized by the idea, that the larger problems of the cities will not be addressed.

Can the idea succeed without the likes of CETA, UDAG, community development block grants, and the Economic Development Administration to complement it? That seems to be the design of the Reagan Administration, for it has planned to eliminate those programs. It is doubtful whether ten or twenty zones scattered across the nation can solve our urban problems. Even if there is economic growth, the elderly, the unskilled, the hungry, the helpless will be cut off from sources of support.

Is the real cause of urban blight government regulations or unbridled free enterprise? The architects of the enterprise zone blame government regulations. They are the major factor inhibiting industrial growth, upgrading of aging plants, meeting payrolls forced up by minimum wage laws, meeting rising property taxes. The defenders of the zones put their trust and hope in an unfettered free market.

Others see the demon as free enterprise. Urban blight is caused by the callous disregard of the private sector for anything but profits. They cite example after example of such disregard. The closing of the Youngstown steel mills, discussed later in this book, is one case in point.

The debate has not ended since all the facts are not in. The history of urban policy has indicated that federal regulations arrived late on the scene, as the illegitimate child of unbridled free enterprise. The purpose of the regulations was to forestall the spread of the blight that occurred during the heyday of industrial development. Would the cities have been in a worse state without them?

From the standpoint developed in this book, it seems clear that weakening federal grant regulations is not the right direction. Federal regulations have brought an end to the horror of child labor, established fire and health codes, brought safety to the work place, limited the possibility of meltdown at nuclear plants, rehabilitated dying neighborhoods, and prevented commercial establishments from encroaching on viable residential areas. There is little or no evidence that conditions would improve were federal requirements reduced or eliminated.

What kind of growth or development is best for the inner city? Economic growth is the purpose of enterprise zones. Is that enough? *Shalom*, as presented and applied here, requires attention to social and economic development. As Edward Humberger suggests in the article cited earlier, was Puerto Rico a success because it generated capital investments and jobs? Manifestly not. The people and the land were in a worse state at the end of thirty years of economic growth and productivity. Humberger claims, rightly in our estimation, that success is a comprehensive process involving local self-reliance and independence, the social development of the area's residents and the creation of community-controlled and self-sustaining local institutions.

Such community involvement has also been recommended by the study, *Source Book on Enterprise Zones*.[2] It adopts the claim of the neighborhood movement that many of the unbearable conditions of inner-city life arise because of a lack of a neighborhood social fabric. It recommends, as does Humberger, that the zone residents be assured equity in the growth of the neighborhood.

The Sabre Foundation study would give neighborhood associations equity in zone lands that are leasable to business. Residents would then have a stake in the zone. They would receive direct benefits from any efforts—reducing crime, vandalism, housing renovation—they undertake to improve the area.

Enterprise zones in their current legislative form fail to recognize the existence of community-based development institutions in the areas that might be designated as zones. To this extent, they have learned little from the lessons of urban history. Neighborhoods survive and remain viable where their residents have a stake in the neighborhood and are involved in its well-being. Growth without development is the difference between a viable city and a ghost town.

The neighborhood movement, basically a grassroots movement, proved that it makes good development sense for residents to play a key role in decisions affecting the revitalization of their neighborhoods. The successes in urban renewal are those that have been based on partnerships of all the parties involved. Community Action Agencies, Community Development Corporations, Neighborhood Housing Services, Urban Development Action Grants were all premised on the idea of citizen participation. The partnership usually included neighborhood residents, local government and representatives from the private sector. Such partnerships were central to Carter's urban policy. It seems to be the only way, in the present circumstances, to assure that residents participate in the shaping of their future. This is a requirement of *shalom* from our perspective, and it is a lack that should be corrected in the enterprise zone concept.

RONALD REAGAN'S BUDGETARY MANEUVERS

The President's urban policy hand is also revealed in the budget cuts of government programs directed at American cities. The same Reagan ideology is operative: "Trust the marketplace." And it has translated into major cutbacks in federal grants-in-aid to state and local governments, labeled a "new federalism."

The cutbacks were expected. Ronald Reagan repeatedly promised as much in his sixteen-year campaign for the presidency. But it is the swiftness with which the cards were shuffled and dealt, and the poor hand dealt the cities that sent shock waves through them that have strained their fiscal, social and economic structures to the breaking point.

The United States Conference of Mayors considers the budget reductions the most serious threat to the existence of the cities in this century. The Joint Economic Committee of Congress conducted a survey of nearly three hundred cities before the Reagan budget cuts took effect. It found that nearly eighty percent of those surveyed projected a deficit in 1981. Already in the red, these cities have limited access to funds to help redress the impact of the deficits and the budget cuts. The *National Journal* suggests that though the budget cuts are bad news for the cities, some will be worse off than others. Most cities will survive. But, it adds, rather baldly, it is the city poor who will be hurt. This should be a cause of concern for the churches.

The same article in the *National Journal*[3] measures the potential impact of the budget cuts on two different American cities. One of them—the Sunbelt's Tampa—is growing; the other—the Frostbelt's Milwaukee—is experiencing the problems of old age. Neither is at the extremes of the growth-decline continuum. They will survive, but each will experience some stress. But, in both cases, it is the poor who will feel most of the post-operative pains of the President's budgetary surgery.

Since they are microcosms of urban conditions in the United States, it would be helpful to look at both these cities closely. Our schema is to view cities as places and as people. As places, the cities are physical environments, built by humans, to support their political, social, economic, and cultural lives. Shakespeare, himself an early lover of cities, noted in *Coriolanus* that "the people are the city." They are large concentrations of people, interacting, developing common interests, seeking common and private solutions to individual needs. No matter what one thinks of the Reagan economic program, one has to admit that the people will be hurt in the short run. They will be hurt indirectly through the physical development of their towns that will be truncated. They will be hurt directly through the eclipsing of needed social services and the imposition of higher taxes and user fees.

TAMPA

Tampa is typical of the fast-growing cities of the sunbelt benefiting from low wages and taxes, government incentives toward new construction, and pleasant weather. Its population—just over a quarter of a million in 1970—will probably grow to 400,000 by the turn of the century. In 1980, its citizenry was 23 percent black and 13 percent Hispanic. About 11 percent of its citizens and those in the surrounding county were 65 or older, which is low for a Florida city.

The county has a large poverty population—about 28 percent of the households had incomes below $8,000 in 1979. The city's unemployment rate in 1981 was about one percent below the national average but particularly high among black youth.

Cigar smokers recognize it as a major cigar manufacturing center become more prominent after the United States embargoed Cuban products. It was also a major banana port. Today, its economy depends on the importation of phosphates and the agriculture that surrounds this urban center.

The federal government has been good to Tampa. It has been receiving about 44 million dollars annually, which is equal to more than one-fourth of its city budget, well above the 15 percent national average.

This city is most concerned about reductions in programs that would support growth such as sewer and highway construction grants, funds for the construction and operation of mass transit, housing rehabilitation funds.

Sewerage treatment is an obvious health need, and expanded facilities are a necessity in growing cities. Seventy-five percent of Tampa's 93 million dollar recently-completed sewerage treatment plant was paid for by the federal government. President Reagan had called for zero budgeting for sewerage treatment grants in 1982. The President now has called for turning these grants over to the states in fiscal year 1984 as part of his New Federalism program. Either way, the impact on Tampa will be significant. The city may not be able to complete a great pipeline to move its sewerage to the treatment plant.

Tampa's bus system is a part of the county's transit authority. Federal aid pays half of its operating losses. It also supports its capital improvement program. Mass transit aid is another candidate for the budgetary machete, putting Tampa into a catch-22 situation. Bus fares are 75 cents. A property tax was levied in 1980 to meet expenses. Raising fares further would discourage ridership, as it has done in many major cities. That would only add to the deficit of the system, increase car and air pollution, generate a need for new road maintenance, and waste limited energy resources.

Community Development Block Grant (CDBG) funds provide for improvements in housing, physical facilities, and social services in areas with concentrations of low-income residents. Cutbacks here leave the city unable to help this population, and the people faced with high interest rates and rapidly rising property values.

According to one of the county commissioners, unemployment among black males is between 50 and 70 percent. CETA is the major government program designed to ease unemployment. Tampa expected to lose 4 million dollars in CETA funds in 1981, a 40 percent cutback which will be 20 percent larger in 1982. This translates into a drop of 1800 low-income participants.

CETA workers here, as in many large cities, staffed important public services. Reductions mean fewer trash collections, more shoddy roads and closed day care centers. And there will be a ripple effect: individuals who depended on child care centers will have to stop working. Where are they then to turn, except to the welfare rolls? Clinics will close because of the cap on Medicaid. Tampa public health sources have imposed a modest user fee—2 dollars per immunization; 15 dollars per prenatal examination. The poor cannot afford that much. An expected drop of 3 million dollars in federal school aid would force Tampa to remove three thousand students from its compensatory education program. In both health and education, needs will not be met and people will not be served.

Contrary to the intention of Reagan's New Federalism, the State of Florida will not fill in the gaps. Florida, probably our fastest growing state, has not been generous with dollars for local government in the past. But, there is another factor to consider. The Reagan budget cuts have fallen disproportionately on states and localities. According to a report in the *Congressional Quarterly Weekly*[4] total federal aid to these jurisdictions dropped 14.8 percent from fiscal 1981 to 1982, and will drop 32.5 percent from 1980 to 1986.

Tampa is being left to its own devices. For cities, that usually means property taxes. There is both a psychological and legal limit to what it can do there. The Proposition 13 mentality, which sought the transfer of money from the poor to the upper classes, is still alive and well and feared by city officials. The polling booths will not be places of solace for tax hikers. In addition, Florida, as most states, has a legal limit on its cities' property tax rate.

The broader picture indicates that Tampa will have an easier time meeting its physical needs through municipal bonds and taxes than in helping its poor, who will bear the burden of federal budgetary maneuvers.

MILWAUKEE

In Milwaukee, the picture is worse because it is an aging and aged city with a shrinking tax base. It is not as threatened as the Clevelands and Detroits and New Yorks of the country. The bond rating of a city is one of the best measures of its financial soundness, and Milwaukee's is excellent.

This city's population has declined from 717,372 in 1970 to 636,212 in 1980. It has a larger minority and elderly population than Tampa. Twenty-four percent of its residents are black and 4.1 percent Hispanic. About 18 percent of its county's population is over 60, and almost all of them are white. 147,000 people are officially poor.

Milwaukee, of course, is the town that beer made famous. It is a major beer producer, but the central element of its economy is light equipment, much of it related to the auto industry.

Central to Milwaukee's future stability is maintaining a strong tax base. Its principal source of revenue is its property tax, which suffers legal and psychological limits. Furthermore, property tax hikes would fall most heavily on those least able to pay, those on fixed incomes.

One way to keep its tax rate stable or expanding is to provide a healthy and growing economic climate to nurture new productivity. That kind of growth would increase tax revenues without tax hikes. Milwaukee has been helped in this area by federal sewerage treatment grants, UDAG, CDBG and EDA programs. All of these have been put in jeopardy. A 10.3 million dollar grant from the Economic Development Administration (EDA) was central to the redevelopment of a major downtown area. Hopes for that development, and its ripple effects throughout the municipal economy, have been dashed against the Reagan Administration's zero-budgeting of EDA.

Milwaukee, like Tampa, has a concern for its sewer system. It is of a kind that indicates the different types of problems both cities are facing. Tampa is short of funds to complete a pipeline to its new sewerage plant. Milwaukee's aging sewer system overflows after heavy rains, dumping raw sewerage into Lake Michigan. Repair estimates are 1.6 billion dollars. Where will it find those funds? The Reagan budgeteers are trying hard to eliminate sewerage grant monies. Wisconsin is facing a deficit of one-half billion dollars and reduced federal aid.

When funds are short, the maintenance of the municipal infrastructure is neglected. It is the urban equivalent of running a car into the ground, with all the attendant expenses as the vehicle is brought to the point of total decay and abandonment.

As with the poor of Tampa, the poor of Milwaukee will bear the burden of social change shaped by others. They will experience the ravages of cutbacks in CETA, Supplementary Security Income (SSI), food stamps, AFDC, education and community services.

A CETA-staffed program that has been successful in dealing with black-on-black crime has been eliminated. Over 7 million dollars in education aid to disadvantaged children will be lost. In all, reductions in community services would cost Milwaukee more than 104 million dollars in 1982. The city's Community Relations–Social Development Commission estimates that more than 200,000 individuals or households will be hurt.

The Reagan budget cuts will dramatically reduce direct federal commitments to the cities. The programs being shorn by his budgetary shears are those that responded to urban needs. The Reagan Administration proposes to reduce federal costs associated with cities and urban areas by eliminating duplicative funding, encouraging the consolidating of funding into block grants, eliminating programs which it views as unnecessary and remanding others to the states. These proposals severely shrink programs that have become part of the social and economic fabric of the cities. Many were good, helpful programs. Some were misdirected. Others were saddled with waste and fraud. The Reagan approach is again one of separating economic and social development. What hope does this approach offer when the history of American urban policy has demonstrated its futility?

The recommended urban aid retrenchments in fiscal 1982 total more than twenty billion dollars. In fiscal 1983, they will be reduced by another 13.2 billion dollars. This represents a significant, continuing scaling back of the federal government's commitment to cities, their residents and businesses. As if that were not bad enough, the cities will be hurt most by the side effects of failures of the Reagan program for economic recovery. Interest rates are at the highest level they have ever been in this country, partly because of the Reagan program. Both of those factors hit cities hardest. Unemployment is highest and more concentrated in the cities. High interest rates make it more expensive for cities to float bonds, keep hotels and commercial buildings from getting built, and dry up the home construction industry.

What all this amounts to is a form of socio-economic triage. The poor have been deemed dispensable for the sake of economic gain.

The churches have to face this question: Is it necessary? Must or ought the poor suffer for the good of the country? What kind of ethics would justify that approach to the people of God's special concern? Is this program penny wise and pound foolish? Will the short-term gains lead to the long-term promises? There are alternatives.

Time after time, cutbacks are justified by the Reagan ideology that the particular programs can be better run and supported by private financing. It is time to take a closer look at that ideology.

IDOLS OF THE MARKET IDEOLOGY

When David Stockman, the Director of the Office of Management and Budget, unburdened himself to columnist William Greider in *The Atlantic*, he said this about the Reagan economic program: "The whole thing is premised on faith . . . On a belief about how the world works."[5] Stockman indicated that Reagan was not a pragmatic politician, one who made decisions as the events presented themselves, depending on the integrity of his political sense to guide his judgment. The president is committed to an ideology, a specific view of how the world works, and it is that view which controls his decision making.

Basic assumptions about cities are bound up with personal, social, economic and political images of what it means to be a person, of how people are related to one another and of how competing interests are resolved. In general, assumptions about urban organization derive from such images or models of human life. It is on this level of models or ideologies of human life that we shall finally have to work out our differences with the prevailing urban policy proposals. It is a contention of this book that the Reagan urban initiatives, and to a lesser extent, the Carter Urban Policy, merely reflect the conventional American wisdom for dealing with urban ills. But, to what model of the good human society are the postulates, if any, in this conventional wisdom wedded?

The guiding principle of the Reagan ideology is "Trust the marketplace." The market has almost the same significance in that phrase as the word God.

Current American urban policy is constructed around the familiar economic notion of an open market. The market model operates like a very large shopping center. In it, a human being is an isolated entity, one of many islands in the great sea of humanity. Each human is equipped with certain faculties and skills, and connected to others by various instruments such as language, work habits, family ties, and the responsibilities of citizenship. Communities are made up of bunches of these isolated humans, each negotiating to maximize its own advantages. The major aim of every individual and community is to increase its wealth (or capital) and to maintain its power over other groups.

There are limits, at least in principle, to what is allowable in the competition for wealth and power. Those limits are set by laws—anti-trust laws, fair trade laws, consumer protection regulations, fair housing acts, for example—placing restrictions on the use of force and fraud in the competitive struggle.

The image of the human being implied here and its political implications have been summarized by C. B. MacPherson, in his volume, *The Political Theory of Possessive Individualism*. According to this theory, human society consists of a series of market relations. What makes a person human is freedom from dependence on the wills of others. The individual is the proprietor of his or her own person and capacities, owing nothing to society.

Freedom, in this model, means freedom from any relations with others except voluntary associations made for the individual's own interests. Individual freedom can only be limited by those obligations and rules necessary to secure the same freedom for others. Political society, a human contrivance, exists to protect the individual's property, person and goods. Its chief function is to maintain orderly relations of exchange between individuals.

This market model of individualism and competing interests made some sense in early America. At the time of the Revolution, the majority of free persons were small landowners, craftsmen, or tradesmen. Economic power and the means of production fell sufficiently into individual hands to warrant such a notion of free exchange. Freedom and economic power or self-sufficiency converged enough to lend credibility to the model. In fact, Jefferson and other founders feared industrial development in the New World because its patterns of organization could endanger this conjunction of freedom and power in the individual. Women, Native Americans and blacks were excluded from this "free market," but the ideology had some credibility and warrant for those in power.

Industrialization, extension of the system of wage labor, managerial capitalism and, in our own time, trans-national, corporate capitalism severed the bond between individual freedom and economic power in America. Economic power became more and more concentrated in national and then trans-national structures.

Richard Barnet's recent study, *The Lean Years*, brings out dramatically the concentration of control of energy, food and human resources in these global structures. Even the so-called "service" sectors of health, education and welfare are now concentrations of power in bureaucratized professions.

It is common knowledge that the escalating costs of medical services are interwoven with the power of the professional elites such as the American Medical Association, who control the health "industry." The very notion of a "free market" becomes ludicrous when one considers the concentration of power in the oil industry between the OPEC countries and the corporate structures of the oil companies. Even national governments such as the United States are losing control over this vital resource for the national life.

Freedom has also been distorted with the dislocation of economic power from individual, communal, and national interests. It has come to mean the power to do what one wishes with one's private style of life. Economic activity for most persons, and now for most couples, simply means a way to gain enough income to survive, and, with good fortune, to maintain a comfortable style of life. Inflationary pressure has meant that the struggle to survive occupies more and more time. Larger sectors of the minority populations, older people, young, and handicapped have been forced into poverty and deprivation. Freedom has become a luxury for those who can gain a foothold in a work sector that is becoming increasingly technical and specialized. To be free now is to have a job.

This amoral market model, which clearly is the operative ideology behind the Reagan political philosophy, has taken its toll on community life during recent generations. The communal fabric of the major cities was renewed in the latter part of the nineteenth century by an influx of immigrant peoples from Europe. These ethnic communities lent a solidarity to local neighborhoods and constituted a mosaic of political groupings for the major cities. Many eroded in time and were not replenished. Those remaining are treated with disdain, rather than valued as national treasures of human interaction.

In turn, black people were forced off the land in the South and drifted into the cities in search of work. As August Meier observed in his study of this migration, it was a movement from one bondage to another, from plantation to metropolitan ghetto. Discrimination in housing, education, health care, employment, and every major aspect of survival eroded these communities. For the blacks, this deprivation continues even more intensely in the 1980s. As summers of racial riots and tension across the nation have demonstrated, metropolitan areas have become centers of racial crisis.

The erosion of communities has been supplemented by the expansion of the service industries of health, education and welfare for whom the poor have become clientele. America is an over-medicated, over-litigated, over-credentialed society. The "free" market has been deformed into an artificial market catering to created needs. Some people are able to benefit from these programs of service, finding opportunities for employment and economic gain through the growing dependency of ghetto and other peoples on these service industries. Thus, the structural deformity of the market model has become the vehicle for the imposition of dependency on whole sectors of the urban population, including large numbers of middle class people whose economic welfare is dependent on mortgages and interest rates.

Hence, it is not only the assumptions of prevailing urban policy which are in question; the comprehensive image of human life and community, of freedom and power which underlies it, the market model itself, is in radical trouble. Fewer and fewer people are really benefiting from the market structure. Even major corporations are finding themselves crippled by global, ecological, and human forces they never anticipated. The dislocations that drive corporations into trans-national conglomerates in order to retain power over resources and markets have forced cities into bankruptcy and despair.

The market model was a novelty a few centuries ago, a novelty which served to release certain economic forces from the restraints of traditional societies and governments. This model may have been useful in its time, especially for releasing certain energies for productive expansion. Its theory of "possessive individualism" is rooted in Hobbesian, mechanistic thought. Hobbes was logical enough to know that the only remedy for such a war of each against all was the Leviathan of absolutist government. This is one alternative before us if we do not achieve a more humane vision. Some despairing critics like Robert Heilbroner have all but resigned themselves to the Leviathan as an alternative to nuclear blackmail and domestic revolt. There may be a better way, but it must be a richer, more authentic and more humane vision than the market model.

THE CARTER AND REAGAN URBAN POLICIES

We have been hard on the urban policies of Jimmy Carter and Ronald Reagan, more so on the latter because it is so out of line with what we perceive to be a biblical vision for the cities. We recognize that both a e similar in their basic assumptions. At the heart of both is the open market model. Reviewing the two approaches to the city, and the history of urban policy, the authors of this volume find themselves in greater agreement with the approach of the Carter Administration despite its limitations.

In the first place, Carter designed the country's first coherent policy. It did not confront the structural and systemic change required for solving urban problems, but it was a step in the right direction. Reagan has signalled that his primary urban program will be enterprise zones. No matter how brilliant the concept, it is doubtful it will succeed without many of the programs that he has abolished.

Secondly, Carter's idea of targeted assistance seems correct. It was his administration which developed the idea. Reagan's claim that all will be helped by improving the economy as a whole has a ring of truth to it. The image he has used is that all boats rise with the tide. But some do not. Some are in such poor condition that they can rise only after receiving special care. That's what targeted assistance means.

Thirdly, the two Presidents have put their open market ideology to work in different ways. Ronald Reagan has thrown the cities out into the open market to fend for themselves. Jimmy Carter developed the idea of partnership and the leveraging of private financing with public monies. The partnership was to be among the government, business and the not-for-profit voluntary sector. True, he did not give enough support to the latter, but the idea required citizen participation in events that would shape their own lives.

Finally, the Carter urban policy introduced some mechanisms for institutional capacity-building at the grass roots level. The Consumer Co-operative Bank gives loans and technical assistance to non-profit organizations that provide food, housing, health care and a variety of other services to elderly and low-income groups. The Neighborhood Self Help program provided funds directly to neighborhood groups for economic development. Both programs are being eliminated by President Reagan, yet they are two of very few examples of federal programs that help citizens to take charge and improve their own lives.

The initiative of the Carter Administration to put in place a coherent urban policy will not be furthered by his successor. While this turn of events is not surprising, something needs to be done to reverse the direction of the present administration. The Carter urban policy was not created overnight. It was the result of a history of work, thought and experimentation.

What is the role of the churches and other voluntary agencies in the present economic situation? We have many suggestions for the churches, some of which have been listed in the Introduction, and others in the final chapter. President Reagan, however, has one of his own. Without apparently consulting with church leaders, he has made an appeal to volunteerism. The care of the poor, he believes, belongs properly to charitable organizations and churches.

The response of charitable organizations to that call has been almost unanimous: It's impossible. Charitable giving cannot meet billions of dollars of direct losses to the poor over the next three years.

Most churches recognize their limitations, yet church response to the President's recommendation has been divided. An article in *Christianity Today*[6] represents a positive response to the President. It sees the current situation as an occasion to "fulfill God's commandments by mirroring the efforts of the early church while reaping the resultant benefits; demonstrate to society the power of love; perfect the social systems." It attests, with some accuracy (since grassroots groups have been cost-effective in the administration of social services), that local church efforts will surpass the efforts of the large government machinery.

In an essay entitled, "Assault on the Poor"[7] Danny Collum details two dangers inherent in the President's call to volunteerism. In the first place, "the approach ignores the structural and systemic causes of poverty." Volunteerism would never get to those roots. Secondly, "To say the needs of the poor should be met by private charity is to say that the basic necessities for a decent life are not a God-given right of each person." It is a way of saying that the society has no obligation for the poor, which indeed is what David Stockman, OMB Director, has publicly testified.

The perspective developed in this book is in line with Collum's clarion call for structural change. Justice, informed by *shalom*, means not only the charitable distribution of goods, but also the means of new human capacity for economic production. *Shalom*-inspired charity is more than service, it means helping people to construct new systems for survival.

Those concerned about the well-being of city dwellers, particularly the poor, should take a close look at all the actions of the current administration. It is difficult to justify attempts to cut the vital safety net of social programs before the growth promised by urban enterprise zones takes effect. Nor is it sufficient to encourage only economic productivity. Social productivity—the capacity of persons to take charge of their own lives and participate in shaping their future—requires attending to. And this is precisely what is being disregarded through indiscriminate budget cutting and selective legislative design.

NOTES

[1]"The Enterprise Zone Fallacy," *Journal of Community Action* (Washington, D.C.: Center for Responsive Government, September/October, 1981), p. 20.

[2]Mark Frazier, editor (Washington, D.C.: Sabre Foundation, 1981).

[3]"What the Budget Cuts Mean for Cities—Lean Years, with Less for the Poor" (Washington, D.C.: Government Research Co., 5/30/81), pp. 960–70.

[4]"Reagan Federalism in Practice," (Washington, D.C., Congressional Quarterly, Inc., October 24, 1981), p. 2047.

[5]"The Education of David Stockman" (Boston: The Atlantic Monthly Corp., December, 1981), pp. 27 ff.

[6]Tom McCabe, "Reagan's Budget Cuts Challenge the Church" (Carol Stream, IL: Christianity Today, Inc., October 2, 1981), pp. 42–44.

[7]*Sojourners* (Washington D.C.: Peoples Christian Coalition, July, 1981), pp. 12–16.

5.

Federal Urban Policy:
Some Critical Issues

IS THERE any hope for the cities? The answer to this vital question depends on whether or not our society has the political will or desire to address the existing urban crisis conditions. The resolution of the long lists of urban woes that we read in the daily newspapers rests on the strength of our corporate willingness to take these issues in hand at the macropolitical level. It ought to be clear that current technological capabilities are sufficient to meet our urban needs. What is lacking is the political will.

Once again, in looking at Western European societies on the one hand and the United States on the other, differences in attitudes towards the city exist which have played themselves out in the political process, and have resulted in a generally healthier situation in Europe. In many European societies there is a political will to devote the necessary resources to tackling urban problems. Throughout most of its history, America has been ambivalent about its cities. Beyond the economic reality of limited resources, there is a prevailing attitude on the part of the citizenry concerning the most appropriate way to use what wealth is available. Rugged individualism and the ideology of the free market continue to dominate the American mentality. Barbara Ward has been able to capture the parameters of this mentality:

> Some of the basic difficulties in open societies stem from the over-concentration on personal interest and self-advancement which, carried beyond a certain point, makes it all but impossible to achieve a proper and general balance of justice and sharing. It is the nature of a large number of basic services to become available to all citizens only if they are provided through public expenditure. . . . But the citizen in developed societies tends to believe that what he spends on the public good through taxation—the 'tax bite'—is less valuable than what he can choose for him-

self. . . . [He is] the first to point to any failure, any disappoint-
ment in public spending as proof that the 'tax bite' is not doing
its job and should be suitably reduced.[1]

Earlier in this book we acknowledged the human capacity to "till the
earth and keep it" as a gift of God the Creator, a sign of God's love for
humanity and the earth itself. Society-building is part of the human task,
and justice for all its members is one God-given requirement of society.
Nowhere in the Bible is poverty treated as a historic inevitability. (Those
who are fond of quoting Jesus on this point—"you have the poor among
you always"—should study the context of the statement in all three Gospels
and especially the context of Mark 14:7: "You always have the poor with
you, and whenever you will, you can do good to them.") Jews and Christians needed only their Bibles, not the latter-day outcries of socialism, to
tell them that human effort, informed by political will, can ameliorate
poverty. In turn, will must be animated by the pulse beat of vision. American cities have developed without much of a vision. We have proposed
shalom, in all its rich implications, as a vision adequate to the historic
need of our cities. This chapter examines some critical urban policy issues
in the context of this vision.

NEIGHBORHOODS: THERE'S MORE TO BE SAID

Carl Holman, longtime President of the National Urban Coalition,
said this about federal urban policy: "I believe that the creation and the
growth of strong, vital urban neighborhoods is key to full revitalization of
our cities and that without a neighborhoods emphasis any urban policy
must founder for want of foundation."[2] The National Urban Coalition
has been a principal and effective advocate for the urban poor. Holman
is aware of what many other urban analysts are not, namely, that the urban
poor live in neighborhoods.

Neighborhoods are not just characteristics of a few scattered ethnic
groups. Neighborhooding is a universal sociological phenomenon. People
live and act together in groups. Land is vital to this interaction. Humans
build not only social groups, but neighborhoods, each of which acquires
its own character, much like urban villages. The neighborhood issue cuts
across racial, ethnic and class lines. Failure to recognize that the needs
of the urban poor cannot be satisfied apart from the neighborhood has
been one of the dominant factors in the failure of many of America's public
housing projects.

The symbol of this failure is the celebrated Pruitt Igoe high-rise complex in St. Louis, Missouri. Hailed as a tribute to modern architectural design when it was erected, it won a prestigious award. Today there are pictures of it in almost every book on housing, but not of the sleek concrete and brick structure with severe architectural lines. The pictures are of the building being blown apart, literally. Within twenty years, it had experienced such social breakdown among its residents that it was virtually uninhabitable.

If the building of neighborhoods requires more than sheer apartment space, it requires more than sheer commerce, too. Holman rightly notes the inadequacy of condominium development, gentrification, and "boutiqueization" in older neighborhoods. A neighborhood is not a bazaar for weekend visitors from the suburbs. It is rather the cell of the urban body-politic on whose health the *shalom* of the city itself depends. The emphasis of the Carter urban policy on neighborhood building was clear though weak. Holman's principle must be expanded rather than eliminated from federal concern.

Many churches have a good track record in the neighborhoods as the source, often the sole source, of funds, support, and services for residents. Most often, these resources have been made available from the wellspring of the churches' mission to the suffering, inspired by the frequent biblical mandates to feed the hungry, cloth the naked, visit the imprisoned.

These same churches need to advocate an urban policy that supports neighborhoods. This appropriate church activity dovetails with the mission of the churches, most of which have stated that their intention is to create community. Neighborhoods are historic communities. They are concentrations of people cooperatively interacting out of a set of overlapping values and concerns.

It makes sense that the churches be concerned about sustaining these historic communities. Urban planners, public policy makers, and industrial, corporate, and business executives have contributed, through self-interest or insensitivity, to the destruction of neighborhoods. Who needs to be reminded of the impact on urban neighborhoods of public policy that encouraged new construction over revitalization? Or of urban planning that split viable neighborhoods with highways, or tore down stable residential areas to make room for shopping malls or new department stores? Or of the internal readjustment caused by the movement of industry from frostbelt to sunbelt, or of the horrors that a Love Canal or Three Mile Island imposes on a community?

The suburbanization of religion in America also played its part in the neglect of neighborhoods. Churches that were not territorially defined put a greater priority on following a fleeing urban population than preserving the urban networks that so drastically needed this support through times of painful social change. The migrating churches forgot the Christian call to justice for all, and failed to see that the new urban immigrants needed the stability, respectability, advocacy that only the established churches could supply. They put nurturing over enabling.

Besides their mission to create and sustain community, another theological factor that should motivate church activity for a neighborhood-founded urban policy is related to the theology of creation discussed earlier in this book. The churches should be concerned about helping neighborhood residents refurbish their divine imagehood, helping them become stewards of a creation which is a gift of God and of a previous human generation. For the most part, Americans have built their cities with confused, inconsistent expectations of both permanence and change in neighborhood structures. Paradoxically, as historian Sam Bass Warner points out, we have celebrated change and mobility as a national way of life but have attempted to fortify certain urban neighborhoods and suburbs against change by zoning-out the industries, the social classes, and the racial diversity that make the city as a whole a workable and livable human place. To "preserve the neighborhood" has too often been synonymous with keeping all "undesirables" out of the neighborhood, even when its residents require just this diversity for their economic prosperity.

Also contradicting the popular suburban goal of neighborhood-preservation has been the system of land-investment and mortgage-financing that have served middle-class aspirations in one generation only to undermine them in the next generation. Neither suburban nor inner-city neighborhoods can be preserved against the relentless tides of metropolitan housing shortages, the resulting rise in land prices, and the increase in taxes and property values that may ironically make some suburban homes too expensive even for their owners. Aiding and hastening these developments, especially over the past fifty years, have been policies of the federal government that have assumed that subsidizing the homes of middle-class Americans will have a beneficial effect on poor Americans to whom middle-class houses eventually trickle down. Warner describes this system succinctly:

> New housing is built for the middle class and the upper levels of the working class, and all others inherit what is vacated by these. Thus the quality of housing in a given city depends directly upon its quantity. If there is a shortage of housing . . . then those least able to pay rents must double up and occupy unfit structures,

and the immediate result is "slum conditions unfavorable to that self-respecting family life upon which the security of our democracy rests."[3]

This surge of the middle classes out of the city into the suburbs is marked by the old tide-lines of deteriorating housing tracts. The deterioration has been hastened by two interlocking programs of the federal government invented by the New Deal of the 1930s: home mortgage insurance for the middle class and public housing for the poor. The one program enabled a considerable number of professional and skilled Americans to "escape" the city into the suburbs and to leave behind their previous housing into which larger numbers of the poor might crowd. The other program segregated the poor, often in a single racial group, into a "housing project" lifestyle that "stigmatized the beneficiaries as second-class citizens."[4] It was as if, with their own government's connivance, Americans had agreed that, by looking at any urban house, one should know clearly whether the occupant were on welfare or not.

The combined result of this system in the American city of the 1980s is not only a more radical segregation of the poor than has characterized most periods of our national history, but also the continued decline of almost any neighborhood's ability to control its own future. In the inflation-ridden economy of the 1980s, one must be very rich and politically very powerful to combat the impact of land-value increases, rising rents, and declining municipal services upon one's own wealthy suburb. Even there the internal economic forces act on the command of governments, corporations, and interests external to the neighborhood. And if this is the case with the wealthy, how much more is it the case with the poor neighborhoods of the city?

Human beings want a say to shape their own future. They want an environment in which a livable future may be possible. The hope for increasing a neighborhood's control of its destiny need not be absolute. Indeed, from the perspective of creatures subject to a Creator, nothing about human intentions should be absolutized, and the reversion of all urban neighborhoods to a "we-first" system of self-determination would be an imitation of the worst side of suburban isolationism. But the neighborhoods of our cities are too much the pawns of forces over which their residents have no say whatsoever. The balance of influence needs redress. That is what the neighborhood government movement is all about.

The principle of this movement might be reduced to the principle of "subsidiarity," says Andrew Greeley: No bigger than necessary. This means that no decision should be made on the federal level that can be handled on the state level, and no decision on the state level that can be dealt with adequately on the municipal level and on the municipal that the neighborhood can effectively control. It contrasts with the "New Federalism," which intends to divest the federal government of all responsibility for cities and neighborhoods. It says that each level of government has its proper role, and that role needs to be carefully defined.

Subsidiarity and human scale are complementary concepts. A reigning myth taken for granted, but yet to be proven, is that bigger is better. It has been effectively challenged by E. F. Schumacher in his seminal study, *Small Is Beautiful*. He demonstrated the use of this principle of subsidiarity in economics. A neighborhoods urban policy is possible because it has been well demonstrated that neighborhoods are large enough to administer programs, solve problems that involve: housing, unemployment, crime, education, economic development, delivery of human services and community credit. A neighborhood whose residents initiate their own solutions to any of these problems will be "self-governing" in significant ways.

Not all problems can be handled on a neighborhood level. Transportation systems, for example, or sewerage and water systems, all require larger administrative units than the neighborhood for adequate management. A neighborhood urban policy means subsidiarity, solving problems on the level where they should be solved. It requires a careful assessment of the weight each jurisdiction in the federal system can realistically bear.

The Carter urban policy, "A New Partnership to Conserve America's Communities," made a commendable start in this direction. It clearly perceived that the magnitude of urban problems demanded the participation of all parties concerned. The "New Partnership" is made up of federal, state and municipal officials, the private sector, and neighborhoods and voluntary groups. (These last two are sometimes referred to as the voluntary sector.) In theory, the neighborhood was raised from client to partner. Neighborhoods were to take part in shaping their own futures.

One weakness of the policy is that it marries by fiat groups that have historically been at odds with each other. Whether or not these groups can work together is an idea that needs to be tested. Neighborhoods are being asked to work today with bankers who yesterday redlined them, bankers with groups they regarded as non-profitable.

Can the partnership work? The burgeoning of Neighborhood Housing Services across urban America suggests the answer is yes, possibly. The Neighborhood Housing Services are legal corporations whose boards of directors are made up of bankers, developers, local government and neighborhood residents. Their mission is neighborhood revitalization based on actual neighborhood needs. They seem to be working, perhaps because they serve the self-interest of the banks who have found urban revitalization suddenly profitable. The neighborhood has little to protect itself other than the goodwill of the participating banking community.

In the Carter urban policy, the neighborhood is the weakest partner. It has just returned from the urban battle scarred by the policies and practice of the other partners who have the resources to take care of their own interests. The neighborhoods do not. Moreover, even the Carter policy provided them with few additional resources.

The Reagan Administration has been insensitive to neighborhood needs in the domestic policy maneuvers it has made on the budget. It has completely eliminated the Office of Neighborhoods at the Department of Housing and Urban Development, and it has chosen to eliminate the one urban program that was directed towards empowerment on the neighborhood level, the Neighborhood Self-Help Program. The program funneled twenty million dollars each year directly to neighborhood groups around the country. Hardly a drop in the bucket of federal outlays, the money was to be used, not only to improve the neighborhood, but to increase the capacity of area residents to shape the future of their neighborhood. It was a successful program. The neighborhood groups demonstrated, as they have many times before, that they can use the federal dollar more effectively than any other governmental or business sector of society.

At issue here is the Reagan Administration's emphasis on the development of physical capital and its insensitivity to the development of human capital, namely, the capabilities of citizens to participate fully in shaping their own and our national well-being. Besides those mentioned above, capacity-building programs that the present administration has attempted to cut, with varying degrees of success, are student loan programs, job training programs and the National Consumer Cooperative Bank. All were to enable persons and groups to take the initiative in shaping their own futures.

For the idea of a New Partnership really to work, neighborhoods have to become the keystone. The most effective way to do this is for the federal government to take the initiative. Once it does, others will follow.

That a neighborhood urban policy is possible, has been demonstrated by the 1979 report of the National Commission on Neighborhoods. This presidentially-appointed commission resulted from the efforts of neighborhood groups intent on determining which federal policies were damaging to neighborhoods.

The Commission, which included neighborhood advocates from the black, Hispanic and white ethnic communities as well as government officials from the legislative and executive branches, published a compendium of over 200 recommendations with this bold purpose: "To reorganize our society—away from the stranglehold of a relative few with a near monopoly of power and money in political, social and economic institutions to a new democratic system of grassroots involvement that allows individuals to have control over their lives."[5]

Unfortunately the Commission Report does not constitute a coherent policy. While it addresses a wide spectrum of problems, it does not establish priorities and has no apparent organizing principle. Nor does it communicate a sense of the relative magnitude of each of the problems it addresses. It is obviously a document that has resulted from a series of compromises made by the Commissioners. The report, however, indicates that a neighborhoods urban policy is feasible. Some of the issues that would have to be addressed are neighborhood reinvestment, neighborhood economic development, neighborhood delivery system for human services, neighborhood self-governance, citizen participation, neighborhood empowerment, the problem of racial and ethnic minorities, community full employment and the legal, fiscal, and administrative obstacles to neighborhood self-reliance.

These, however, require an organizing principle. A neighborhoods urban policy could be organized along four dimensions suggested by Dr. Stanley Hallett of the Center for Urban Affairs: tools, techniques, resources and authority. Fundamentally what the neighborhoods and cities need are not big programs that would provide large amounts of goods and services. This would keep them dependent. What they need is access to the appropriate techniques, tools, resources, and authority to provide for themselves. Policy developed along those lines would enable urbanites with a range of effective capacities to manage many of their own affairs.

In addition, the principle of subsidiarity would ensure the necessary pluralism that urban policy requires. While it is resisted mightily by entrenched forces in public policy, pluralism in public policy is largely a matter of common sense. It merely recognizes the existence of regional, racial, ethnic, and economic differences. It recognizes, for example, that the same program or method that would solve the problems of San Jose, a city in the midst of flourishing economic growth, may not begin to deal with the needs of New York or Cleveland, or any other city.

Pluralism acknowledges that different racial and cultural groups, while they share certain values, have value systems that are organized according to varying sets of priorities. Ethnic writers point out that family may be the primary value for one group, while land may be of prime importance for another. Some groups put the relationship between person and things first; others, the interpersonal relationship; still others, the relationship between the individual and the group. Each of these value systems would give a different shape to public policy formation, and they need be given full sway. Humans have a right to actualize their humanness to the fullness in open social interaction. This, along with the principles described above, could be developed into an urban policy that is sensitive to the justice requirements of *shalom*. It would enable the urban poor to shape their own lives and future. It would enable them to acquire power in negotiating national political debate. Then it would no longer be necessary for them to see themselves "as men and women coping with the city and not as participants in its building."[6]

ISSUES IN THE "NEW PARTNERSHIP": PRIVATE AND PUBLIC SECTORS

A function of government is to regulate the economic, environmental, and social behavior of private enterprise in a manner that protects the interests of the wider public. Government intervention, unfortunately, is often depicted only as a constraining force on private enterprise, as a brake on corporate greed. Seldom is sufficient attention paid to government's role in protecting and safeguarding the private sector, or in stimulating economic activity. Yet, many regulatory agencies were created not only with the intention of protecting the public from the wayward practices of private enterprise, but also to provide a stable and, sometimes, less harsh competitive environment for private enterprise.

Government, especially on the federal level, has intervened in economic activity in a variety of ways.

(1) Government intervention has been used to provide goods and services the private sector cannot provide such as expenditures for military hardware and social welfare. National defense is provided for through the Defense Department, while the Department of Health and Human Services plays a key role in making human services available for the needy. Even staunch advocates of free enterprise accept this function, especially in the case of military expenditures. One of the regrettable bits of ideological blindness in President Reagan's budgetary planning is that military protection is among the few unquestioned obligations of the federal government to the nation as a whole.

(2) In some countries, government has intervened to take over a few functions of the private sector. In some cases, government runs the railroads, supplies the electricity, or pays the medical bills. In its classic form, this is socialism whereby the government owns and controls the major means of production and distribution, even those that could be profitably operated by the private sector. The United States has not moved far enough in this direction to be called socialist.

(3) Government has intervened to take over those sectors of the economy that the private sector can no longer operate profitably. This kind of intervention, sometimes referred to as "socializing the losers," or "lemon socialism" might become a reality in the United States. Federal support of Amtrak, the railroads, parts of the steel industry and other failing enterprises, are all steps toward "lemon socialism" as are government bailouts of segments of the aerospace or auto industries.

(4) The American federal system structures governmental intervention into the citizen's life in complex, multi-leveled ways familiar to all students of the Constitution. Current Reagan Administration budget policy makes much of a "return to state and local responsibility" for government help to the lives of citizens. Rhetorically this sounds similar to the principle of subsidiarity; and in principle there is nothing sacred about the particular level of government that one may choose to meet a human social need. The policy question is whether that level can and will meet the need. One of the lessons of the 1930s is that the states of the United States are less likely to meet some needs inside their own borders than is the federal government, which has access to the resources of the nation as a whole.

At stake here is both a philosophical and an economic issue. Philosophically, in his 1980 campaign, candidate Reagan made it clear that he opposed asking the citizens of Sioux Falls to pay taxes for the support of mass transit in Los Angeles. Carry that logic far enough, and one gets the argument that led to the American Civil War of 1861–65. Presumably that war "decided" that the parts of the American people were "one and inseparable." It is appropriate therefore that the federal government should use the taxes of one region to support the needs of another. Justice requires an exchange of benefits in such a distribution, and it may also require the subsidiarity that funnels some federally-collected tax monies to the control of state and local governments. But that is where questions of the resulting state and local fiscal strength come in. It is one thing to prefer governmental action at the level closest to the people, it is another to expect local governments to depend on their own resources. It is yet another for a national government so to reallocate its own resources that it takes resources from locales in service to other national interests. This, in effect, is what has happened in the Reagan budget, whose basic contrast with previous budgets has been its transfer of monies from social programs to national defense. Longtime Republican and supporter of the Reagan Administration, Mayor William Hudnut III of Indianapolis, Indiana, raised just this complaint in late 1981 when at a meeting of the National League of Cities he brought out into the open just how frustrated state and local officials have become over the administration's refusal to make significant cuts in military spending. "The nub of our argument is simple," he said. "Two thirds of the cuts made in the budget so far have come from the 15 percent of the budget that contains money for states and localities. We're being asked to do more than our share."[7] In this context, the military budget of the national government is a powerful negative intervention into the texture of relations between state and local governments and their citizens. Far from strengthening these grassroots governments, the new defense-minded national administration is depriving them of power. More important, it is depriving them of the ability to meet human needs to which they have long been committed.

(5) Fundamental to the Carter urban program was the principle of financial leveraging. It represented the way government can intervene in the private sector by stimulating specific economic development (in partnership with private enterprise) or redirecting economic growth to achieve particular social ends. This has been referred to as the public/private marriage. Like any form of wedlock, it has its good and its irksome points.

The word "leverage" has gained some bureaucratic prominence in the past few years. Most accurately, it depicts the use of public funds to stimulate innovative private capital investment. The venerable technique of "matching grants" whereby the granting institution will supply funds in proportion to money raised from other sources is a form of leveraging. Sometimes, however, the word "leveraging" is used to cover up the declining amounts of government funds available for projects.

In the Carter urban program, leveraging had been invoked to direct government monies to create a new partnership between the public and private sectors. Because the private/public marriage was so central to the Carter policy, and because we believe it should influence all future urban policy, a closer examination of the concept is warranted. It appears that while the marriage is necessary in a capitalist society, it is limited in what it can accomplish.

There are structures already in place which throw light on this marriage, namely, the "public authorities," which are hybrids of the mechanisms of the public and private sectors. Many authorities operate bridges, airports, buses, and other public means of transportation such as the Port Authority of New York, the Chicago Transit Authority, and BART in San Francisco.

These public authorities were created by legislative action in order to bypass the bureaucratic machinery of politics and government. They are not bound by regulation nor are they subject to the political budgetary process. Their primary function is to perform specific tasks such as the regulation of public transportation. Unencumbered by the political process, they possess certain privileges of government, including tax-free status and the ability to sell tax-exempt bonds. While receiving both indirect and direct government subsidies, the public authorities depend upon the private market for capital.

In an excellent critique of the social performance of public authorities, Annmarie Hauck Walsh noted that their reliance on private investment has had a skewing effect on their development. Most authorities undertake only those projects that promise reasonable rates of return. Thus their service to the public is conditioned by a project's profit margin. Operations that would serve the public interest are avoided if they cannot produce sufficient revenue to satisfy potential bondholders. Walsh points out that as a result, authorities favor physical development over responding to social needs: highways over mass transit, school buildings over student coun-selling, industrial parks over small business assistance, support of new housing construction over rehabilitation and low-income rental units.[8] This suggests that government monies can be directed to projects more favorable to private profit than public interest.

Because of the privileges granted to them by government, public authorities have enjoyed some advantages over the public and private sectors. Because of their independence from the political budgetary process, they usually have operating flexibility, unencumbered with civil service regulations that might prevent efficient management. Both these assets allow them to move more rapidly and creatively than a government agency. Their tax-free or low-tax status and ability to sell tax-exempt bonds give them an appeal to investors that the private sector envies but does not enjoy.

But there are also self-perpetuating tendencies, the sacrifice of social responsibility to profitability, the equating of profitability with the public interest. As the career of Robert Moses in New York illustrated so dra-matically, vast amounts of power can be accumulated by the managers of these "public" authorities, which in fact are not accountable to any public judgment at all. Private/public partnership can be an effective instrument to get some things done, but social objectives and goals can become greatly influenced by the criteria of profitability.

Government intervention into economic affairs can provide the necessary context for economic growth, it can stimulate specific economic activities, and it can redirect economic growth to places of greatest need. For example, the Interstate Highway system could only have been possible through the aegis of the federal government. It is an infrastructure which leverages economic activity such as new housing construction, shopping malls, industrial parks, secondary roads, commercial developments. There are, however, several proposals to consider that are usually ignored in such economic planning.

Government funds should stimulate economic development in areas of greatest social need and in a manner that provides maximum social benefit. This would provide a hedge against the encroachment of profitability into the public interest. It would also oil the wheels of social and distributive justice. Such an approach would call into question tax exemptions and the "trickle down" theory to stimulate economic growth.

There is a need for an economic impact analysis to be done prior to funding a project. Unlike the typical cost-benefit analysis that deals with aggregates, this analysis should consider the distributional aspects of economic growth. Who pays the costs and who receives the benefits? The economic impact analysis has to be done by the public sector, for the public interest is its special concern.

Earlier in this book, the need for citizen participation in the political process was stressed. Another area that needs serious revamping is the role of the citizens in economic planning. Citizen participation in basic economic planning is sorely needed if democracy is to be extended to the economic arena. Not much has been done to foster this, especially in projects where large amounts of private investment funding are employed. Many of the regulations requiring citizen participation have been or are being rescinded by the present administration. The promotion of an economic impact analysis and citizens' involvement in economic planning are elements virtually foreign to private investment decision-making, although that is beginning to change. Both of these will make any project seem less attractive to private enterprise. The private sector is wary of excessive government regulation and work that does not produce a profit. If the project has a high risk, business will demand a high rate of return on its capital as a condition for participation. Private enterprise can be expected to participate at a modest rate of return only if the risks are very low. Lowering those risks can be costly for government, but it will probably be one of the prerequisites for private sector participation. The business community fears a serious capital shortage, and has other, often more profitable, investment opportunities.

The familiar "turnkey" technique (by which the government initiates a project that is then turned over to the private sector) might not be the recipe for dealing with urban woes. This is a foundation mentality of funding that has only recently spread to government.

Often there simply are no sources other than the original funders. Consider, for instance, the rent supplement program. Ongoing government subsidies are needed in order to allow people to take advantage of private housing opportunities. Just what would the unemployed, the elderly, those on welfare, do if this money were withdrawn?

Government initiation and private sector continuance of a socially beneficial project is sweet in theory, but often unrealistic in practice. That posture would promote a migration toward those economic ventures that are profitable. Unfortunately, many serious social problems are not profitable to solve. That is one major reason for serious social problems.

In many instances, therefore, the private/public marriage has to be a lasting venture. Such a marriage will have its strains. Both partners will eventually have to assess whether it is worth staying together. This the private sector will do routinely; the public sector needs to do likewise. There are questions the public sector should ask. Is the government supporting a venture that it could more profitably do by itself? If the private sector withdrew, what course would the government take? Would it continue even if it could do so less effectively? Or, would the entire project be killed in the political process? These are not unimportant questions when the public welfare is at stake.

The Carter urban policy relied heavily upon the public/private sector marriage. Whether or not the social limits of such an arrangement have been fully recognized is not clear. The Reagan Administration has, for all practical purposes, eschewed the entire idea, choosing rather a "supply-side" bias favoring industrial productivity.

Ultimately, it is not sufficient for government to try to redirect the flow of private capital. It needs to have some control over that flow. This will seem like socialism to some, but what is being spoken of is not socialism in the traditional sense. Karl Mannheim noted that the dilemma was not capitalism or socialism. In the United States, he pointed out, society is ordered by the cumulative effect of a series of independent private decisions. The cumulative pattern is based on the suboptimization of individual decisions, and not on the optimization of the national welfare. If the government can set the policies for which goals are to be met, the private sector can be called upon to use its genius to help the nation achieve them. That involves a large role for the public sector in economic planning, while it allows the operating flexibility and management skills of the private sector to have full sway. The genius of the public sector lies in its ability to get the private sector to participate out of its own self-interest.

One proposal is to regulate corporate relocation by requiring a corporation that is moving out of an area to pay some of the costs for ameliorating the social impacts of its exodus. Legislation on the state level would be ineffective; it might heighten the economic competition between states. Only national legislation will suffice. Some argue that such legislation will accelerate the outflow of multinational capital from the United States, an argument that leads to regulating the flow of multinational capital. Another way to move in that direction is to seek the establishment of public investment banking institutions as the National Consumer Cooperative Bank or the aborted National Development Bank as alternatives to private money markets for the financing of public enterprises. These deserve further investigation.

The issues are complicated both on an ideological and technical level. Creative private/public marriages are delicate balancing acts. Slogans about "free enterprise capitalism" or a "socialist reconstruction" are unhelpful and will further strain discussion already polarized. The essential contribution of Christian ethics and the churches to the discussion must be in their insistence on the ability of a rich country to structure its economy for doing justice to all segments of its citizenry including the poorest. The basic argument, from the Christian perspective, will always be over which system serves best the cause of justice.

LAND OWNERSHIP: AN OVERLOOKED ISSUE

The city's chronic problems of poverty, crime, slums, joblessness, and blight stem in large measure from a serious imbalance in the ratio of land to people. The imaginative and often heroic measures launched to improve cities are frequently undermined by a basic injustice in land tenure arrangements.

Land is more than some soil for farming or support for buildings. It encompasses all natural resources: rivers, oceans, coal, oil, and other minerals beneath the surface. Among the most valuable and productive lands are urban sites where the majority of people live and work. Without equal access to land, equality of opportunity is a sham. The widespread denial of equal access to land spawns major social and economic distress.

Even though the Jews had just fled Egyptian slavery, Moses feared that they might nevertheless enslave themselves and others if they ignored the primary land-people equation. He therefore institutionalized a periodic redistribution of the land in the Jubilee year every half century as a means of preventing the division of society into landed and landless, master and servant, rich and poor. The mechanisms spelled out by Moses, geared to a time when families could easily pack up their tents and belongings, are not adaptable to today's society. It is not certain that the precepts of the Jubilee were put into practice in biblical times. Yet, the underlying philosophy is even more imperative in an urban culture and modern equivalents of the Jubilee need to be shaped.

Because of their homeland's size and large unsettled areas, Americans until recently considered land problems a peculiar concern of other countries. In the eighteenth and nineteenth centuries, Europe had old civilizations with rich cultures and numerous magnificent cities. Yet the downtrodden and persecuted peoples of the Old World streamed to this land that, in the modern vernacular, would have been called backward and underdeveloped. The newcomers were attracted by what they lacked on the other side of the Atlantic: access to a continent's resources. Once freed of feudal, landlord-dominated systems, they were no longer satisfied to remain as serfs and peasants. They were drawn by the open land and shaped by it. The wealth of land, its vastness and inexpensiveness, led them to take it for granted and forget its importance.

Settlers brought European land ownership theories and practices with them. Spaniards tended to preempt vast acreages. For the most part, however, early land grabbers left a great deal for others. While some owners caused hardships along the Eastern seaboard by holding out for high rents and sale prices, the frontier, with free or cheap land, was an escape for the poor. Where landlords and employers were too greedy and made conditions too harsh, their tenants and hired hands could and did head for the west.

Native Americans, however, did not fare so well. Like Moses they believed that land was a gift of the Creator to all people. The notions that some could exact payments from others for use of the earth, and that one generation could bargain away the birthright to the land of future generations were foreign and repugnant to them. The newcomers were too busy dispossessing the red "savages" to learn this land ethic from them.

The seemingly endless expanse of forests, plains and town sites fed

America's land hunger through periods of great agricultural, industrial, and urban expansion. The twentieth century suddenly found the country basically all fenced in. Those at the bottom rungs of the ladder were increasingly at the mercy of those who had arrived first. When poverty festered, those in power turned down the spigot of immigration, set up barriers against foreign trade, and looked with hope to the new demigod of technology. Meanwhile, economic prosperity boomed. The New Deal, the Fair Deal, New Frontier, Great Society, and New Federalism presided over what appeared to be a long period of prosperity.

Beneath the surface, however, urban problems were worsening and they continue to do so. Unemployment was "solved" by officially declaring that full employment implied a jobless rate of 3 percent, then 4 percent, then 5 percent and higher. The higher-than-average unemployment rates in the ghettos were ignored. The goals of decent housing and livable environments for all Americans led to a slew of federal programs, but some of the cures were as bad as the disease. Housing that used to cost people 15 or 20 percent of their income now wrings out 35 percent or more. Rental construction came to a dead halt in many cities during the 1970s, making prospects for housing the poor even more bleak. Cities that sit on the most valuable real estate in the nation are pleading poverty, hovering on the brink of bankruptcy. Business, industry, and residents continue to flee the city, sprawling into suburbia and exurbia.

Fueling these problems are a distorted land system and a tax system that favors the misuse and abuse of land. To understand these distortions, one needs to know how land values are created. There are three factors to consider.

First, all the people of an area, by their very existence, are prime generators of land value. Population pressure creates demands for work and living space. The more people in a city or metropolis, the higher its land prices.

Second, all the people, as taxpayers, contribute to land value through government activities. Schools, firehouses, streets, police, sewer and water lines, parks—the whole gamut of public facilities and services—enhance neighborhoods and are converted into higher land values.

Third, inherent qualities, fertility in farmland, scenic views, and advantageous locations in cities make certain land attractive. Natural endowments have been properly characterized as "the common heritage of humankind" by the people who have been drawing up an international Law of the Seas.

Landlords often create values on the land. But the value of the land itself is almost exclusively a product of social action, population pressures, and God-given qualities. These land values belong to all the people, yet we subscribe to a system that gives the lion's share of land value to a small minority. Over half of the country's agricultural land is now farmed by tenants. Giant coal firms have been absorbed by even larger gas and oil companies. The prime commercial and industrial sites in cities are held by increasingly wealthy individuals and corporations. Even home ownership is questionable. Savings and loans associations, insurance firms, and banks hold mortgages and represent a concentration of the equity in the nation's housing. By and large, our landholding system is redistributing wealth from the poor to the rich.

Washington, D.C. is completing a highly praised subway system. When completed it will be 101 miles long, extending deep into suburban Maryland and Virginia. It is meeting with such success that the opening of just three new stations along the route has increased the ridership of the young system by 17,000.

Land development around the stations of Metro has been remarkable. The Dupont Circle area, abandoned by the middle class in the late 1960s, has blossomed overnight into a vibrant commercial and residential area populated by the new, young, middle class. Convenience stores and boutiques selling speciality items have sprung up all around the station. An area once known for only two restaurants is dotted with cafes, natural food restaurants, bars.

Three pocket cinemas have opened catering to a clientele that favors foreign films and the likes of Woody Allen. Rents have doubled and tripled. Efficiency apartments are renting for $400.00. Condomania is subdividing every large building within walking distance. One-bedroom apartments, costing anywhere from $24,000 to $45,000 once, have doubled in value in eighteen months. Two-bedroom apartments—not houses—have been sold for between $175,000 and $200,000.

This scenario has been replayed around station after station. Yet the Metro system is constantly on the verge of bankruptcy. User fees cannot be made high enough to support it. The area governments (the District of Columbia, Northern Virginia, Southern Maryland) are constantly looking for creative new ways to finance the project. The private investor, not the public, is benefitting from the leveraging created by Metro, by the value the peopling of downtown Washington, D.C. has brought to the land.

A just system of private property would rest on the valid principle that people are entitled to reap what they sow, to retain what they produce, directly or indirectly. The private siphoning-off of publicly created land values does not conform to this principle. Moreover, when society fails to recapture and recycle the social values in the land, government is forced to turn to the very people who were deprived of their share of land values, overtaxing them to meet public expenses. Rampant landlordism is antagonistic to an enterprise system. It stifles more initiative than it permits.

The federal government fosters landlordism by giving favored treatment to profits from land values, called the "unearned increment" by economists. For example, gains in land value are taxed far more lightly than income from wages and salaries.

State and local governments, through the property tax, are major distorters of the land system. The property tax is actually two taxes of very different kinds and very different effects, glued together as if they were one. One tax is on land values, the other on improvements—homes, office buildings, stores, barns or other structures—on the land.

The land tax is one of the best taxes, the tax on improvements one of the worst. The land tax is good because it has the ability to return to the public what the public has created. In this situation, the one who is using the land is paying a "rent," a tax commensurate to the value given to the land by the public. Where the land tax is high enough, and where it is strictly proportional to the differential advantages pertaining to each site, it helps put all of society on an equal footing without constantly moving people about. To view land this way, of course, is to take some exception to the notion of private property as an absolute. It is to put, over against that notion, the social-economic facts that contribute to land value.

The improvements tax is detrimental, almost ludicrous. It says, in effect, that the more you improve your house or business property, the better you maintain it, and the more people you employ in these activities, the more society will penalize you for your efforts. Conversely, if you let the roof cave in, create a neighborhood eyesore, or let your site go into utter disuse, the assessor lowers the property valuation so that your annual taxes will be less than those on adjacent well-used sites. In some cases, neglect is rewarded even further by subdivision into multiple rental units which increases the value of the property without ameliorating its physical condition. Indeed, the very deterioration of overcrowded housing may hasten its condemnation with inflated compensation for its rental value.

In most localities, land values are taxed too lightly and improvements too heavily, the reverse of what justice and common sense call for. Land values tend to rise at a faster rate than almost anything else. In the three decades after 1949, the consumer price index rose 300 percent. During the same period, the price of the average new house rose 500 percent. But the land under that average house rose 1275 percent!

Because the annual increases in site values are usually far greater than the annual tax, the incentive to hold land for its future value rather than for its present productive use is substantial. This incentive is magnified by the high tax penalties imposed when owners try to put land to good use. This helps explain why so much central city land is held in minimal use— surface parking lots, slum housing, stores with empty upper floors, and the like. Such uses are known in the real estate trade as "taxpayers" because they yield enough income to cover taxes and other holding costs while the owners wait for their site values to rise.

Land speculation in the heart of a city denies urban developers access to the most productive sites. At less suitable sites, their productivity and labor force are reduced. Seeking cheaper land, businesses invade residential areas or they go beyond the city limits. Disruption of neighborhoods, unemployment, sprawl in the countryside, and wasted urban resources are the fruits of land speculation.

A common but incorrect impression is that most blighted urban land is a sore on the market, an outward sign of the owners' distress. In isolated instances this is the case. But potential buyers find that most blighted land often is held by wealthy owners who are holding out for ultra-high prices.

Under the right kind of property tax—high on land and low or non-existent on homes and other buildings—these high urban land values can be the salvation of the city:

- By tapping the great store of value at their very doorsteps, cities can revive local treasuries. Cities can then offer a decent level of basic services, including good schools and better crime protection.
- Taxing these high land values can provide the leverage for bringing idle sites into use. As the site tax rises, to pay the tax bill, the owner would be under pressure to make use of the site's potential or sell to someone else who wishes to put it to appropriate use.
- This, in turn, can restore full employment to cities. Vacant sites average 25 percent of all privately held land in the hundred largest cities. Bringing these and the underused sites out of cold storage can open up a great new frontier at the centers of metropolitan areas. Proper public policies, reversing the present situation, can give landusers the upper hand over landholders.
- Creative use of land values can restore competition, vitality and quality to the housing market. When builders are no longer penalized in proportion to their construction investments, and when

owners are no longer penalized for keeping buildings in good repair, rental and other units will be profitable to build. With a greater supply of dwelling units, there will be a tendency to suppress increases in rents.

• Perhaps most important of all, the equitable distribution of land values will help restore a sense of social justice to American communities. Tentacles of misguided land policies reach into many aspects of metropolitan life. Yet, because intellectual and political leaders have been slow to articulate the causes and remedies, despair and pessimism are widely felt.

Urban problems are too complex to be ascribed to any single factor. But it seems clear that the land question has been among the major missing ingredients of recent strategies to help cities.

THE REGIONAL FACTOR IN URBAN POLICY

President Carter's Commission for a National Agenda for the 1980s turned out to be bad news for the citizens of the northeast and the midwest. The commission redlined that quadrant of the nation, claiming that public policy should be reoriented to assist migration to the sunbelt. Were this to happen, the consequences for the nation and the citizens of the northeast and midwest could be drastic. It would mean the further deterioration of the major urban centers of this region and the economies of the thousands of towns and villages whose lifelines play into them. While economy does not define the essence of the person, or circumscribe the whole of the human personality, it is inextricably woven into the fabric of our political, social, cultural, psychological, and religious well-being. The economy supports and strengthens these more crucial factors in social interrelationships.

It is our national good fortune that the urban policy recommendations in the commission report have been rejected by Carter and by prominent spokespersons of the Reagan Administration. The underlying issues of the commission's report were geographic disparities and inequities in urban policy.

There has been a marked reluctance among urban policy makers and analysts officially to recognize the need for pluralism in public policy, but regional favoritism has become a factor in its implementation. Since Franklin Delano Roosevelt declared that southern poverty was a problem of national importance requiring concerted federal attention, there have been numerous federal programs that have abetted the development of the entire sunbelt region. There have been beneficial programs in the areas of rural electrification, interstate highways, water policy, port developments, defense siting policies, corporation taxation policy. The growth of the south has been supported and paid for by the northeast and midwest through its tax dollars and its political support of these programs. From 1975 to 1979, the eighteen state northeast-midwest cumulative deficit in its federal balance of payments was 165 billion dollars. In the sunbelt, the ratio was reversed. As Sam Bass Warner observes about Los Angeles, the modern growth of that city can be largely accounted for by the huge investments of the federal government during and since World War II in defense industries, highways, and airports. Los Angeles is a major example of what national planning can achieve in affecting the growth of a metropolis.

Also reversed are the needs of both regions. The image of the south has changed from one of slow-moving cities and aging plantations to that of burgeoning growth. The fastest growing cities in the nation (San Jose, Phoenix, Fort Lauderdale, Houston, for example) are in the sunbelt. The popular image of the sunbelt city is the "Dallas" which serves as background for the soap opera. The image of the north is closer to the crime-infected cities with aging buildings, dirty streets, large concentrations of the poor and indigent suggested by the names and content of such movies as *Fort Apache*.

That is the image of the cities. The perception is, alas, often different from the reality. That the frostbelt is in the midst of industrial decline is largely a myth generated by the way the statistics are read. The traditional methods of predicting economic decline distort reality and foster the myths of decline. When economists measure growth, they look at the rate of growth. Cities in the south are growing faster than cities in the north because they started out small. They need only to grow a little to increase their growth rates sharply. A large developed city may grow a great deal, but will show a sluggish growth rate. A more realistic way to represent growth is to look at the absolute increase in income rather than the rate of growth. The economy of New York is expected to grow by 55 billion dollars during the remainder of the century, while burgeoning Nevada, called one of the fastest-growing states in the Union, will only grow by 8 billion dollars over the same period. Furthermore, by economic indexes such as industrial wage rates, per capita income, and capital base, the cities of the northeast and midwest still enjoy various advantages over the south and west. From historical and ethical points of view, equity in the allocation of wealth among the regions is overdue. The point is that the northeast and midwest have healthy economies which are suffering from certain fundamental inequalities which can be corrected to the avoidance of human costs.

The south and west have experienced a tremendous growth in population, but the correlation between population change and economic strength is relatively weak. Examination of employment, gross personal income, and per capita income indicates that on the whole the larger metropolitan areas are growing economically rather than declining.

The dynamics of urban policy are exacerbating the situation, however. One of the important ways that cities grow is not so much by increasing the size of the industry that resides in their limits and employs their citizens, but rather by attracting new business to replace those that move or die. Aging cities are unable to attract new companies because of higher taxes, land costs, labor costs, energy costs, and an image of decline. The federal tax code has favored new construction at the expense of rehabilitation in the older sections of the nation. Federal pollution control regulations have made the cities with the highest concentration of population and industry more dependent on the use of expensive sulphur-free oil. Deregulation of oil prices has increased the cost of heating homes and factories in the northern region of the country. The list is practically endless. Personal taxes are higher because wages are higher, but this is compensated for by the higher standard of living. Until this year the south has experienced a huge increase in defense expenditures. Over the past two decades, Massachusetts and New York have lost an average of about 50 percent of their defense employment, while California now has more military personnel stationed there, with all the attendant benefits, than all the northeast and midwest states combined.

From a purely technical point of view, the suggestion of the President's committee was wrong because the boom of the south is bound to end. The sunbelt is unlikely to grow as fast as it has because it is working from a larger base. The limited supplies of water in the sunbelt cannot continue to support the growth that has flourished in the last twenty years. There is liable to be a sharp increase in wages as labor unions continue to make inroads in the non-union south.

As cheap energy becomes scarce, the great coal deposits of the northeast and midwest will put them on a more equal footing. With increases in population, the south, if it does not take things into hand, can expect decreases in quality of life due to congested highways, air and water pollution, sprawl, limited housing production.

It would be unjust and contrary to the vision of *shalom* for northeasterners to gloat over these possibilities. This vision suggests an alternative to the path suggested by the *Agenda for the 80's*. Rather than repeating the regional chauvinisms and inequities of the past, the country needs policies of social conservation that protect declining areas from the ravages of inter-regional competition. It would be ironic indeed if, through population shifts and comparative economic advantages, the northeast now experiences its own version of reconstruction. From the point of view of the south, remembering the north's industrial monopolies and differential freight rates, this may be poetic justice. But it is not real justice.

The Commission recommends a strategy of adjustment, implicitly opposing the alternate strategy of revival. A revivalist strategy seeks to aid cities to deal with the problems caused by age, slow growth, and spotty economic development. The strategy of adjustment often takes the guise of being people-oriented rather than place-oriented. One of its slogans is to bring "people to jobs" rather than "jobs to people." It ultimately means uprooting people from their ties of place, kinship and culture—distorting and destroying communities—for the sake of a few economic values that can be had in other ways. This strategy comes under what Peter Berger calls the "calculus of pain." It covers over the trivia of individual human suffering with the patina of progress. An event is justified, even though it brings about great suffering, because it leads to another more compatible with, not necessarily the needs of the individual sufferer, but with the goals of the policy-makers. Put in terms that the present generation must suffer, denying itself for the sake of some future classless society, it is an idea many Americans would say smacks of Marxism. It makes one generation a means to the alleged good of another. Ethically considered, every human generation has its own worth, and is not merely a means for the benefit of the next.

Berger has suggested a principle in the formulation of public policy that needs to be invoked: policy should seek to avoid the infliction of pain. Where it does, it requires a justification in terms of moral rather than technical necessity.[9] Such a moral justification may apply, for example, to the requirement that one human generation limit its consumption of natural resources so that they may remain available for the next generation.

The strategy of adjustment may be technically rational, but, because of the pain it inflicts on the lives of many, may be morally unjustifiable. In addition, it fails to recognize the importance of such non-economic values as self-determination, assembly and association, social intercourse, family and cultural ties.

Urban policy needs to respect these values as it recognizes the realities of regional differences. An urban policy technically viable and in keeping with the exigencies of *shalom* should be predicated on the idea of balanced growth. This would require an intricate, close-grained diversity in policy with enough flexibility to give each section, region, community the support it needs to meet its problems of growth or decline.

EFFECTIVENESS IN URBAN POLICY

In addition to debating policy strategy, there has been in the last few years increasing attention to effectiveness in domestic policy implementation. Urban policy is no stranger to this quest.

Any discussion of the effectiveness of national urban policy must initially proceed by acknowledging some existing parameters. Many current constraints concerning effectiveness are summed up in the question, How do we know if the policy succeeds? This question of yardsticks for measuring effectiveness is an important one. It directs attention to strategies and results, as well as to some underlying vision that the policy is designed to bring about. Each constraint is germane to any calculus of effectiveness, but we must begin to look more closely at the areas within which effectiveness must be sought.

The first area concerns goals or symbolic strategy. One common argument is that the federal government has articulated a sufficient number of goals regarding a healthy urban future. What is needed now is effective implementation of programs designed to accomplish the oft-stated goals. There is a good deal of truth in this position, but regarding the cities and the nation's urban future, it is not quite as simple as that. In American society, there is not only a confusion of purposes, but a radical lack of an overarching symbol or metaphor for cities to inform and direct policy purposes. Some suggest that the major aim of any national urban policy must necessarily be the promotion of life in denser, compact, heterogeneous, diverse, complex settings, characteristics which anti-urban attitudes cause the American public to reject. The major task of symbolic effectiveness is the forceful development and articulation of cogent purposes of cities in contemporary America.

One need not be so pessimistic in order to see that effectiveness in the choice of substantive strategies is problematic. The Carter urban policy did choose several strategies that have not really been tried. Reagan reversed that choice, eschewing most of the problems and issues and focusing himself narrowly upon the idea of urban enterprise zones. President Carter's Commission for a National Agenda for the 1980s opted for a "people's" strategy over "place" strategy. There has not been any widespread public debate over these opposing strategies and it is needed.

National urban policy is a key presidential issue for several reasons. First, the Electoral College configuration makes cities count larger in presidential than Congressional voting. Second, no matter how cities are realistically defined, there is no major population constituency for a national urban policy. Elected officials can be expected to articulate policies for urban constituencies, but it seems that only presidents can bring a coherent urban policy into focus. Further, where no public consensus exists on the need for new policy, efforts at policy guidance are a preeminent presidential task.

Presidential effectiveness does not cease with the statement of policy goals. Further political effectiveness is required in managing or overseeing the relevant executive agencies, the federal budget process, and in myriad follow-up activities with Congress. Of all the major actors at the federal level, Congress is the most problematic in terms of developing effective political strategies for national urban policy.

It must be noted that suburban Congressional districts have outnumbered central city districts since 1974. This trend is likely to grow in the future. However, in Congressional voting on urban issues, the political party affiliation of the members of Congress better explains their voting behavior (Democrat, pro-urban; Republican, anti-urban) than a number of socio-economic characteristics of their districts.[10] Unfortunately (and this says something about Carter's effectiveness with Congress) a Democratic president could not get most of his urban policy programs passed by a Democratic-controlled Congress.

Moreover, regionalism is of rising importance. There is a regional pattern of urban hardship (northeast and midwest), although the sunbelt has a share of urban distress. This regionalism is beginning to take the shape of nascent coalitions in Congress (like the Northeast-Midwest Congressional Coalition, begun in 1973), with governors (Coalition of Northeastern Governors, Southern Governors Conference and the Southern Growth Policies Board, and the Western Governors Policy Office), and with associated staffs and policy analysis organizations (Council for Northeast Economic Action, Academy for Contemporary Problems, and the National Economic Research Institute).

Finally, the proliferation of single interest groups and PACs (political action committees) makes it even more unlikely that Congress is a primary site for urban policy innovation and effectiveness. Members of Congress are vulnerable to the PAC's in electoral terms, and many if not most of them do not have any urban policy interests. Enrichment, distributional, or entitlement policies are the most attractive to Congress and add to rather than subtract from the number of recipients of federal aid. As far as Congress is concerned, urban policy is likely to continue to be haphazard, occasional, and indirect, with any major change awaiting chance, crisis, or consensus.

Discerning strategies for administrative effectiveness in the Executive branch is almost as difficult as for Congress. The agencies represented on the Urban and Regional Policy Group (URPG) which initiated the Carter policy indicate the scope of the task: HUD, Commerce, HEW, Labor, Transportation, and Treasury. Throw in a couple of other agencies with claims on urban missions such as Interior (urban parks), Agriculture (FMHA), EPA (environment, air, water), the OMB and White House Domestic Policy Staff, and urban mission is found throughout the federal government. The sheer number of agencies with some claim to urban interest and purpose does not make the task of devising effective administrative strategy simple.

Coherence, consistency, and coordination are the hardy perennials of the requirements for administrative policy effectiveness. These desired qualities approach "motherhood and flag" in their ubiquitousness and in the legion of their adherents. Yet, with urban policy it is difficult to see how these can be substantially achieved.

First, there are competing claims for jurisdiction in gauging performance. Second, any managerial span of control is inherently limited. President Carter's Interagency Coordinating Council was not very visible, had little seniority or prestige, and did not produce generally recognizable breakthroughs in urban policy delivery.

Third, Carter's potentially most dramatic and far-reaching proposal for administrative effectiveness, a reorganization of domestic agencies into a new Department of Development Assistance, quickly became a political casualty. Two years were spent in developing this proposal. It was not even offered to Congress by the Carter Administration because other reorganizations were judged to have priority and because of anticipated difficulty with Congressional passage.

Obviously, all actions aimed at effective policy implementation inevitably take some period of time. There will be few immediate, highly visible effects of any national urban policy, so that acting for effectiveness and gauging effectiveness will have to be judged in the long-term.

In the areas examined above, citizens who wish to pursue an effective national urban policy would be well advised to do the following:

First, carry on focused debate and argument in every available forum aimed at clarifying the symbolic issue and articulating the essential purposes of cities in American society.

Second, seize every opportunity to make national urban policy a presidential electoral issue. Make urban policy a test for all presidential candidates in every way possible.

Third, fight to keep urban policy issues alive with Congress; try to define the essence of the issue in terms other than special interest groups; support emerging Congressional coalitions wherever possible since they may be the vehicles which keep the urban issues most alive.

Fourth, insist that administrations work to relieve the constraints on effectiveness by establishing necessary tools such as a system of Urban Accounts, some agreements on the best policy units, measures of city hardship, and poverty; insist on a higher visibility of administrative actions, including more and better information; insist on periodic evidence of agency performance and evidence of enforcement of the President's Executive Orders.

This is a small catalog of actions that need to be taken for greater effectiveness of national urban policy. This list ignores policy implementation locally yet it requires enormous work in a wide variety of forums. One of these forums is the church.

NOTES

[1] *Home of Man*, p. 126.

[2] Testimony by M. Carl Holman Before the Subcommittee on Housing and Community Development, Committee on Banking, Finance and Urban Affairs, August 10, 1978.

[3] Sam Bass Warner, *The Urban Wilderness* (New York: Harper and Row, 1972), pp. 223–24.

[4] Ibid., p. 225.

[5] The National Commission on Neighborhoods, *People Building Neighborhoods: Final Report to the President and the Congress of the United States*, March 19, 1979, p. 17.

[6] Warner, *Urban Wilderness*, p. 55.

[7]*New York Times*, December 3, 1981.

[8]*The Public's Business: The Politics and Practices of the Government Corporations* (Cambridge, Massachusetts: MIT Press, 1978).

[9]*Pyramids of Sacrifice* (New York: Basic Books, 1974), p. 139.

[10]Demetrios Caraley, "Congressional Politics and Urban Aid: A 1978 Postscript," *Political Science Quarterly* (New York: Academy of Political Science, Fall, 1978).

6.

Toward a Just Urban Policy

WE HAVE used the word "policy" often. It is time we gave it more careful definition.

A *policy is an intentional course of action by government or by some other institution.* Our primary concern is with public policy or governmental action.

A policy usually is set forth with a set of symbols which invoke social purposes, ethical justification, and perhaps religious sanctions. It appeals to a set of goals and value priorities. It identifies directives for action, organization(s) charged with implementing those directives, and a body of constituents affected by the action. While a policy normally presupposes consistency in implementation, it is also typically designed to cope with anticipated social changes which will test its effectiveness. These characteristics suggest a more or less conscious, deliberate, rational, and coherent program to solve a serious problem, or at least to limit the damage caused by the problem.

By such a definition one can doubt that the United States has ever had an urban policy. We have seen how belatedly the federal government dealt with the problems of cities and how slowly its leaders have come to conceive of cities as the objects of something more than piecemeal action. On almost all the elements of the above definition, American society seems ill-equipped to make policy concerning its cities. In our history and in our contemporary national life, we display a general lack of understanding of cities and their purposes as human communities; a profound disagreement over the symbolic meaning and goals of city life in world history; uncertainty over even the most accurate unit of analysis for addressing urban problems; and deep political and structural inability to implement with consistency a policy proposed by one level of government but requiring the cooperation of another.

THE NEED FOR SYMBOLIC CONSENSUS

The most serious of these underlying questions is that of symbolic meanings of the city. Americans seem to lack significant symbols or metaphors with which to organize their thinking about current urban phenomena.

Purposes and symbols are crucial to analyses of urban phenomena and articulation of cohesive policy. William Alonso made this point in a recent examination of population de-concentration, "Symbolism will play an important role in the way we think about these issues . . . Over the coming years, we shall be searching for new images to give meaning to current population trends, and they will be a major force in the shaping of diagnoses and policies."[1]

While we sense no contemporary overarching purpose for cities, there has been no lack of purposes imputed to cities historically. These have ranged from places of residence for god-kings (Thebes and Babylon), to centers of imperial power (Rome), common defense (early forts at crossroads) to economic development (trade, industry, labor force), centers of human interaction (transportation, communications and citadels of technological success), to American acculturation (immigrant socialization), creation of unique American political forms (city political machines) to being the primary locus of "post-industrial" society in the development of services industries.

Two purposes currently asserted as reasons for saving our cities are that cities nurture the essentials of civilization and attend to its diffusion for all citizens. Moreover, cities are becoming the major conservators of land, energy, and other resources.[2]

Yet even the cultural purpose is now in question, whether from the influence of electronic communications, the rapid building of state networks of community colleges outside of major urban areas, or the closing of city museums, libraries, and other cultural attractions in major cities due to fiscal cut-backs.

As to the cities' conservation role, the Carter urban policy emphasized it, but opinion polls at the time showed an energy crisis was not believed to exist by majorities of respondents. Gasoline consumption continued to rise, urban fringe and non-metropolitan new development and settlement patterns continued apace. Only in 1980 and 1981 did the public take measures to curb its energy consumption.

Major public opinion research soliciting the images of cities in the minds of American citizens has revealed basically a set of consumer attitudes toward cities in contemporary society. A Louis Harris study, executed for the Department of Housing and Urban Development in support of urban policy formation, discovered: "The image of the large city that emerges from these data is that of an economic, cultural-intellectual and recreational 'service center,' but not of a desirable residential center." This notion is reinforced by city activity patterns also presented.[3]

These attitudes and behaviors demonstrate that a majority of the American public think of major cities only as "shopping centers" for different bundles of goods and services. Such attitudes and behaviors, of course, not only contribute significantly to fiscal disparities in the provision of public goods and services (e.g. museums, public safety), but betray little or no awareness of metropolitan interdependence on which a new intergovernmental partnership would be predicated nor show any sensitivity to any larger purposes for cities.

As with the confusion over purposes for central cities, in recent years there has been a proliferation of symbols and metaphors about cities. A brief survey reveals journalistic and other media images of Cleveland, Newark, and New York City as tottering on the brink of financial disaster, hence, synonyms for irresponsibility or unlivability. Other symbols have proliferated: the suburban era; cities as sandboxes; cities as reservations; the need for a Marshall Plan for cities; various "no-growth" strategies; the biological metaphor of the life cycle, now emphasizing the "death" of cities; Niebuhr's "doctrine of salvation through brick" as applied to federal urban aid programs; new interpretations of central city "revitalization," "renaissance," or "Europeanization" which posit a reversal of present urban patterns of decay and which falsely suppose that European cities have no such problems.

Few symbols emphasize the interdependency of people in metropolitan society. The Carter urban policy's label, "New Partnership," which was designed to illustrate interdependency, did not capture public imagination as an overarching symbol, though popularity is no sure test of a symbol's ultimate adequacy. In fact, feelings of metropolitan interdependency are explicitly rejected in the dominant attitudes of the two-thirds of the American population that are suburban and non-metropolitan dwellers. Their attitudes and actions exhibit strong preferences for isolation from central cities, which belies their real interdependency.

The biological metaphor of the life-and-death cycle calls attention to symptoms of death in older central cities, deterioration in low property values, high occupancy turnovers, accelerated vacancy rates, inadequate housing, and high proportions of low income residents. While a potent image, this is profoundly unbiblical. The presence of poor people is seen as a symptom of death rather than life. Above all, what is missing from this list of purposes and symbols is the idea that a central vocation of American cities is the achievement of justice for their citizens, many of whom are the poor and minorities.

In the history of American industrialism, cities have been the destination of millions of immigrants and migrants in their search for the "American dream." In America's cities, the largest proportions of American blacks, browns, and ethnic minorities along with the nation's poor have settled in this pursuit. There, the poor and minorities have been structurally, systemically obstructed from realizing the "American dream." Public and private authorities are both implicated in perpetuating systems of injustice; cities are implicated.

That cities and the nation must engage in the vocation of achieving justice for urban citizens flies in the face of many societal trends. Industrialism, particularly manufacturing, will no longer be the flywheel driving economic development of urban society. Technology may become the major force and national trends are toward spatial de-centralization. That these trends are collectively anti-city does not nullify, but rather reinforces the city as a symbol for justice.

WHO ARE THE CONSTITUENTS OF THE CITY?

Which cities? What poverty? There are many conflicting statistical and conceptual ways of describing contemporary urbanism. A plethora of definitions is one of many obstacles to developing coherent national urban policy. Some agreement on units would seem to be one prerequisite to applying standards of justice to any such policy.

It is often said the United States is an urban nation. In many ways that is true, but in other ways that statement is a result of statistical definition. Consider these facts:

- Approximately 38,000 local governments receive general revenue sharing funds.
- The metropolitan areas of the United States contain 22,185 local governmental units (of all types) out of a total of more than 72,000 such units in the whole nation.
- Of the approximately 20,000 incorporated municipalities in the United States, over two-thirds have less than 2,500 residents and only 6,500 have more than 2,500.
- There were 288 Standard Metropolitan Statistical Areas in the

United States in 1980, i.e., areas with a central city population over 50,000.

- In 1980, of 225.5 million Americans 27.2% lived in non-metropolitan areas outside of urban places, while 29.4% lived in cities over 50,000; 25.1% of the nation's population lived in cities of 100,000 or more; about 29.4% of the nation's population (about 67 million) lived in central cities of SMSAs.

To say that almost three-quarters of the nation's population is urban is true according to census definitions, but it is a trivial truth at best. There are distinctions between urban, non-metropolitan, SMSAs, and urbanized areas. Of those in metropolitan areas, more people live outside central cities than live within them. And about 30% of people in SMSAs actually live in rural, not urban, places. Their economic and political dependence on cities, however, is a fact that cannot be denied. From this perspective, we are indeed an urban nation.

So the national urban population can be categorized in many ways. It is the nature of that categorization that matters most for purposes of making national urban policy, and for applying standards of justice to it. Does the policy apply equally to all 20,000 incorporated places? Does it aim primarily at the majority of cities (the 13,422 municipalities under 2,500 in population)? Or, at the majority of people in cities (the 33% in municipalities over 50,000)? Or, at the numerical minority of Americans (28%) who live in large cities?

One way to answer this question was undertaken by analyses underlying the 1978 Carter urban policy. The President's Report focused on four major sets of demographic and socio-economic changes which have deeply affected the present and future of the nation's cities: the shifts in population, employment, energy conservation, and lifestyle. These analyses found, with respect to the national population, de-concentration is occurring at an accelerating rate over the past 15 years. There has been a loss of central city population, an inter-regional migration toward the south and west, a halt of black migration to non-southern central cities, a reversal of the rural-to-urban migration pattern, growth of non-metropolitan areas, a drop in birth rate, and rise in household formation rate. Between 1970 and 1975, the northeast had a net job loss; most new jobs were found in the south and west. There has been a non-metropolitan job location shift, and the manufacturing sector is no longer the driving force of urban development.

In short, during the 1970s the nation has seen the interruption or reversal of several long-term population and economic trends that many people assumed would continue indefinitely.

Additionally, there have been a number of aggregate studies of the nation's cities attempting to define and measure city "hardship," "decline," and "distress."[4] A number of independent scholars have examined the incidence and distribution among cities of such distress factors as unemployment, per capita and family income, education levels, crowded and sub-standard housing, poverty rates, dependent population, population loss and growth lag, age of housing, race. Two things are most significant about these studies. First, they have independently produced essentially similar lists of the distressed cities in the nation. Second, a number of these phenomena clearly are interrelated in a number of large central cities across the nation.

Cities ranked high in distress factors are predominantly but not exclusively major central cities in the northeast and northcentral sections of the country. Related analyses have documented secondary findings such as gaps between distressed cities, present financial resources and their service responsibilities, and mis-matches between the service needs of city residents and services available.

The first characterization of urban demography of basic policy importance is a taxonomy of distressed cities broadly defined. "Distress" becomes even more germane as the primary category the more coincident it is with high and disproportionate numbers of the poor and racial minorities in cities. The primary unit for national urban policy formation and subsequent analyses must be all the nation's cities that share those characteristics: high on one or more distress factors, high minority or poverty populations.

This choice has numerous implications. Briefly, the most important are the following:

First, distressed large (100,000 or more) central cities in metropolitan areas are chosen because there is significant evidence of their distress. Moreover, these places are where people who have a disproportionate share of personal and communal socio-economic problems live.

Second, by this measure these units are likely to be primary for the foreseeable future. Pending any explicit, drastic federal relocation policy, which is highly unlikely, people and conditions of distress are likely to be central for the next few decades at least.

Third, this choice of a primary unit is not to ignore totally other possible units. Other units (such as SMSAs, urban counties, even megalopolis or urban field) may become more urgent in policy terms in the near future. The choice of large central cities has more clearly defined problems at present than these others, however, and more policy-relevant information available. This choice of primary unit is therefore definite, but provisional. It is definite as the best choice to focus attention and policy now and in the near future. It is provisional in the sense that it could be superseded by another unit over time.

Only a myopic urban policy planner would overlook the geography of central city problems. Central cities are not independent principalities, like Monaco or Lichtenstein, with resources to solve their own problems. They are politically, economically, socially, and fiscally implicated in metropolitan areas, including suburbia and exurbia. The governments of central cities usually lack the authority to cross the jurisdictional lines dividing these areas. The necessary resources are simply not in the central cities themselves. The achievement of equity in the distribution of jobs, housing, and education increasingly necessitates addressing metropolitan areas. Equity does not stop at central city limits. Central cities, however, are the starting point and primary referent for addressing such questions.

Fourth, this primary unit has important political and policy implications. It means focusing on a minority (about 25%) of the American population. There are, however, no readily apparent, stable, cohesive political majorities for whom this minority is the primary political referent. This fact raises salient questions concerning strategies of political effectiveness for any national urban policy.

GOALS FOR CHANGE: THE CHOICE OF CONSISTENT POLICY PRIORITIES

Another set of circumstances is important as a prelude to national urban policy. This set may be titled the historical effects of recent federal social policy. There are four major effects that bear on any national urban policy effort.

First, in the past forty years we have had a plethora of social policies, not specifically aimed at cities but spelling out national goals which incidentally could benefit cities. We have full employment acts, full and non-discriminatory housing acts, health acts, education acts, anti-poverty acts, community development acts, and so on. As a national society we have accumulated a large number of goal statements urgently relevant to the health of cities, even though they were not initially urban in character.

Second, with the growth in the past quarter century of federal domestic programs, we still have no system of federal Urban Accounts. We do not know systematically how well or badly cities are benefitting by the existing array of federal domestic programs because federal agencies do not keep data in any urban format.

Third, societally and governmentally, we do not have an agreed-upon definition of poverty, urban or otherwise. Instead, we have a number of competing definitions, all based on different assumptions or program requirements. These are only the best-known or widely used definitions, each with a different dollar income figure for an individual or a family: Bureau of Labor Statistics (BLS), Supplemental Security Income (SSI), Medicaid's medically indigent, food stamps, U.S. Bureau of the Census, Aid to Families with Dependent Children (AFDC), Comprehensive Employment and Training Act (CETA), assisted housing (several programs). If we cannot agree on what it is, how can we expect to do something significant about it?

Fourth, even if rudimentary consensus can be achieved on goals, the federal debate over means is more divisive than ever before. A *New York Times* news story on aid to the poor for home heating fuel illustrates the latest case. "The reason (the measure is likely to fail in Congress) is that no one has been able to develop a foolproof method for distributing money to people in proportion to their need. Some Congressmen think the middle-class and the rich should be eligible for fuel subsidies. Some think the money should go just to those who heat with oil; others want people who use gas or electricity to be eligible. Some want the grants to be weighted in favor of people living in the coldest climates; that does not sit well with politicians from the South and Southwest."[5]

This example is merely symptomatic of a deep break-down in the consideration of means to implement social policy. Welfare reform, changes in Social Security benefits, tax revision, hospital cost containment, national health insurance have or are about to succumb to a federal inability to confront the "means" question responsibly. This situation, of course, has implications for any urban policy.

SOCIAL POLICY, URBAN POLICY, AND THE QUESTION OF RELIGIOUS MEANING

More generically, then, in summing up the circumstances for a national urban policy when considering the current situation of cities in the American political economy, we confront the rhetorical question, "Is the cup half empty, or half full?" After all, there is an impressive legacy of governmental reform, both local and national, and until recently, there has been a great expansion of federal domestic programs, including specific urban ones, over the last four decades. On balance, what does this mean for future national urban policy?

Several years ago, Robert Lampman, analyzing anti-poverty policy in a retrospective on the Great Society, suggested that, even if all the anti-poverty programs tried in the 1960s had not fulfilled their goals, they left one indispensable, indelible impact on all domestic policy.[6] Lampman argues that they made the question "But what does it do for the poor?" a mandatory test for any future domestic policy. While this may not be a demonstrable legacy, it is a plumb line for testing urban policy by the norms of biblical faith. For Mr. Lampman the cup is empty, but the structure is still intact for it to be filled again.

Two more perspectives can be juxtaposed here. Diane Ravitch, in a recent article, begins:

> Since 1960, American society has been transformed by a quiet revolution. In response to the unrelenting pressure of a militant civil rights movement, the courts and the Congress dismantled a racial caste system embedded in law and practice for generations . . . In a relatively short time, the results of these policies (civil rights and social welfare) have been impressive. Since 1960, the number of poor people has dropped from 39 million to 25 million (from 22 per cent of the population to 11.8 per cent, according to the Bureau of the Census). Efforts to expand educational opportunity have substantially narrowed the gap between the educational levels of blacks and whites . . . The ultimate goal— a society without poverty, injustice, or bigotry—has not been attained, here or in any other nation; but progress toward that ideal has been made in the past two decades.[7]

For Dr. Ravitch, the cup is half full.

The opposite perspective is found in another recent paper, "Toward Revolution in Urban America: Problems and Prospects."[8] These authors, using social class analysis, examine the progress the nation and its cities have made in the decade 1968–1978 in implementing the Kerner Commission Report. They find evidence on some key social indicators that conditions in central cities, particularly for blacks, have gotten worse. Unemployment is higher for all blacks, and particularly teenagers, than in 1968. When combined with the high inflation rates of the 1970s, they find no evidence of reduced poverty rates over the decade. For Meranto and Mosqueda, the cup is half empty and draining. As Ravitch says, "Radical critics insist that liberal social policy in a capitalist economy can never improve the lot of the poor, because its true purpose is to deceive the discontented masses."[9]

In a semi-official exchange concerning the present existence or persistence of an "urban crisis," T. D. Allman argued that there is no more "crisis" and that the vestiges of one will take care of themselves, while a Carter Administration HUD assistant secretary and staff argued there was enough of a "crisis" left, at least to justify the Administration's urban policy.[10]

No doubt, evidence can be adduced for each of these positions. This analysis will not resolve the discrepancies in comparisons. Nevertheless, the choice of perspective, the meanings attached to the present circumstances of cities is of some importance for generating national urban policy. The context of meaning given to social facts shapes action and remedies. It is sufficient for this analysis that all perspectives show too many distressed cities and too many impoverished people residing in them. Need continues to outweigh current performance. No matter what other perspectives must also be invoked, the question, "What does it do for the poor?" remains the question to be asked of any urban policy from the perspective of the Hebrew-Christian ethical tradition.

WILL STANDARDS OF JUSTICE BE APPLIED TO NATIONAL URBAN POLICY?

Interpreted in familiar contemporary terms, a biblical standard of justice means advocacy of the cause of the country's poor, a drive toward greater equality in distribution of material resources for the poor, pursuit of healing rather than destructive social acts, and building community relationships.

The Carter urban policy, as a beginning reference point, had a mixed record in terms of these standards. The question, "Was the policy *adequate* in terms of the proportion of federal budget devoted to it?" has several answers. One is, manifestly, "No," since the severe problems of people in central cities still abound. Other answers depend on readings of the budget.

Another, more complex though indefinite, answer is "We don't know." We do not have a budgetary system of Urban Accounts with which to measure. A third answer would have to depend on defendable estimates of adequacy. A fourth answer would begin by acknowledging that budget dollars are only a partial, but insufficient measure of federal governmental purposes with respect to cities. Equally important as dollars, if not more important, is the question of uses to which the dollars are put. Here again, accurate measurement is difficult.

Thus, at the present time, we can only begin to analyze tendencies. The goal statements or principles of the New Partnership tended to be in line with the standards of justice, particularly the "people-oriented" and "place-oriented" policy elements. The debate over and execution of means of policy implementation, particularly by Congress, continue to fall far short of the standards, however. The "targeting" strategy to most distressed cities has been significantly diluted in several policy programs. The emphasis on interdependence of the partners has not been significantly realized, particularly with respect to states and neighborhoods.

In particular, there is little or no movement toward a wholistic definition of urban problems within the federal government. Bureaucratic turf battles and program definitions continue for the most part. Forms of federal aid to cities as cities continue, generally, to be indirect rather than direct. An "economic development" strategy rather than an "incomes" strategy predominates, in the existing array of urban programs, in which government-to-government transfers greatly outweigh government-to-people support. Indirect aid does little to foster the growth of a sense of community in cities.

A policy emphasis on revitalization and rehabilitation of central city structures, and on conservation, may begin to promote healing and overcome the legacy of destructiveness. But this policy emphasis is merely at the beginning rhetorical stage.

The reduction or elimination of program elements bearing directly on income redistribution for the urban poor such as in CETA and supplemental fiscal assistance is directly contrary to the above standards of justice. As the first extant case of national urban policy, then, the Carter Administration and Congress made only extremely modest beginnings toward establishing a just policy.

In the immediate future, cities and American society face new problems such as drastic budgetary cutbacks, dwindling energy sources, and renewal of old problems such as inflation and recession. There remains the question of whether the American public and federal government will continue to remember cities in significant policy terms. There are several dangers. There is no significant national political majority/constituency for cities; the federal government and attentive public has been extremely "faddish" in their consideration of domestic issues over the last decade or so; the new problems are likely to be just as intractable as the old ones and hence will divert attention from cities except as peripheral issues.

The Congressional Black Caucus responded to President Carter's national urban policy with a list of five principles it felt were essential to any urban policy which is to receive support of black Americans. They are:

1. The Federal Budget must be reordered so as to provide adequate resources for revitalization.
2. Physical development of housing, public facilities, and transportation must be focused on people living in areas of concentrated poverty, must provide job opportunities to those persons, and must not displace them from their neighborhoods.
3. Tax policy and other federal expenditures must support the revitalization of cities rather than continue to undercut central cities while building up suburban areas.
4. Transportation policy must be reoriented so as to bring lower income persons to jobs which have moved out of the central city rather than moving their wealthier suburbanites to their inner-city jobs. There must be at the same time movement of jobs back to the inner-city.
5. Consolidation of human services for more effective delivery at the state and local level must be done in a manner which promotes jobs for residents of areas of concentrated poverty.

The National Urban League's response to the Carter urban policy was in basic agreement with these principles and enumerated a number of detailed recommendations based on them.[11] These principles are still valid, and, in light of the budgetary maneuvers of the Reagan Administration, need to be vigorously advocated.

The issue of establishing and implementing a just national urban policy will continue to be before American society, as will the choice of a central symbol for our collective life. The performance of public policymakers, entrepreneurs, and academicians must be called to account continually by vigorous applications of standards of justice. A balanced federal budget is an insufficient symbol of a just national urban policy. The standards of justice must endure for this and every age.

POLICY GOALS FOR THE CHURCHES

Almost every worthy list of goals for society must include a set of urban goals, because the cities are the warp of the national fabric. Those that follow do not pretend to constitute a comprehensive listing of the elements of the good community. Rather, the focus here is on a narrower set of high-priority matters that seeks to address some of the most critical problems and shortcomings of the American city today.

Listing an item as a policy goal does not necessarily imply that its attainment is primarily the responsibility of government. In some cases, federal, state and local governments may indeed have major roles to play. In others, the people themselves, acting as individuals and in voluntary organizations, may have the key functions. In still other cases, success may be achieved through a combination of public and private action.

(1) **A Coherent Urban Policy:** To those imbued with the churches' historic concern for the problems of people in pain, the development of a coherent federal national urban policy may come as a surprise. But dealing with any one problem without attacking its parenting complex of problems is like yanking out one blade of crabgrass. It will soon be replaced by another, rooted in similar causes.

Fundamentally, a coherent urban policy is a matter of commonsense in a system of government with interacting and overlapping levels. A national urban policy would provide a framework for government approaches to city development, and for coordination of these with non-governmental activities. Only a coherent urban policy will secure a fair deal for the urban poor, and this is why the development of one should be of chief concern to the churches.

(2) **Jobs for All:** Involuntary unemployment is a social maladjustment of the first order. All people have an equal right to food, clothing, shelter, as well as the things of the spirit. It is possible, of course, to redistribute the wealth produced by others, giving it to those who are denied the chance to earn their own living. On an emergency basis, this is often essential. On a permanent basis, it tends to be paternalistic and deprives recipients of their dignity as images of the divine Creator. For all members of society to experience their own dignity and to have control over their own lives requires that each have the full opportunity to work.

(3) **Decent, Affordable Shelter:** The majority of Americans are well-housed, but millions of urban families are confined to ugly, squalid places. No one-to-one correlation exists between housing conditions and happy, meaningful lives. The love and understanding essential to wholesome families sometimes are abundant in the midst of poverty and absent in the midst of affluence. Yet, living in dwelling places that are overcrowded, unsafe, vermin-infested, frigid in winter and unventilated in summer poses severe handicaps for the nurturing of children and the maturation of families.

Several generations of governmental housing programs still leave a big gap between that ideal and reality. Our declared national goal is "a decent home and a suitable living environment" for every American. Prospects for improving housing conditions of the poor appear grim as inflated rents and sales prices are driving retirees and others out of acceptable housing, and housing assistance programs are cut drastically.

(4) **Sane Approaches to Health:** Americans have grown to expect physicians and hospitals to provide miracle cures for almost any ailment. They have become inured to preventive health care through eating and living habits and even their mental attitudes. In the cities, medical costs are rising at double the rate of inflation, millions have no regular source of medical care, or are without any means to cover their health care costs. Many people are covered by insurance programs that pay for extensive, even questionable, medical expenditures, while others are deprived of basic care or forced to suffer catastrophic financial losses when illness strikes. The challenges to find new approaches to healthful living, to devise economic safeguards for those who experience health misfortunes, and to strike a proper balance between society's investments in prevention and in heroic attempts at cures are all as critical as they are difficult. Health means not only the absence of pain and infirmity, but also physical, social, and mental well-being.

(5) **Strengthened Neighborhoods:** Neighborhoods are human scale communities. Revitalized as communities of concern and caring, neighborhoods can be antidotes to the isolation and social alienation that face many city dwellers. Neighborhood assumption of responsibility over local matters would put into effect the principle of subsidiarity and the active participation of urbanites in their own future. Neighborhoods as the path to self-help and decentralization require federal and local government funding to further their aims. Federal help is needed to help neighborhoods mobilize their own resources. They need to be wary of being co-opted as instruments of centralization by those upon whom they may become dependent. Decentralism should be endorsed as a balancing force, not as an alternative to larger government, because localism at times has aligned itself against social progress while the federal government has led the forces against inequities. Other opportunities for empowerment may, for example, take the form of food co-ops, employee-operated businesses, mutual provision of child care and other social services, development of small-scale technologies, cable television communications, and the humanizing

of financial institutions by expanding their neighborhood contacts and activities.

(6) **Justice in the Welfare System:** Discrimination due to race, sex, nationality, creed, economic class, age or other distinctions is abhorrent to a biblical mentality. Every effort needs to be made to sweep away practices that prevent people from being treated as equally worthy in the sight of God, the law, and their fellow humans.

Welfare frequently is set forth as the remedy for discrimination and injustice. Institutionalized welfare in which persons are put in a permanent condition of dependency tends to be demeaning and debilitating. Often it reinforces the prejudices that separate people from each other. What most powerless and dependent people need is the removal of the social obstacles that hinder them from pursuing their own interests and from developing their own talents to the fullest.

Welfarism, as a system, is viewed by some as living off the public dole, as a "something-for-nothing" lifestyle. Strangely, such sentiments in America are typically directed against the "unworthy poor" but rarely against the "unworthy rich." Prestige and respect are seldom withheld from the rich whose wealth often results from heredity rather than hard work. Welfare needs to be defended, while the society makes a concerned effort to assure ample job opportunities and equality of access to job markets. This should reduce the necessity for welfare among those who want to work and who have no physical or mental disabilities.

Society has an obligation to those who have disabilities and handicaps or who suffer misfortune. Welfare should be designed largely for this sector, and it should be offered with dignity and a minimum of red tape. Where it is provided to those who could become self-supporting, the aid should be clearly temporary and given in such forms that open doors to jobs or other paths that break the grip of dependency.

(7) **Compact Energy-conserving Land Use:** The flight of residents and business from central cities to the metropolitan fringe has tended to polarize the urban poor and the more affluent suburbanites. It has splintered urban areas governmentally, leaving jurisdictions to wrestle with problems that extend far beyond their borders. It has led to tax disparities and fiscal crises for older cities. All these need to be reversed or mitigated.

The present energy crisis presents further reasons for containing urban flight. Cities that are reasonably compact conserve energy as compared with the dispersed suburban and exurban development patterns. This is because city residents travel shorter commuting distances, rely more on mass transit, live in townhouses and apartments which consume less energy than single-family homes, and use public services and facilities that are more energy-efficient because they serve larger concentrations of people and buildings.

The new social frontiers are in the cities. Existing sprawled land-use patterns developed over the past half century cannot be undone. But every effort should now be made to fill in the unused spaces in existing cities and older suburbs, halting the invasion of precious farmland by urbanization. Cities can be opened to appropriate uses at acceptable prices if taxes that now make speculative landholding profitable are revised, and if the many federal and state programs that have been biased toward new out-of-city development are turned around or neutralized.

Meanwhile, cities should intensify efforts at weatherizing existing buildings and hasten the transition to renewable energy sources. Compact cities also can be made more livable by increasing integration efforts— reversing the recent trends to segregate housing by income class, to keep dwelling units out of commercial areas, and to bar village-type commerce from residential neighborhoods. Creative mixes of compatible land uses will help revitalize cities.

(8) **Safety and Security:** Crime is unquestionably a major city problem and is a chief concern of urbanites. It is an obvious symbol of the breakdown of community, *shalom*, in urban life because it reduces persons to objects for the satisfaction of one's needs. Attempts to deal with crime through policing alone will not suffice. This will only continue to assure the polarizing of the community. Resolving some of the underlying economic problems of cities should help set the stage for more law-abiding attitudes. Community crime control programs have shown remarkable success and should be encouraged.

In a country founded at a time when 90 percent of its citizens lived on farms, whose Constitution mandates legal control of cities to states rather than the federal government, and whose cities have grown more in conformity with land laws and markets than with any other law or plan, it is not surprising that fifty years of federal urban programs have failed to solve major human problems in our cities. Nor should it be surprising that one lesson of these fifty years, as read by many voters in the 1980 national election, should be that "Washington cannot solve all our problems." Government itself cannot solve them all, but neither can isolated individuals and institutions solve them. New collaborations and deliberations among many persons, institutions, and interests of city life remain to be invented and explored. Among the collaborators must be the churches, to whose role in the search for a just urban policy we now turn.

NOTES

[1]William Alonso, "Metropolis Without Growth," *The Public Interest*, 53 (New York: National Affairs, Inc., Fall, 1978), p. 85.

[2]Subcommittee on the City, Committee on Banking, Finance and Urban Affairs, U.S. House of Representatives, *Proposition 13: Prelude to Fiscal Crisis or New Opportunities?* (Washington: U.S. Government Printing Office, 1978), pp. 34–36.

[3]Louis Harris and Associates, Inc., *A Survey of Citizen Views and Concerns About Urban Life* (Washington, D.C.: U.S. Department of Housing and Urban Development, 1978), p. 5.

[4]Major "distress" studies include: U.S. Congress, Joint Economic Committee, *The Current Fiscal Condition of Cities: A Survey of 67 of the 75 Largest Cities*; Harvey Garn, et al., *A Framework for National Urban Policy: Urban Distress, Decline and Growth* (Washington, D.C.: The Urban Institute, 1978); Richard Nathan and Charles Adams, *Understanding Central City Hardship* (Washington, D.C.: The Brookings Institution, 1976); Committee for Economic Development, *An Approach to Federal Urban Policy* (New York: CED, 1977); William G. Coleman, "The Future of Cities: Contrasting Strategies for the Haves and Have Nots," Prepared for Conference on Reorganization, Woodrow Wilson International Center for Scholars, Smithsonian Institution, September 1977.

[5]*New York Times*, October 21, 1979.

[6]Robert J. Lampman, "What Does It Do for the Poor: A New Test for National Policy," *The Public Interest*, Winter 1974.

[7]Diane Ravitch, "Liberal Reforms and Radical Visions," *New York Times Book Review* (New York Times Co., September 16, 1979), p. 3.

[8]Philip Meranto and Lawrence Mosqueda, Delivered to the American Political Science Association Annual Convention, 1979, p. 3.

[9]Ravitch, op. cit., p. 3.

[10]See, *inter alia*, T. D. Allman, "The Urban Crisis Leaves Town," *Harper's* (New York: Harpers Magazine Co., December 1978); U.S. D.H.U.D. Urban Policy

Staff, "Whither or Whether Urban Distress—A Response to Allman," Working Paper, Office of Community Planning and Development, February 1979; Robert C. Embry, Jr., Assistant Secretary for Community Planning and Development, U.S. D.H.U.D., Statement before the Joint Economic Committee Subcommittee.

[11]See National Urban League, *National Urban Policy: A National Urban League Assessment*, August 1978.

7.

The Churches' Role in Shaping

American Urban Life

FOR CHRISTIANS to claim a vital role in the redemption of American cities is to call for a new objectivity in perceiving church influence in the public sector. It is to require historical and institutional perspectives which provide a dynamic context for new church strategies in cities. It is to appreciate Abraham Lincoln's wisdom: "If we could first know where we are, and whither we are tending, we could better judge what to do, and how to do it."

THE CHURCHES AND THE BUILDING OF CITIES IN
AMERICA: 1607–1980

The discovery of where we are requires knowledge of where we have been. We earlier acknowledged the roots of the Christian movement in the historic Hebrew people, as a people subject to an ancient, yet unrealized vision of *shalom* on earth. We forget who we are if we forget that biblical vision.

We remember that among the people who founded the United States were religious people, mostly Protestants, carried by visions of the City of God to a "New World." Sociologically considered, the Christian movement has long been a predominantly urban movement. As the great German sociologist Max Weber said:

> During all periods of its mighty external and internal develop-
> ment, it [Christianity] has been a quite specifically urban, and
> above all a civic religion. This was true during Antiquity, during
> the Middle Ages, and in Puritanism. The city of the Occi-
> dent . . . has been the major theater of Christianity.[1]

The Puritans who settled the east coast of America in the pre-industrial seventeenth century proudly identified themselves as citizens of towns and cities.[2] The first charter of Jamestown in 1607 speaks of spreading Christianity and bringing "the infidels and savages . . . to human Civility." Governor John Winthrop, twenty-three years later aboard the *Arbella*, urged his fellow passengers to build a Biblical "City upon a hill"; and with true Puritan doctrine, called them

> to seek out a place of Cohabitation and Consorteshipp under a due forme of Government both civill and eccleasiasticall. In such cases as this the care of the publique must oversway all private respects, by which not onely conscience, but meare Civill pollicy doth binde us; for it is a true rule that perticuler estates cannott subsist in the ruine of the publique.[3]

Winthrop envisioned a "Holy Community," in which individuals, the church, and all citizens had a common interest in "doing justice, loving mercy, and walking humbly with God," as prescribed in Micah 3:8. This was a Christian social vision as carefully thought out and as politically structured as any in Western history. As historian Sam Bass Warner characterizes them, these early Puritans "carried in their heads the specifications for a good life and a decent community, and for a time they were able to realize them" in their small towns, "the most completely planned of any American settlement" in history.

> The genius of the township system, distinct from later planning ideals and achievements, lay in its crude organization of freedom and opportunity in group, not individual, terms. More strongly than in the tightest urban ethnic or racial ghetto or in the closed union or in the inbred family corporation, the unity of land control combined with a common village and religious experience to force men of the time to seek change only in group terms.[4]

"Change in group terms" is a definition of politics, and what people decide together to do, especially in relation to scarce resources like land, is the stuff of social policy. No human construct is more expressive of politics and policy than the *polis*, the city that humans build. These early Americans, in short, had a clear, powerful urban vision. They were heirs to centuries of Christian identification with the life of cities; and they believed that they could build towns and cities that would embody elements of the ancient prophetic social vision which we have called *shalom*. However diluted that vision was to become in the ensuing two centuries of Christian church development on American shores, this stubborn social principle remains basic in American history: "the care of the publique must oversway all private respects."

But that was a principle which the subsequent centuries would see subject to increasing, erosive attack by other generations of Americans, Christians among them. The Puritans planned their towns under the illusion that they could convert their children to their religious vision, keep control of the political order against future immigrants, and discipline their own hunger for landed wealth. On all three counts they failed to anticipate future history. Their children were obeying the imperative "Go west" long before Horace Greeley coined the advice. Cheap land drew a second generation of colonists perpetually away from the homesites of the first. These latter-day settlements, consisting of individual families occupying their own farms, turned American colonial society into a patchwork of estates. Owning land became the essential economic expression of personal liberty for Americans. It was not strange that Thomas Jefferson should have adopted most of John Locke's famous summary of the purposes of government as the securing of every citizen's "life, liberty, and property." For many of Jefferson's contemporaries, "owning property" and "pursuing happiness" were indistinguishable.

As Warner observes, the almost-absolute sense of the rights of private property is the one element of early Puritanism that survived all the major dilutions of the Puritan spirit in subsequent American history. Individual right to control the uses of land became the "given" of all American town-planning and urban political decision, installing in political power in every town "men who saw the duty of government to be the defense of private property."[5] Above all, the legal institution of property rights hobbled the ability of citizens and governments to make collective decisions about their transitions from farm to city living. Decades before the industrial revolution made cities profitable places for mass manufacturing, the cities of the east coast encountered the conflict between the individualism of land ownership and the social nature of human life in cities.

> Cities attempted to resolve the conflicts between the integrity of each small plot and the growing interdependencies of the city in two ways: by establishing networks of public services in the streets to bind together individual parcels, and by expanding the regulations of private behavior outward from the old common-law base. As early as the epidemic of 1793, Philadelphia discovered that each section of personal property could not safely support a private well. That year, yellow fever killed four thousand residents, a twelfth of the population.[6]

Private wells tapped into a single underground water resource is a vivid image of an institutional pattern that has shaped the American city from its beginning. The problem of pure water for his beloved city was so great for Benjamin Franklin that he willed a share of his wealth to the perpetual improvement of the Philadelphia water supply. In the following century, the interconnections of people's lives in cities multiplied on a scale unimaginable in the first two hundred years of American history: cities became centers of industrial production, marketplaces for world commerce, centers of supply and finance of the continental westward movement, and the places where art and education were expected to flourish. Each of these developments was the product of human social interaction, but culturally speaking, "We have remained what we were as farmers: a nation of small proprietors, jealously protecting our individual property rights as if they were the cornerstone of our civil liberties."[7]

Individualism in American culture fed and directed the surge of industrialism in the nineteenth century. Industry was first an urban phenomenon in Europe and the United States. It was a phenomenon for which the churches of neither continent were spiritually, intellectually, or institutionally prepared. Either by their marriage to a land-tenure system that clustered their political and economic interests around the rural "parish" or by their easy approval of the individualistic entrepreneurial spirit of the new capitalists, the churches of the new industrial cities found themselves alienated from the new working classes of the cities. It was what Pope Pius XI called the "great scandal" of the nineteenth century. English theologian David Edwards has similarly written: "The greatest defeat of modern Christianity was its failure in the industrial revolution." In the twentieth century, Edwards says:

> Christianity's institutional failure is likely to vary with the size of the city. A visitor wishing to see the continuing strength of the ecclesiastical tradition should go to Herefordshire and not to Birmingham, to Brittany and not to Paris, to the Middle West and not to New York.[8]

In the United States, the accommodation of urban churches to the middle and upper classes was accompanied by the agrarian fundamentalism of the frontier. In time, that essentially Protestant individualism of rural and small-town America became a dominant ideology even in many Catholic and Protestant city churches. It is still promoted in Billy Graham crusades, typically held in central city convention halls. Catholic fear of the religious heterogeneity of the city resulted in the privatizing of a predominantly social European religious experience. It also has tended to sanction the twentieth century version of the American Dream: moving to the suburbs means moving up the social scale and forsaking the un-pleasant problems of central cities.

As both cause and effect throughout the nineteenth century, the spirit and activities of religion in a changing America were largely centered on the life of the individual. The "great awakenings" of the eighteenth and nineteenth centuries saw millions converted to Protestant church mem-bership, to the Old Puritan emphasis on individual personal experience to the relative exclusion of the old emphasis on building human com-munity. Admittedly, the churches had some social excuse for their captivity to this individualism. Cut off from official relation to government by the Constitution of the new nation, competing with each other for their share of new members in a largely "pagan" population, and baffled by the varieties of religious experience among immigrants seeking jobs in the new industrial cities, white Protestant churches of nineteenth century America sought to cope with urban pluralism through episodic charity and appeals to individuals that they believe the gospel and join the church. These emphases betrayed an incapacity to relate the Christian faith to the full range of the people and problems of the cities. Seldom in human history have either politicians or religious leaders had to cope with so rapid a collision of dreams, with such an onslaught of cultural diversity centered increasingly in cities. This collision continues to the 1980s, when Amer-ican cities continue to be hosts, sometimes unwilling, to the peoples of the world.[9]

Humanly speaking, then, it was understandable that no nineteenth century church movement proved capable of institutionalizing its vision of a church, a city, and a nation comprised of "all sorts and conditions" of humans. Having followed immigrants to these shores, church after church followed the same immigrants in an internal migration typified by the movement of the inner-city church to the suburbs. For example, Charles Stelzle's *Christianity's Storm Center: A Study of the Modern City*, published in 1907, vividly portrayed the retreat of Protestantism from lower Manhattan. Forty Protestant churches had abandoned neighborhoods below 20th Street while 200,000 immigrants had moved in. Stelzle put the onus on both the churches and business greed.

> The filthy slum, the dark tenement, the unsanitary factory, the long hours of toil, the lack of a living wage, the back-breaking labor, the inability to pay necessary doctor's bills in time of sick-ness, the poor and insufficient food, the lack of leisure, the swift approach of old age, the dismal future—these weigh down the hearts and lives of vast multitudes in our cities. No hell in the

future can be worse to them than the hell in which they now are.[10]

The settlement houses, religion-labor coalitions, cooperative urban parishes, and civil rights-empowerment movements of later decades may be viewed as extensions of these somewhat marginal phenomena of social prophecy by churches at the turn of the century. They have found inspiration in both papal encyclicals and Protestant social creeds.

That word "marginal" is deliberate. There has never been a time when the dominant churches of America have made social justice for the city an effective priority in their own institutional decisions, not to mention the political life of the nation. There has been a chronic failure to think and plan strategically for the welfare of the city as a whole or for those people most victimized by the nation's industrial and commercial institutions. "Urban mission" has been viewed largely in terms of church survival and charitable projects, not engagement in the political struggle for power over urban and national priorities.

By standing aside from many of the political and economic struggles that have shaped the nation and its cities, the churches have built and preserved themselves institutionally at the cost of falling into political and economic molds little resembling a "holy community."[11] Religious organizations repeatedly have spent themselves securing and protecting turfs of their own, accepting as given the institutions that nudge and maneuver around their perimeters. Theologically, the churches have been so busy becoming American that they have had little energy left over for thinking deeply about the difference between being American and being faithfully Christian. Sam Bass Warner eloquently describes the easy shaping of religious identity to fit the contours of changing ethnic and class identities in the history of the immigrants and their children in the American city:

> All American families share a remarkably uniform urban experience, an experience compounded of class, ethnicity, and religion. The pattern is migration, followed by the ghetto or the slum or just hard times in the city, and this is succeeded by the eventual emergence into a stable income position, be it good or bad (for many it is good), then the church and the suburb. Behind the migrations lay tribes, villages, or family farms, depending on whether the family memory went back to Africa, Europe, or the rural United States. But as each family lives through its experiences in this country, each one passes through the acid of the city which burns off the special qualities of the past. In this corrosive environment Sicilian villagers become Italians, and Italians become neighborhood Catholics; Alabama farm boys, black

and white, become slum family men, and family men become builders of Baptist or Methodist churches. . . .

The most enduring ethnic cultural institutions in American cities have proved to be the churches, so that over the years or generations ethnic loyalties become merged into religious loyalty. Simultaneously job, income, housing, and neighborhood teach the class structure of the city, so that in time—for some a few years, for others a generation or two—a class and religious culture determines the orientation of all city dwellers. [12]

The attempts of the churches to carry on an aggressive mission to the metropolis from 1850 to 1980 must not be overlooked. There were the great revival meetings of the Second Awakening that successively drew Finney, Drummond, Billy Sunday, and Billy Graham to the city auditoriums; the settlement house movements that sought to meet the physical and cultural needs of inner city immigrants; the urban seminaries, like Union and McCormick, founded to train ministers for the "great and growing" metropolis;[13] the rise of the Social Gospel, Protestantism's great nineteenth century attempt to grapple with the industrial issues of child labor, women's rights, union organization, and the scandal of poverty in a rich society; the early participation of Catholic priests in asserting the rights of inner-city working people to decent housing, limited hours of work, and schools for their children; the aroused Protestant conscience of urban government reform programs that sought to rescue countless city halls from the predations of Tamanny Halls across the land; the liberal minorities in many churches that welcomed the federal government's new concern for jobs and housing for the poor in the cities of the nineteen-thirties; the new inner-city ministries in East Harlem and Westside Chicago in the 1950s; and the early support by many local Catholic churches of the neighborhood movement. All of these historic movements expressed the commitment of many church leaders and constituents to the needs of cities and their citizens.

But in almost every case the commitment was flawed, as if the leaders of the movements lacked either the theology or the empirical perception to take the whole city as object of missionary witness and service. The revivals of the mid-nineteenth century, while producing new religious impetus to such causes as the abolition of slavery and the rights of women, continued in a post–Civil War version that was strangely lacking in social conscience. Most of the famous revivalists of the past hundred years have preached a gospel to individuals with little explicit social concern at the heart of their message. The urban seminaries, few in number compared with their institutional sisters located in town and countryside, demon-

strated in their changing locations an uncertainty as to whether they belonged to the world of the city, the world of the university, or the world
of the suburb. The vocal criticism of urban industrialism, raised by Marx
and by the Social Gospel preachers, little dented the settlement houses'
preoccupation with food, clothes, language lessons, job-searches, recreation, sewing classes, and other personal services to the daily survival of
the immigrant millions. For all their theologically-correct concern for the
downtrodden members of the new industrial society, many Social Gospel
preachers remained socially identified with the well-educated rather than
the downtrodden, and a second generation of Catholic priests left their
preoccupation with the rights of working people to join the twentieth-
century trek of American Catholicism towards middle class suburban respectability. The urban reformers, as Lincoln Steffens' story makes clear,
attacked personal corruption in city hall without attacking the structures
of the city that often accounted for the growing wealth of the reformers—
such as the prices of urban land and the racial exclusions of urban residences. In addition, the "muckrakers" had the characteristic Protestant
weakness in politics of the conviction that "honest government" was possible chiefly through honest people without resort to the compromises and
interest-balances of ward politics. For the most part, church leaders in the
1930s gave little support to the federal government in its first incursions
into urban housing and community planning. Large majorities of Protestants, in particular, have sided with the adage of "The best government,
the least government," down to 1980. Even the bold new attempts to
fashion an urban ministry in the Harlems and west sides of the cities after
World War II had ambivalent support from seminaries, church bureaucracies, and the local churches. Following the people to the suburbs was
again the programmatic priority of all churches. Their strategists gave little
systematic attention to a religious and political ministry. To have remedied
decay would have been to examine the economic dynamics, the political
powers, and the cultural presumptions that produced it. It would have
been to ask why people of diverse national origins have such difficulty
living together in some neighborhoods of our cities. Did questions of
adequate housing for poor people, civil rights for racial minorities, and
job opportunities for the unemployed enter Sunday morning sermons in
the 1950s? Sometimes, but neither ministers nor congregations had grown
up to understand how, supremely in the life of the modern city, the lives
of people intertwine and intersect empirically in ways that would have
surprised even John Donne. In a city, there is no strict separation of physical

structures like streets and water mains, institutions like government and churches, and ideas like "justice" and "the good life."

To ask about this intertwining is to take the whole urban community as a field of religious and ethical concern. Let us look briefly at the empirical difficulty and possibility of such a concern on the part of the churches of this country in terms of "assets" and "liabilities" which the churches bring to such a venture.

CHURCH ASSETS AND LIABILITIES IN URBAN POLICY

Assets	Liabilities
1. Humane values	1. Anti-political bias
2. Congregational presence	2. Congregational idolatry
3. Regional polities	3. Incongruous polity boundaries
4. Racial inclusiveness	4. Racial separatism
5. Institutional experience	5. Preoccupation with church
6. Wealth	programs.
7. Educational institutions	6. Capitalist elites
8. Communications media	7. Anti-intellectualism
9. Lay leadership	8. Narcissistic habits
10. Urban pastoral experience	9. Church-domesticated laity
	10. Demoralization of city pastors

These parallel columns suggest the ambiguity of the churches' power and institutional resources. The assets add up to a much more imposing stock of resources than many would recognize. But the liabilities associated with or negating those assets are also more formidable than is commonly perceived. The obvious key to effective church strategy in urban policy is to exploit the assets and to overcome the liabilities.

1. With regard to **values**, the churches have a rich treasury of teachings appropriate to the urban struggle. Such values serve to motivate and empower Christian action. They include: the sanctity of personal and community life, the imperatives of justice and compassion for the poor and the oppressed, the interrelationships of all peoples, a ministry of reconciliation which can confront conflict and estrangement and can bring a new wholeness to human relationships.

But these values are considerably offset by the anti-political bias of most churches, which often means neglecting issues of justice for the sake of "spirituality"—or preferring the relief of individual plight to a more effective and preventive approach to complex and endemic problems—or

insisting on "nurture" as the precondition of an involvement which somehow never develops. Worship, pastoral care, evangelism, Christian education, missions, and even social action have, all too typically, been so
conceived as to avoid controversial political issues, even when the very
survival of city, nation, and world is at stake.

2. **Congregational presence** in urban communities has often meant
a witness of identification with the city, caring for those in special need,
sharing the opportunities and the burdens of urban living, commitment
to the city's future. Almost alone among the institutions of the city, the
church has multiple locations in virtually every neighborhood and organizational ties stretching across the city and the world.

But there is also widespread congregational idolatry which assumes
that the local church or parish is the "real church." This tends to mean
a preoccupation with church building and maintenance to the neglect of
community concerns, denominational relations, and ecumenical cooperation. Too many congregations corrupt the integrity of faith into self-
centered judgments about priorities, issues, and actions. Instead of becoming strategic outposts for redemptive mission, many local churches
become defensive enclaves retreating from their social environment.

3. **Regional polities or groupings** can bind urban and suburban churches
together in common strategies for mission. Presbyteries, dioceses, districts
offer unique non-governmental frameworks for action on metropolitan
problems and needs. Broader, less parochial viewpoints become possible
in such regions.

But the polity boundaries of denominations too often are related
incongruously to secular political boundaries in states and metropolitan
areas. In fact, ecclesiastical boundaries typically defy rationality, they are
sometimes used to avoid concerted action and to rationalize exclusivism,
especially in political matters. In many cases, the greater wealth and professional prestige of suburban churches find imperial expression in paternalistic dominance over the more disadvantaged churches, as well as in
avoiding or resisting such proposals as commuter taxes which would bring
greater equity to metropolitan revenues.

4. Denominational and ecumenical structures have made notable
progress toward **racial inclusiveness** in governing bodies, staffs, pronouncements, and programs. Multiracial church agencies have become increasingly resourceful in relation to urban minorities. Here and there, local
congregations have developed heartening models of racial inclusiveness.

But the racial separatism of most local congregations remains, reinforced by the white flight and visible weakness of churches in central cities

where minorities are concentrated. Tokenism angers minorities and exacerbates tensions toward extremism, hardening positions and limiting communication. Cosmetic actions for racial justice produce unrealistic expectations and deny the true depth of needs and concerns. Assumptions about racial dissimilarities rationalize congregational exclusiveness, abandonment of missions to the disadvantaged, and passing responsibility for urban ministry to unprepared clergy and unequipped congregations. Racial categories also obscure economic and class similarities which transcend ethnic excuses for discrimination.

It is a mark of the retreat and defensiveness of many white city churches that perception of social realities tends to become more and more distorted. In one northern metropolis some years ago, a newly arrived inner-city pastor was given remarkably different political pictures by beleaguered Protestant clergy. One old-timer warned him, "The Catholics have taken over this town." Another solemnly whispered, "The Jews pretty much run City Hall." And a third offered this briefing, "The colored people have all the power now." Only with time and more studious analysis did it become apparent that white suburban Protestants maintained a disproportionate share of control over the city's economic and political life.

5. The churches have accumulated a vast store of **institutional experience** in operating congregational and urban organizations and services, including hospitals, orphanages, community centers, and skidrow missions. Many of these have been passed along to secular institutions.

But these projects and services have frequently resulted in proprietary fixations by the churches on the maintenance of their own charities to the neglect of systematic political concerns. The transfer of management to secular agencies has too often been accompanied by disinvestment in the city. Whether preoccupied with their own urban programs or abandoning the city, churches have been only feebly represented in public struggles over urban policy.

6. The churches of America remain the **wealthiest** of all religious institutions in the world. They hold billions of dollars of properties, pension funds, other investments, operating budgets, and personnel. The total stewardship capacities of America's individual Christians, congregations, and denominations are an immense reservoir of financial power beyond the resources of most national governments. In 1980 the Southern Baptists recorded contributions of almost two and a half billion dollars; the United Methodists, one and a half billion; and the United Presbyterians, three quarters of a billion. Of the 48 billion dollars in charitable giving recorded in the United States in 1980, almost half (46.3 percent) was contributed

to religion; and most of these latter dollars came from the cumulative individual gifts of the 60 million or so individuals who go to church on a typical American Sunday.[14]

But capitalist elites tend to dominate church governance and to impose ideological constraints upon the church. For example, proposals for the investment of pension funds in socially-redemptive urban enterprises have commonly met narrow "prudence" as to how churches should earn their income. Too often church investments are bound to the biggest American corporations. There is also such a high percentage of the churches' capital investment in fixed assets like church buildings that strategies for institutional change and timely response to social crises are virtually precluded.

A common pattern of funding of urban ministries is the paternalistic arrangement under which limited short-term support is offered with the stipulation that those ministries will soon become self-supporting. The economic realities in such urban settings often combine the exodus of upper and middle income groups, the influx of lower income and welfare families, increasing unemployment, and rapidly rising taxes and rents. In short, prospects of self-support may be declining in the face of ecclesiastical expectations to the contrary. The actual stewardship achievements of some inner city congregations may be heroic on any fair standard of judgment but may meet with censure or cut-offs from funding agencies, thus hastening institutional demise in central cities.

7. The churches have developed and maintain thousands of **educational institutions**, including colleges, universities, and seminaries. These institutions offer bases for training leaders of church and society. Urban studies in basic curricula and continuing education programs have been established in some of these institutions.

But the anti-intellectualism of much church life orients most American Christians away from the complexities of economic, social, and technological problems, even in most seminaries. Agrarian fundamentalism continues to be a dominant force in the church at large. The transfer of new learnings and leadership models is impeded by lack of effective communication between secular and church structures. In educational institutions themselves, fragmented teaching and research often precludes coherent analysis, theological integrity, and bold experimentation in responding to institutional challenges to church and society.

8. The extensive array of **communications media** in the churches includes periodicals, educational materials, broadcasting and film agencies, and personnel from the secular media. A fundamental characteristic of Christian mission is communication of the word of faith and of judgment

to society. The media offer unique opportunities to feature urban and other public issues.

But many, if not most, religious media are addicted to narcissistic habits. They are house organs to promote the special interests of the churches' internal life. They tend to be inadequate instruments for candidly reporting, analyzing, and criticizing those special interests. Their non-political posture with regard to the life of the church itself is reinforced by a failure to expose Christians to the most basic political and ideological conflicts of their society. Suburban and rural images of the church and of Christian families tend to dominate and urban policy is neglected.

9. The churches are vocationally represented in secular institutions by **lay leadership** in many fields of vital importance to the welfare of the city. Government, industry, banking, commerce, labor, health, education, social work, real estate, journalism and other professional sectors are strategic vantage points for viewing justice and injustice in society.

But, American churches have typically preferred to nurture "church-domesticated laity, tamed and caged by the church" (Johannes Hoekendijk), instead of strategies for empowering the ministry of the laity in the world of work and citizenship. Daily work rarely gets the attention accorded to the housekeeping tasks of church maintenance. Vocational responsibilities for social justice are seldom nurtured. Yet the decisions of bankers or realtors or physicians largely determine the quality of life for whole communities or regions.

10. The churches, especially in their clergy, have acquired over many generations a rich fund of **urban pastoral experience** through daily ministry to city persons and families and communities which is unique in its wholistic exposure to the human realities of urban life. In many cases, that ministry represents a profound vocational commitment to the urban struggle and has provided precious personal satisfactions.

But many clergy see an appointment to a city pastorate as a demotion or a punishment. Ecclesiastical status and rewards often do not favor inner city ministries since suburban churches offer higher salaries and more comfortable family living. Advocacy of liberal and minority causes often taints city priests and pastors with an untouchable "radical" label and lack of peer support makes urban clergy more vulnerable to burned-out careers. In short, the demoralization of urban pastors is a very serious institutional weakness in most Christian denominations.

There is no intention to suggest that the liabilities cancel all the assets of the churches in the urban arena. We only insist that realistic perspectives be developed concerning urban policy strategies. The assets will be vividly evident in the models of urban ministry described in the next pages.

COALITIONS OF WITNESS, WORK, AND POLITICAL CHANGE

Urban policy in America includes federal policy, state policy, county policy, and municipal policy. Some of these layers have no other connection with each other but others are entwined with each other. Some of the layers are mutually supportive; others smother those below.

Our thesis is that urban policy is in the province of the churches' mission. But the function of the local church varies in relation to each layer of urban policy. We focus here on illustrations of urban mission undertaken by local churches. In all of the following cases, we are dealing with the dynamics of building coalitions.

History offers some interesting examples, particularly among the great cathedral-like "downtown churches" of the turn of the century, of the solitary impact of individual churches on government policies. Often these churches had held sway in the political arena while denying the validity of religion's encroachment into the world, affirming its proper sphere as the salvation of souls or the conversion of sinners. Such churches had political influence because of the size or prestige of their constituency.

This picture has been considerably altered, at least since the civil rights struggles of the 1960s. Individual churches of varying size and denomination have come to the pragmatic conclusion that their social mission can only be accomplished through coalitions because the voice of an individual church is relatively weak among the tumult of special interest voices and urban problems are larger than any one church. Blight affects large segments of the city irrespective of church lines. It is resistant to Band-Aid treatments applied by individual practitioners.

Some flourishing coalitions have been developed by churches around the country in the past decade. Some of them are familiar to urban activists. The Birmingham Neighborhood Coalition (Toledo, Ohio), Communities Organized for Public Service (San Antonio, Texas), Michigan Avenue Community Organization (Detroit, Michigan), The Northwest Community Organization (Chicago, Illinois), Greenpoint Williamsburg Coalition of Community Organizations (Brooklyn, New York), Missouri Delta Ecumenical Ministry (Southeastern Missouri) have successfully used community resources to attack area-wide social problems.

The development of effective urban policy calls for the same type of coalition-building on the national level. The problems those organizations address are ultimately intractable to piecemeal action on the local level. Urban policies can only be dealt with through systematic coordination. Successful church strategies have to be aimed at systemic change, malleable only to macro-social actions.

An important example of the development of this type of strategic thinking is the anti-redlining movement. The churches cannot take credit for it, but they were early participants in it. The movement became national when local groups realized they could not change pernicious bank policies which denied home mortgage and repair loans to local urban residents unless they effected new national legislation. It took seven years of national coalition-building, but in 1976 Congress finally passed the Home Mortgage Disclosure Act. The act requires banks to make their lending policies public, enabling community groups to take action on the basis of these disclosures. Later, the Community Re-investment Act was passed. It requires that banks make known their investments in the local community. An indication of the power of these acts is that the banking community lobbied furiously and unsuccessfully to prevent the renewal of the Home Mortgage Disclosure Act in 1981.

Ultimately, coalitions require a style of working that is at variance to the mode of operating of most local churches. Church groups can rapidly become expert at it.

An interesting example of positive church involvement in the city is Adopt-A-Building. Begun in 1970, it serves the residents of the lower east side of Manhattan, who refer to it by the Hispanico-American neologism, "Loisaida." In terms of devastation, rubble, decay, and deteriorated quality of life, Loisaida is only surpassed by the South Bronx. It has about 30,000 residents, almost evenly divided between whites and minorities (blacks and Hispanics).

Interfaith Adopt-A-Building, as it was then called, originated in 1970 as a network of all the churches and organizations in East Harlem. Its central purpose was to train clergy and laity to organize tenants to improve housing conditions in the area. Organizers worked as volunteers that first year out of the Interfaith City Mission Society office. Through the accumulation of funds through small grants and donations, they established a city-wide organization, but they discovered that they were not ready to manage an organization with that large a scope. Around 1974, Adopt-A-Building became a neighborhood-based organization, with a clear idea of its territorial limits, its housing stock, and its target problems.

Initially, its main work was tenant organizing. It helped residents in deteriorated, often abandoned, buildings to acquire title to the buildings and to rehabilitate the buildings themselves. Adopt-A-Building grew to a staff of 110 employees by the end of the 1970s with a budget of just over one million dollars. Among its material accomplishments are the preservation of the neighborhood community, skill-training in rehabilitation, building management and maintenance, community ownership of low and moderate income housing, on-the-job training, improvement of neighborhood security, development of youth leadership, increased local participation in city government, and development of the cultural characteristics of the neighborhood.

Loisaida was once a neighborhood where strangers feared to walk, where debris and sewerage littered the streets, where the housing stock resembled that of a war-torn city, where people stopped reporting crimes to the police. Today, things are different. It is still very much a city neighborhood, plagued by the problems of air and traffic pollution and diminishing municipal services, but it is also a neighborhood with a future. There are signs of hope. It has over two hundred tenant-owned buildings, vegetable gardens, new pocket parks, a plaza for cultural activities, sealed empty buildings, resurfaced streets and sidewalks, and citizen participation in crime control.

Beyond these, there are other more elusive achievements to be noted. The residents of Loisaida developed their own capabilities by acquiring new skills and techniques and improved the quality of their own lives. They became centers of collective power with a vision of hope.

Adopt-A-Building developed from being a reactive to being a proactive organization. Its initial priority was to react to urban decay by tenant organizing. Gradually its strategies shifted to defining a territory and designing plans for the future of the area. It moved from short-term accomplishments to the development of long-term goals on the basis of residents' expressed needs.

The organization, whose leaders came from the neighborhood, discovered the need to move beyond physical rehabilitation and organized town meetings where residents made concerted decisions about the future of their neighborhood. It encouraged explorations in the oral history of its old and new immigrants. It built a new community center, presented locally written dramas, inaugurated a series of neighborhood festivals, all with the intention of getting the residents more deeply involved in their own and in each other's lives. Realizing that decisions made in city hall, Albany, or Washington, D.C. affected their efforts, they sought ways to participate in the larger governmental structures that affected their lives. Neighborhood residents won membership on the municipal community board. They also joined other groups who were lobbying for public policy change on the local and national level.

Most of this might not have happened without church participation. The churches played an initiating role that was facilitated by their position of stability and acceptability in the community. They lent financial support at the crucial early steps, and continued the support throughout. They gave it a vision profoundly related to *shalom*. To the credit of these churches, they were able to put the organization into the hands of the people.

One religious lobby has given this definition of its mission:

> People in political ministry accept their responsibility for changing these (social, economic and political) systems, for getting at the roots of injustice. They believe that the systems are potentially transformable, and that political action is an effective tool. For this reason, they focus their energy on legislation, believing that reorienting public policy is a force for incremental systemic change. . . . It is a way to move step by step from how society is now to a preferred world. It enables people to be practical about their vision. As they attend to what is possible now—immediate, effective structural changes—they also move toward eventual overall systemic change. Their activity is more than reform, a minimization of injustice in existing structures. It is an attempt to restructure society itself.[15]

A good example of this strategy in operation in an urban context is the National Low Income Housing Coalition.

A recent issue of the *National Journal* said about Cushing Dolbeare, the President of the National Low Income Housing Coalition, "Many housing insiders attribute the victory (over the middle-income housing legislation) to the shrewd lobbying tactics of Dolbeare, whom they consider one of the most effective housing lobbyists."[16] Dolbeare, the article went on to say, attributed her success to the support of low income people themselves.

All this praise was for an organization with two full-time staff persons and an occasional part-timer. They represent a coalition of individuals and organizations whose purpose is education, organization, and advocacy for decent housing, suitable environments, adequate neighborhoods, and freedom of housing choice for low-income people. They are concerned about all people for whom decent housing is unaffordable, but the urban poor is their first priority. Though they supported the idea of middle-income housing legislation, they resisted the proposed middle-class legislation because it intended to take money directly from low-income housing programs.

In the United States there is no other public interest, consumer-based national organization focussed solely on advocacy of low-income housing programs. How does it operate? It follows low-income housing needs and programs closely. It alerts its members and others in its national network to actions that need to be taken up in Congress or by the Administration. It develops policy positions, testifies and works on Congress and the Administration to get them adopted.

Some of its tactics are apparent in another of its recent successes. In November, 1979 HUD's budget for assisted housing was to be cut to about 185,000 units for fiscal year 1981. The Coalition and its members spearheaded the efforts to get President Carter to reconsider these decisions. On December 12, it presented Vice President Walter Mondale with a letter for President Carter urging an increase in the number of units funded for low-income people. The letter was signed by 66 national organizations, and 448 state and local groups, representing every state in the union. Vice President Mondale was visibly impressed with the range of support for low-income housing demonstrated by this letter, and agreed to see that the President read it personally. President Carter later decided to increase HUD's low-income housing programs up to 300,000 units, a 23% increase over the 1980 appropriation, enough for 60–75,000 additional units.

In addition, the Coalition worked on the following low-income housing issues: low income energy assistance, the Uniform Relocation Act, extension of the Home Mortgage Disclosure Act and the Fair Housing Act, the Housing and Community Development Amendments of 1979, and Section 8/public housing. Church leaders were among the founders of N.L.I.H.C., and the organization is another example of church contribution to a change in national urban policy.

We have presented a vision of justice and *shalom*. We have suggested certain policy alternatives in the political, social, and economic areas. A strategy that exemplifies both nerve and steadiness of purpose is the church response to the shutdown of the Youngstown Sheet and Tube Company by the Lykes Corporation in Youngstown, Ohio. It is an instance of church action in an all-but-hopeless situation to use resources to create a new future. The strategy is significant not so much for its method, but for the scope and content of church involvement. Here, the churches moved beyond their traditional social services, even beyond community organizing, to issues of public policy and economic redevelopment.

The history of the closing of the company has been told in many places. Here is one brief account, which displays its human consequences.

"The Lykes Corporation acquired Youngstown Sheet & Tube in 1969. For eight years, Lykes milked Youngstown Sheet & Tube of its assets in order to acquire cash for corporate growth in other fields. In 1968, the combined debt of Youngstown Sheet & Tube and Lykes was $192 million. By 1970 it had grown to $609 million and Lykes had become a conglomerate. In the early '70s Lykes failed to utilize available cash to modernize Youngstown, using it instead to acquire other companies—a phenomenon becoming more common as conglomerates come to dominate the national and international economy.

"When Lykes announced the closing in September (1977) it blamed cheap imports, environmental requirements and government price restraints. A careful review of the facts indicates that poor management practices and the draining off of profits and cash reserves for non-steel purposes were more crucial factors. . . . When Lykes acquired it, Youngstown Sheet & Tube was a healthy company. In the ensuing eight years, Lykes' policies of heavy borrowing, siphoning off assets, mismanagement and neglect have left YS & T an expendable part of a sick conglomerate.

"Campbell is a small suburb of Youngstown where most of the shutdown facilities are located. Last year (1977) the city took in $1.5 million in income taxes, 90% of the total generated by YS & T. Property taxes make up 60% of the town's general fund, and 90% of those property taxes come from Sheet & Tube. The Ecumenical Coalition estimates that the ripple effects from the 5,000 layoffs will result in the loss of an additional 10,000 jobs. Assuming that each of these jobs is a primary income source for a family of three or more, as many as 50,000 persons will be *directly* affected by the closing. Statistics are impersonal, but they have consequences in human lives. The economic insecurity and loss of human dignity which ensues from the closing will be reflected in an increase in marital breakups, alcoholism, depression, adultery, racial antagonisms, crime and suicide. This is not idle speculation. Studies have demonstrated what individual-oriented therapists and caseworkers have often overlooked—that there is a direct connection between 'personal' problems and economic conditions. As the Ecumenical Coalition puts it, Lykes' decision to close the plant 'is the result of a way of doing business in this country that too often fails to take into account the human dimensions of economic action.' "[17]

Both the size and the suddenness of the layoffs caught everyone by surprise. Traditional government, labor and business circles were paralyzed. Local politicos took to blaming foreign imports and the inflated state of the economy. The United Steelworkers initially offered only a shrug of the shoulders and counselled resignation to the situation.

Local religious leaders, however, stepped quickly into this vacuum. Within a week of the announcement of the shutdown, Bishop James W. Malone of the Catholic diocese of Youngstown and John H. Burt, Episcopal Bishop of Ohio, initiated a series of actions to evaluate the situation and formulate a response. An ecumenical coalition was put together. It rapidly concluded that this was not an issue just of steel or of jobs, but of urban decay and community disintegration. Their response was to consider public policy and economic alternatives, namely, worker/community ownership of the mill and the development of related public policy. Their approach was thoughtful and cautious. They ordered a feasibility study to determine the possibilities and pitfalls of such an alternative, and to develop a plan for implementing whatever action was deemed feasible.

The Carter Administration demonstrated an initial enthusiasm and interest in the project and made a feasibility study possible through large grants from the Department of Housing and Urban Development and the Community Services Administration. But, before the study was completed, Attorney General Bell approved a merger between the Lykes and LTV Corporation, without specific requirements to facilitate the efforts of the local community. Lykes/LTV put a number of obstacles in the path of the workers.

The completed feasibility study concluded that the plant could reopen and show a profit by 1982. But, the community of workers would need 300 million dollars in federal loan guarantees, similar to those given to Chrysler. President Carter denied the request.

The Ecumenical Coalition stopped operating officially as a coalition a few months later. The member churches, individually and cooperatively, continue to supply support and aid to the community because the human tragedy continues to spread. U.S. Steel closed two huge works in November, 1979, putting four to five thousand more workers out of work. Attempts at legal remedies and further appeals to the Carter Administration to execute a similar worker/community-owned mill failed.

Four years after the closing of the Youngstown plant, a combination of worker initiative and personal sacrifice, family resourcefulness and government action, has diminished the human tragedy of this sudden change in one community. By 1981, of the 200 workers who lost their jobs, 1,200 had taken early retirement at 50 percent of their previous income, 1000 skilled workers had found jobs elsewhere, 4,200 were being retrained at government expense; and only 600 were unemployed and without promise of employment. These facts demonstrate that the job market can adjust to dislocated workers, that industrial and union programs can improve justice for workers, and that government can do something to make economic dislocation more tolerable. But, if our vision allows us to treat even 600 unemployed steel workers as expendable for purposes of economic efficiency, then we are far from *shalom*.

Both vision and strategy underwent a testing in this event, and what the churches tried to do here may be as instructive for the future as what they succeeded in doing. What they did and tried to do can be summarized as follows:

1. It was an effort to move beyond the traditional urban model of Christian service to one of enabling, empowering and empurposing. The churches were motivated by the accepted and worthy Christian concern for the amelioration of suffering. They realized, however, that Christian services to alleviate the pinch caused by the new, disastrous social milieu were not adequate to the situation. At stake was not the suffering of a few, but the viability of the community itself. They moved beyond the assuaging of symptoms to the altering of causes.

2. The Coalition advocated the development of new economic and public policy alternatives. The churches questioned established economic doctrine upon which current public policy is based. They called for a study of economic alternatives. Their worker/community ownership model included local self-help, local control, widespread worker and community participation, the development of new steel technology, energy conservation, environmental protection, and meeting public needs. The Coalition also asked for concomitant public policy change, requiring administrative and legislative action to:

- provide federal aid for modernization of existing steel facilities in severely impacted areas where steelworkers already live.
- facilitate government purchasing policies to provide preferential treatment for communities in deep financial trouble.
- encourage increased use of steel to meet human and community needs.
- seek changes in economic policies which unfairly pit region against region for jobs and economic growth, which encourage the development of conglomerates and neglect the needs of older and urban communities.[18]

Such strategy can change the character of workers from passive victims of economic decisions made in the distant executive suites of the corporate world to owners, shapers of their own future and sharers in the profits of their own work.

3. The effort was ecumenical. Issues of injustice are impervious to denominational lines. Strategies of empowerment, empurposement, and public policy change are larger than the capabilities of individual churches. The religious leaders of Youngstown and Ohio recognized this. The membership of the Ecumenical Coalition of the Mahoning Valley included leaders from the Catholic, Protestant, Jewish, and Orthodox communities.

4. The Coalition filled the institutional gap. Institutions are anchors. They provide stability, recognition, and continuity. Without institutional support, the workers would have been treated like a loose association of malcontents. Traditional institutions were paralyzed. The Coalition undergirded the workers movement with the institutional support it needed to make substantial progress and gave the movement respectability. Churches do this by their missions and goals when these are perceived as altruistic by the larger society.

5. The churches supplied the workers with an ongoing religious network. A network is a ready audience, available to hear problems, take action, make financial contributions, lend moral support. All churches are part of one. Initial steps were taken with the help of funding from national denominations. The network also gave evidence of a broad base of support for the revitalization efforts in Youngstown. It developed a mechanism whereby persons could open up special bank accounts in their own name and control, but which served as a pledge backing the re-opening of the mill.

6. The churches also served their traditional educational role. They issued a pastoral letter pointing out that it was not just a question of jobs or the sufferings of individuals, but of the broader issues of the destruction of community and communal well-being, of social justice and corporate responsibility.

> The purpose of economic life is to serve the common good and the needs of the people. . . . [Their] rights include the right to useful employment and to decent wages and income, the right to participate in economic decisions and even ownership, the right to bargain collectively, among others. These rights carry with them the responsibility to labor honestly and productively for the common good. . . . Government is required to preserve and defend human rights when private action fails to insure them. Economic institutions, although they have their own purposes and methods, still must serve the common good and are subject to moral judgment.[19]

7. As an extension of traditional educational roles, the Coalition became heavily involved in broad public education. The Coalition realized that its goals, objectives, and the details of its proposals, needed to be understood by the public at large in order to recruit their necessary support and cooperation. Briefings were conducted with business, political, religious, labor, media, and community leaders to explain various types of ownership, financing ideas, the availability of local capital, management possibilities. There were several large meetings for Youngstown citizens, different groups of steelworkers, and business people. Feature articles were published and editorials encouraged in various journals and newspapers. National media coverage was supplied by television networks and news magazines.

8. The Coalition also used its political clout. The churches represent a constituency, which they do not necessarily control but over which they exercise a moral suasion and which gives them a ready ear. Politicians and public policy makers recognize this. They like to be seen standing next to Pope, bishop or minister, they support family legislation for this reason, and they are sensitive to issues concerning the future of Israel. The Coalition was able to get many local and state politicians to take a public stand on the issue during an election year. It was also able to call on its network to participate in letter-writing and telephone campaigns to politicians.

9. The Coalition functioned as catalyst and resource. The churches initiated actions, brought together various groups, educated the public, generated funds, supplied motivation and a vision. They had the wisdom, however, to recognize their own limitations in economics, steel production, finance, and law. They carefully sought out and gathered together a team of experts in those areas, and declared themselves ready to assume a less conspicuous role when the project was ready to stand on its own.

10. The churches supplied financial assistance. This traditional role for the churches was applied in an untraditional way—to support grassroots action. Grassroots action means people seizing control of their own lives and shaping their own future. Funds are often not available for this type of activity. Conventional funding sources look for innovative projects that operate within the safe perimeters of accepted economic, social, and political doctrine. Grassroots groups often challenge these assumptions. Frequently, churches are the only source of funds for this kind of activity. In the Mahoning Valley, this proved to be the case. Many, but not all, of the traditional funding sources perceived the turn of events as socialism, not as a form of worker capitalism.

•   •   •

How does the work of the Coalition measure up to the strategy assumptions stated at the very beginning of this book? It is clear that the overall strategy was motivated by human suffering and the deterioration of community well-being. The strategy was also empurposing. It had a vision, it took stock of the potential and capabilities of the workers, and attempted to create a situation in which they would be able to take control over their lives and decide how to deal with their own problems.

Finally, the strategy was directed to issues of public policy. At stake was the future of a viable urban community. Conventional fiscal policies, industrial policies, employment policy, intergovernmental policy were unable to deal with the problems that shook the community to the breaking point. For this reason, the Coalition took the direction it did, and advocated public policy change. Its goal was to empower the local community.

This strategy is a microcosm of a neighborhoods-based urban policy. It has the same intention, though the concrete goal of worker capitalism may not be the answer that fits the crises of a total national and international economy.

OTHER STRATEGIES

No list of church ministries or social strategies can be complete, but the other major church efforts to deal with the human challenge of urban America fall generally into these seven groups: (1) Hearings, (2) Staff Offices, (3) Lobbying and Networking, (4) Task Forces, (5) Assessment and Planning, (6) Seminary Education, and (7) Study Centers. In recent years, one of these approaches has tended to include, or lead to, others. This is a development natural to many a successful effort at social change such as when church people move from an initial commitment to feed hungry people in their neighborhood to do research on the conditions which cause people to be hungry to form coalitions for political action to change basic laws and social policies.

(1) **Hearings:** Roman Catholics and Episcopalians have used a "hearings" format to understand urban and other social problems. Roman Catholic meetings have covered a large range of issues: justice in the church, women in the church, ethnicity and race, family, human rights and global justice, political responsibility, parish and neighborhood, community and personhood, equal opportunity and economic justice. The Episcopal Church's

hearings were targeted directly at urban problems and concerns. For this reason, its process will be briefly described here.

The Episcopal Church, recognizing that it is inextricably interwoven with the life of the cities, chose the hearings format to assure the widest possible participation of church members in the assessment of the urban situation and the role the Church should play in exercising its Christian mandate. To accomplish this, a series of public hearings were held in seven urban centers beginning in 1977. In each case "listening" board membership included bishops, representatives of the minority community, and urban experts. They heard testimony from a wide range of people who share urban concerns.

As a result of these hearings, and a felt need on the part of some bishops, clergy, and lay persons, the Urban Bishops Coalition supported the establishment of the Episcopal Urban Caucus. The Caucus' program is based largely on the insights gained from the hearings.

The Caucus is a movement within the Episcopal Church to stand with and for the poor in urban areas. It seeks to influence the structure of the church as well as to minister to the needs of the poor in cities. This attitude is reflected in a fine working paper of the Bishops Coalition "The Challenge for Evangelism and Mission." It calls the church to the frontiers of public policy: to shaping public policy in regard to the arms race, nuclear proliferation, haphazard urban development, the flight of capital from the cities, unemployment, and the nurturing of citizen participation in the search of a new urban economic base and structure. While most of the operating funds come from diocesan and other church sources, the Caucus was not established officially by the church, and has an independent existence from it.

(2) **Staff Offices:** Attrition affected many of the national urban staff offices of many churches during the last decade. The tide is turning. Staff offices with urban concerns are beginning to reappear.

The Office of Urban Ministries of the United Methodist Church is one that held its own throughout the decade. It has three foci: urban church development, urban community development, and urban mission development. The office is involved in strategy development, training, consultative services, and financial resourcing. The development of a just national urban policy is seen as the framework of possibility and constraint for whatever else the church wants to do. The office has advocated full employment, housing and community development, community economic development, and opposition to various urban forms of racism. It also has been engaged in building the capacity of local churches to carry on a ministry in these areas of concern.

(3) **Lobbying and Networking:** The Washington Interreligious Staff Council (WISC) is a cooperative association of the professional staff of major Protestant, Catholic, and Jewish groups in America. WISC attempts to provide an ethical dimension to public policy debate. Through its newsletter and telephone network it interprets public policy decisions to its constituents and communicates their concerns to policy makers in Washington. It has task forces on United States food policy, foreign policy, military spending, housing, health care, criminal justice, and similar issues.

One of its member organizations is NETWORK. A registered congressional lobby, NETWORK has members throughout the nation organized to bring constituent pressure on local congresspersons to vote in favor of legislation they support.

Political observers have said of the eleven full-time employees of Network in Washington, D.C.: "They know their issues, they know what they have to do, and they do it." Their choice of issues is surprising because they do not fit the politician's stereotype of a church organization. In 1980, they were working for the passage of the revised Fair Housing Act, the Home Mortgage Disclosure Act Amendment, and the Equal Rights Amendment. They opposed the development of the MX missile system, the continued licensing and construction of nuclear reactors, and budget cuts in domestic social programs. These are the issues and positions that were decided by its 4,500 members.

As a political lobbying group, contributions to Network are not tax deductible. A tight budget requires its executive director to make an annual salary of just over six thousand dollars. Many of the staff receive only half that much. It supports itself through membership dues and donations. Roman Catholic nuns are among its major supporters. As an organization providing Washington decision-makers with continuous, informed, timely communication from a cross-section of American Christians, Network is a uniquely effective religious invention.

(4) **Task Force:** Task forces often take different shapes because they are usually temporary groupings organized around a specific objective. Because of the broad agenda of most church groups, task forces tend to proliferate. The Task Forces on Urban Mission and Ministry of the United Presbyterian Church in the U.S.A. and the Presbyterian Church in the U.S. have set

up a productive strategy which parallels the "hearings" tactic of the Episcopal and Catholic Churches.

The task forces used a team approach to solicit grassroots participation in the formulation of an urban mission statement for the Presbyterian Churches. To accomplish this, carefully trained teams of two were sent to twenty-six cities to study the nature of local urban problems and to inquire about appropriate church responses. On the basis of these data, an urban policy statement was written that envisions the city as a just, inclusive society in which persons are nurtured, supported, and affirmed in its rich diversity. While not as pointed a public policy statement as that of the Episcopal Caucus, among its recommendations are these: focussing judicatory activity on public policy, the political education of the local congregation, better urban ministry planning, and the establishment of a joint Urban Mission Office.

(5) **Assessment and Planning:** Some churches have developed technical plans for accomplishing their urban mission. A 1977 plan by the Lutheran Church in America's Division for Mission in North America (DMNA) has been used as a model by others. A strength of the plan is its recognition of the city as a network of communities and systems. These include neighborhoods, the political system, the economic system, the cultural system, the commercial media system. Also included are the education system, the legal justice system, the professional support systems. Within these, it recognizes a large class of cultural and social groups. For each of these groups and systems, it lists broad church objectives.

In general, this plan seems to be more oriented to social service and the interior life of the church than to public policy development or advocacy. This is unfortunately true of some of the plans which preceded it. The strategy, however, is a commendable and important one. To repeat a thesis of this book: careful planning is one way to insure that poor people shape and share in the commonweal.

(6) **Seminary Education:** A large proportion of Protestant seminaries founded in the nineteenth century were rural by location and educational intention. Only a few seminaries like Union in New York were conceived as urban institutions from the start; and some like McCormick now in Chicago followed the westward-moving tide of migration from frontier to town to city before identifying with a metropolis. Many Protestant and Catholic seminaries remain today in small town or rural locales, and few have

developed curricula strongly oriented towards the training of ministers for city churches and an urban mission.

The most powerful influence on the training of future urban ministers, perhaps, resides in those city congregations where effective ministry is already occurring and where seminary students serve as interns or part-time ministers. The "clinical" or practice-centered component in education exercises great power on the forming of students for their future professional roles. Moreover, theological schools located in great crisis-ridden cities orient their students to urban problems by the convenient— and inconvenient—methods of subway riding, apartment living, and rubbing elbows with "all sorts and conditions" of people on the streets.

Only a few American seminaries, however, have changed their theological curriculum structures to address urban life and mission in more than episodic fashion. Faculties in cities like Boston, New York, Washington, Chicago, Atlanta, Dallas, San Francisco, and Los Angeles have individual members who teach courses in this area of concern; but seldom is their work coordinated with that of their colleagues. One exception to this generalization is the Seminary Consortium for Urban Pastoral Education (SCUPE) in Chicago. Founded in 1976, it seeks to prepare students for urban ministry in a combination of extensive evangelical theological study with long-term supervised training in some aspect of an urban church ministry. Courses address such topics as biblical approaches to urban culture, the social structure and political processes of urban black communities, economic development of a community, and the organization of neighborhoods. Among the skills which the program seeks to cultivate in students are:

- Acquiring a working knowledge of the system, issues, and demographics of a large city.
- Communicating with people from a variety of ethnic and racial backgrounds.
- Analyzing an urban neighborhood to identify needs, concerns and resources.
- Identifying the existing lines of authority in an urban church.
- Developing working relationships with community social agencies.
- Writing funding proposals.
- Working with community organizers and organizations.
- Addressing major social issues from sociological, theological and practical ministry perspectives.
- Identifying signs that a church is declining because of neighborhood transition and working constructively with that church.

- Analyzing and critiquing the use of technology as a means of building or destroying community life in the city.
- Working with the political, economic, and social structures of an urban society so that these systems are influenced by values of God's kingdom.

As custodians of the theological tradition of the Christian churches, seminaries are obligated to link that tradition to the contemporary Christian mission. Seminaries can help the churches cross the frontier between their old urban fears and new needs of people. For the achieving of a theology and a ministry adequate to the life of cities, seminaries will doubtless continue to need the practical experience of city pastors, congregations, and missions. Even more, all will need each other.

(7) **Study Centers:** The best of intentions sometimes produce questionable accomplishments. Government programs intended to alleviate housing problems have contributed to the deterioration of neighborhoods. Church service programs intended to alleviate suffering have contributed to the dependent client status of those they intended to help.

Knowledge follows interest, and most research and theories are shaped by the values of the theorizers. Church-run and church-supported study centers are necessary to insure that their values and perspectives come into play in the research process. With the well-being of the urban poor as a plumbline, for example, such a study center would aid in the solution of fundamental problems by:

- Analyzing government and private programs for their adequacy to empurposement and well-being of the poor.
- Mapping alternative approaches and perspectives in public policy.
- Examining church programs to insure they are producing the desired effect.
- Sifting through the information from urban research projects around the country.
- Insuring that church groups receive a hearing in public forums.
- Weighing potential differences in intention, effect, and costs of various programs.

Policy research is best conducted by organizational units that specialize in such research but are sufficiently independent of deadlines and constituency pressure to allow critical analysis. Aside from the Churches' Center for Theology and Public Policy, there is no church study center that deals directly with issues of urban policy affecting the lives of millions of the urban poor. The Center has a staff person working exclusively on issues of urban policy and an urban policy panel which meets several times each year. Panel membership includes policy makers, theologians, social ethicists, church activists, political and social scientists. The panel is unique. It is the only group of experts with a religious or theological interest meeting on a regular basis to deal with issues of urban policy. Panel and staff are concerned with the development of a coherent urban policy and the empurposement of neighborhood and community residents.

One of the significant findings of the Church Women United Urban Causeway was the discovery of many dedicated people in public agencies who wanted the help and support of church people. These "lay ministers" are often neglected by the churches with their priority concern for training church personnel. Professionals in their fields can be helped by church-supported study centers which deal with public policy issues on a technical level.

NOTES

[1] H. H. Gerth and C. Wright Mills, editors, *From Max Weber* (New York: Oxford University Press, 1946), p. 269.

[2] Cf. John Garraty, *The American Nation* (New York: Harper & Row, 1966), p. 24.

[3] "A Model of Christian Charity," in *American Christianity*, ed. H. Shelton Smith, Robert T. Handy and Lefferts A. Loetscher, vol. 1 (New York: Charles Scribner's Sons, 1969), p. 100.

[4] Sam Bass Warner, Jr., *The Urban Wilderness* (New York: Harper & Row, 1972), p. 12.

[5] Ibid., p. 20.

[6] Ibid., p. 25.

[7] Ibid., pp. 27–28.

[8] *Religion and Change* (New York: Harper & Row, 1979), p. 63.

[9] Donald W. Shriver, Jr. and Karl A. Ostrom, *Is There Hope for the City?* (Philadelphia: Westminster Press, 1977), p. 18. Cf. pp. 18–23.

[10] Quoted in C. H. Hopkins, *The Rise of the Social Gospel in American Protestantism, 1865–1915.*

[11]For further exposition of this term, especially in the context of Calvinism and Puritanism, cf. Ernst Troeltsch, *The Social Teaching of the Christian Churches*, vol II, pp. 590 ff. (London and New York: The Macmillan Company, 1931).

[12]Warner, *Urban Wilderness*, pp. 156–57.

[13]From the Constitutional Preface of Union Theological Seminary, New York City, 1836.

[14]*Church Financial Statistics and Related Data* (New York: National Council of Churches, 1981).

[15]*NETWORK Quarterly* 7 (Washington, D.C.: Network, Summer, 1979), B3.

[16]*National Journal* (September 20, 1980), p. 1558.

[17]"Save Youngstown: Save America," *JSAC Grapevine* 9 (New York: Joint Strategy and Action Committee, January, 1978), p. 1.

[18]Pastoral Letter: "A Religious Response to the Mahoning Valley Steel Crisis," November 29, 1977.

[19]Ibid.

A Postscript-Conclusion

IT IS easy to demonstrate the limits of power religious organizations have to influence public policy in the United States. It is even easier to demonstrate the limits of their wisdom, moral rectitude, and capacity to "practice what they preach." The authors of this book, on the basis of their faith in God, have little faith in the ability of the churches, or any other human institution, to solve all human problems. In the final analysis, a famous word of Reinhold Niebuhr still holds:

> Nothing that is worth doing can be achieved in our lifetime; therefore we must be saved by hope. Nothing which is true or beautiful or good makes complete sense in any immediate context of history; therefore we must be saved by faith. Nothing we do, however virtuous, can be accomplished alone; therefore we are saved by love. No virtuous act is quite as virtuous from the standpoint of our friend and foe as it is from our standpoint. Therefore we must be saved by the final form of love which is forgiveness.[1]

We have tried in this volume to demonstrate that faith in God neither denies nor obscures religion's concern for the everyday world of human affairs. To the contrary, religious faith orients believers to this world, gives them a sense of its direction, and impels them to pursue in their own actions a future already promised the world by its Creator.

Whatever steps are taken in the next few years in the United States to confront certain urban problems, we need new vision and new direction among people who shape political decisions on all levels of our national life. We have to rethink our models of human purpose, human community, and human responsibility. We have to clarify our assumptions about what is real, desirable, and possible for human beings. Such clarity will be all the more essential in an era that some have foreseen as "lean years" for the American people. We have to rethink what justice means for a people who are giving up their dreams of unlimited national affluence. We have to decide if wealth for some is worth purchasing at the price of poverty for many, at home and abroad. We have to decide if Jesus was empirically correct when he resisted material temptation with the words,

"Human beings do not live by bread alone." The authors believe that in saying this in the context of his own hunger, Jesus confronted demonic power with a spiritual truth of utmost practical relevance for the material life of humans. What does it profit a person or a society to gain utmost wealth at the price of losing justice, compassion, and joy of soul?

We have claimed modesty for the mission of the church to America's cities, but have opposed the kind of modesty that cloaks the sins of doubt and little faith among the churches. If, "where there is no vision, the people perish," vision becomes a central ingredient of our very survival. What institutions in American society are more charged by their own charters with the promulgation of a convincing vision for the whole society than the churches? Can the churches ignore the prolix realities of the cities without falling into false spiritualism? The Christian faith concerns a Creator who refuses to be above it all, who enters the creation as a creature to bring this great work to completion in a *shalom* above all that humans—including Christians—are likely to ask or think.

The authors of this volume confess our abiding temptation to think too small about the vision and the tasks that belong to church people in this urban society. We have tried to state the theological, the political, and the urgent practical case for large involvement of the churches in America's search for a more just human life for the people of our cities. The reorientation of a public policy requires getting at the roots of injustice. Religion is very much a matter of the deepest roots of all human things. Therefore, the incursion of religion into the search for better social policy need not be pretentious; it may be the only way by which policy and religious faith achieve authenticity.

We Christians are told in our primary document that "faith without works is dead." In our time, faith without public works of *shalom* will be especially dead. Only by serving the whole Human City and the wholeness of all its inhabitants, will we point them to "a city with foundations, whose builder and maker is God."

NOTES

[1]*The Irony of American History* (New York: Charles Scribner's Sons, 1952), p. 63.

APPENDIX A:

Claiming the Media for Doing
Justice in the City

THE RECENT phrase, "the electronic church," suggests that there is clearly a new way of being churched, the congregation being linked not by physical presence around the preached and sacramental Word, but by microwaves bounced off an orbiting communication satellite. Some of the larger, traditional churches have begun to enter the field with a great deal of alacrity, but the phenomenon of the electronic church has not benefitted yet from the theological analysis it desperately needs. Here we recall Marshall McLuhan's cogent pun, "the medium is the massage." The medium affects the one who uses it as well as the one who receives the communicated message. Television is not changing the churches as much as the churches are changing themselves by their use of the medium. This ought to be a focus of theological discussion, lest the churches unwittingly act themselves into a way of being that is not faithful to their own self-understanding.

That necessary discussion cannot be pursued here. Our concern is that the medium itself is potent for the work of justice, which is the work of the church. This possibility has become clear more so since the medium brought politics into the pulpits. Before then, the churches used television principally for evangelization or doctrinal exposition.

Obviously, the drift of this book is not in the same direction as that of the majority of television preachers. But the possibility for television leads us to present two perspectives on the uses of television for the future of cities. The first case, "Television and the Image of the City," analyzes the impact of the content of television's message about the city, decides it is wanting, and suggests more positive communication. The second case, "Television and the Shape of the City," describes the benefits to the city were the citizens to become producers instead of merely consumers. It suggests organizing television's potential through citizens' information centers.

TELEVISION AND THE IMAGE OF THE CITY

Modern technology has had a direct impact on the development of the American city. Air-conditioning, for example, has made southern urban climates more tolerable, and has ameliorated their growth. Urban experiences on television tend to be negative. Numerous crime programs, all of which have an urban setting, contrast with the idyllic settings on *The Waltons* and *Little House on the Prairie*. Network news hardly does better. Its coverage is crisis-oriented: crime, traffic accidents, fires, nature's catastrophes. Where is time given to the processes of city hall, or the school board, or neighborhood revitalization efforts? The impact of these images on the American population has been broad and pervasive, and warrants close examination.

Historically, the city was experienced directly. Not only its avenues and markets, its waterways and industry, but also its forums and council chambers were open, accessible, points of direct experience and encounter. The city was not just a place in which individuals pursued their private interests, but an object of concern, pride, and affection. Civic purposes had a directness and immediacy born of encounter, contention, and common action.

Today, the experience of the city is most frequently mediated through electronic communication, notably television. Television has become the window through which people *see* a selection of experiences, carefully chosen to keep their attention. They do not interact directly with the subjects of those experiences. Their judgment about them is second hand or made for them by the program producers.

Television is a giant amplifier which multiplies certain sights and sounds several million times. In the multiplication, a remoteness develops that makes it possible to share in violence and love, surprise and danger, intimacy and action on a grand scale through an aseptic screen that provides the home viewer the protection of perception removed from action.

In the process, the city itself as an arena of encounter, with real conflict and risk, but also the possibility of genuine contribution and achievement, becomes remote. Indeed, the perception of the city as a dangerous place, a view which television fosters, becomes a factor in further withdrawal from encounter with the city. The self-reinforcing power of the image created by television reduces further the inclination to take the city seriously as an object of affection and an arena for action. The consequences are that the practice of civic responsibility suffers, the normative foundations of city life fall into disarray, and, with them, the genuine possibilities for city life are diminished.

The centrality of television in the lives of Americans requires that we ask, How can television do a better job of presenting the city? Are there ways in which interpretations of the city can be communicated by television that will build affection for the city, enlist people in action on behalf of the city, explore important questions about city life in ways which stimulate encounter and enlist action?

In order to pursue these questions, it is useful to remind ourselves of key factors that have shaped the evolution of television and its relationship to the city. Television evolved after the film industry. Technically, it provided immediacy to a medium which required a freezing of action, a delay during preparation of the presentation, and an elaborate staging of the events which were to be captured. The film industry had evolved to provide eye-catching entertainment which gripped the emotions through carefully arranged sequences. The heavy hand of the producer was unavoidable, and the most successful were the ones whose hands were best disguised.

With television, however, it became possible to provide immediate coverage of events in progress. The most obvious application was to sporting events, where the camera could be unobtrusive. But even here the events themselves are carefully staged to achieve hoped-for dramatic effects. The result has been a growth in the general level of knowledge about the details of game rules, strategies, and skill, an increase in attendance at the games, and frequently a dramatic increase in the number of persons who are willing to play the games themselves.

When it has come to television portrayal of other aspects of city life, on the other hand, similar positive outcomes are difficult to find. Some are notable, and may be instructive.

1. The Army-McCarthy Hearings of the 1950s brought before a large national audience one of the most dramatic encounters in our national life. These hearings combined immediacy, encounter, serious discussion of issues, powerful personalities, and a dramatic flow of events with the knowledge that the outcomes were not only significant but also in doubt.

2. The "Missiles of October" of the 1970s was a dramatic recreation of a flow of action in 1962 with careful attention to accuracy that provided a window for the nation into a situation in which the future of our national life was in doubt.

3. The "Watergate Tapes" was a dramatic recreation of actual conversations which had been taped, and enabled a national audience to pursue the meaning of a set of events which had been hard to lift off the printed page.

There are difficulties which account in part for current television coverage. For example, the visual immediacy of TV tends to lead to the depiction of events or episodes which are short-lived and visually exciting. Houses and factories burn down in a few short dramatic moments. Immediate confrontations are more easily caught by the camera than are the slow processes of legislative action or the growth of bureaucracies. The scene of a crime or auto accident is more apt to get coverage than a meeting of the local school board. Directness of relationships is often oversimplified. Actions are presented as the result of one cause. Someone's decision has direct and obvious consequences. The governor refuses to sign a bill, and schools are short of funds. Nurses go on strike, and a hospital is shut down.

Dramatic personalities make for good media. People identify with visible individuals who act out their parts, become heroes or villains, and give emotion to events. Mayor Richard Daley becomes the personification of the city of Chicago. Gloria Steinem, with her slick upper-middle class style, becomes the symbol of the liberated woman.

Many of the important dynamics of the city are difficult to capture through these immediate, direct, personal relationships. Patterns of action by large numbers of people over long periods of time are critical for understanding the city. And there are many variations in between the immediate, the direct, the personal, and the long-run, indirect, and impersonal which require attention to understand what the critical choices and opportunities for action are in the city.

To the degree that this is the case, a challenge is posed for the managers of the television media. The challenge is to find ways to interpret the city which enable citizens to understand that wise action is needed and effective action is possible. Three types of television treatment of the city might be developed to deal with these issues, each of which has distinct problems and opportunities. They will be referred to as: The Prism, the Problem-Solving, and the Panorama approaches.

The Prism approach looks for the dramatic event or confrontation in which a number of forces in city life come together, and are explored in the course of an unfolding drama.

Illustrations of this approach might include dramatic recreations of events such as:

- an important court case, where basic patterns of urban development are brought into the courtroom.
- an important municipal decision, such as the choice some cities are making of whether or not to invest in older neighborhoods.
- an important citizen referendum where advocacy would need to be developed, giving viewers an opportunity to judge, for example, whether or not investment should be made in a deep water tunnel system government officials or urban planners might want to construct.

The Problem-Solving approach would look at the dimensions of some major urban problems, explore alternative definitions, and perhaps tell the story of the variety of ways in which people in different neighborhoods or institutions are trying to deal with the problem.

Illustrations of this approach might:

- examine problems in meeting the basic requirements for food, energy, shelter, water, air, and waste management, and explore alternative technologies for use in city neighborhoods.
- examine health, education, and security, the limitations of large bureaucracies in meeting these needs, and the alternative ways which people in city neighborhoods are finding to meet these problems.
- examine the flow of resources in urban regions, and the problems of investment and credit deprivation in many city neighborhoods, with an exploration of the various forms which urban re-investment is taking.
- examine the problems of authority, or its absence, powerlessness, as people try to get handles on institutions and resources needed to deal with neighborhood problems.

The Panorama approach would develop the longer sweep of dimensions and trends in city-building. It might use a contemporary version of the "Civilization" or "Cosmos" series in which a narrator walks viewers through visual reconstructions of the life of the city.

Illustrations of this approach might include:

- the major forces of technology, resource availability, and population growth which contributed to the growth and form of the modern industrial city.
- the changing patterns of governance of the city as they have been tried, tested, and modified through time.
- the interactions of ethnic groups in the city, how they have contended with each other, struggled for their places in the economic

and political mosaic of the city, and contributed to its religious and cultural richness.

• the struggles to deal with the problems of scale in the city between large and small systems of commerce, industry, governance, and association; the role which technology has played in these struggles (including television) and the prospects for new choices, including the prospects for neighborhood, and audience interactive television.

TELEVISION AND THE SHAPE OF THE CITY. *

Charles Najinsky flipped to the local news section of the town newspaper to find this advertisement staring out at him:

Fairmont Community College announces the opening of a Citizens' Information Center for the use of persons interested in community issues like the following:
    —effect of new industry on residential property values
    —zoning law and its effect on your neighborhood
    —improved municipal services: garbage, water, sewage
    —impact of unemployment on Fairmont
    —preservation of green space
    —air and water pollution
    —citizen desire to get acquainted with differing national culture
The Center has been financed on an experimental basis by a coalition of the college, the State of New Jersey, and three local religious bodies representing the Jewish, Protestant, and Roman Catholic faiths. A major aim of the Center is to put citizens interested in similar problems in touch with each other. Call 988-2561 for further information.

For at least five years Najinsky had watched the paint peeling in his neighborhood. His wife had already suggested that they sell the house before his retirement to avoid being caught here forever. "Well," he said to himself, "let's give it a try." He called 988-2561.

"We're building a file of people in each residential section," said the woman on the other end of the line. "When as many as six persons express an interest in a similar problem, we send a letter to them, with all the names, addresses, and telephone numbers. Would you like to register your name, address, and telephone number with us?" Najinsky thought a moment: would the whole thing get to be a hassle? "I guess so," he said

*This section is taken from Donald W. Shriver, Jr. and Karl A. Ostrom, *Is There Hope for the City?* (Philadelphia: Westminster Press, 1977), pp. 165–73.

dubiously. He put down the phone wondering if anything would ever come of it.

More did come of it than he had expected. Seven names appeared on the letter which arrived two weeks later. One of them was a casual acquaintance from the box factory where he worked. Another he had met one Sunday at Mass. The other five were strangers. But that very night, one of the strangers called to ask him if his living room was available for a get-together. "Sure," he said. "Let's make it Wednesday night."

Five men, four women, and three young children came. Most of them lived in their own homes, but two families were renters, and one of these was black. It was the first time a black couple had ever been in that living room—a fact that pushed Najinsky close to calling off the whole deal. But before the evening concluded, their mutual concern for the neighborhood won out. The nine adults agreed to divide into two groups, one to study zoning and industrialization laws, the other to conduct a telephone poll of residents of every street represented by some family in the initial group.

Only three months later, the results began to startle Najinsky and (what they came proudly to call) the "Fairmont Fair Deal Association." Forty homeowners and fifteen landlords had decided to paint their houses. A cooperative arrangement for the purchase of paint had been worked out at 40 percent of hardware store prices. A retired grocery store manager in the neighborhood had been enlisted as a mini information center for bulk purchases of several items such as grass seed, snow shovels, and roofing materials. In the meantime, largely through the help of the Citizens' Information Center, they discovered that zoning law permitted "medium industry" to locate in Fairmont and restricted all but a few neighborhoods to twelve-family apartment buildings. Builders were urging the county government to remove all restrictions on the size of apartment houses, and there was even talk of large purchases of current low-density residential tracts for this purpose.

"What we've got to decide," said Najinsky at an open meeting of the Association at the synagogue, "is whether we want this town to remain a place where you can get to know your neighbors." (His wife, Lola, said later to him with a laugh, "A year ago, Charlie, you didn't know any of the people at that meeting. You don't know anybody just by living in a place.") The upshot of the meeting was a series of delegations to the planning commission, the county board, and the president of a large residential construction company. In the midst of all this, a delegation from Foamcut, Inc., in the person of the latter's executive vice-president, paid a visit to the officers of the Fair Deal Association: "The Federal Government is financing the purchase of the area of the South Bronx in which our present factory is located. They expect to build an apartment complex and some office buildings there. We're thinking about moving to New Jersey, and to Fairmont in particular. We are committed, by the way, to bringing as many of our present workers with us as possible. Some of them are having their residences cleared away too. You should know that a hundred and fifty of our workers are black or Puerto Rican. I'm wondering if, as an Association, you'd work with us to be sure that they can be housed in this community."

"Well, I guess we'll think about it," said Najinsky. "We'd have to think a *lot* about it before we tell you." The comment led to adjournment of the meeting.

Actually, Najinsky felt that there wasn't much to think about. Just when they were beginning to develop some real stability and spirit in the community, outsiders wanted to push the place downhill again. He'd almost stopped thinking about it, when he was invited one Sunday after Mass into Father O'Malley's study. "You know, Charles," said O'Malley, "your work with the Association is something we all can be proud of. It's the one thing we've done in this parish with the Protestants and the Jews that really makes sense. But I have a problem for you to think about. I don't want an answer from you right now, but I want you to think about it. A social worker from the South Bronx came to see me this past week. Her name is Harrisene Little. She was brought up there, loves the people there, is doing some remarkable things to help them. She came to me out of concern for thirty men and women who work for Foamcut, and who want to continue working with the company if and when it moves to Fairmont. They can't commute from the Bronx, and they would like very much to walk to work. They can pay modest rents, and they could live in any of those twelve-family apartments which the builders are willing to put up here. Everybody knows what a bombed-out area the South Bronx is. This would be our chance to help bear the responsibility for improving the lives of the people who live there. Would you consider working in the Association to get the cooperation of people on this thing? The Association could easily become a tool for locking up this community against people different from ourselves. As a Christian I don't want that to happen. I hope you'll think very hard about it."

That was the only kind of thinking you could do about it: hard thinking. Riding home in his car, he grumbled to his wife: "This Association thing just gets me in deeper and deeper. I was beginning to enjoy living here, but I can see one big hassle coming out of it now. I wish that social worker would just stay in the Bronx. What business does she have coming all the way over to New Jersey to see O'Malley? This thing is getting out of hand. Why don't they leave us alone?" Lola Najinsky left his question hanging in the air.

The forces insulating citizens, institutions, and locales from each other in American urban society are legion. The modern city is a highly differentiated society, if nothing else. Its split-upness is more easily experienced than its integrity. All through this study we have insisted that religious faith yearns toward the integrity—the peace, the wholeness, the salvation—of persons and communities. The threat of modern urbanism to integrity in all senses is immense. Charles Najinsky has begun to experience a form of integrity renewal. As his path crosses that of Harrisene Little, he stands at a critical point: Will he expand his network of urban community and responsibility, or will he retreat into one of the differentiated ghettos which the metropolis itself makes only too possible?

The question is posed to him as part of a process which the churches of Fairmont initiated in concert with a local college and a state government. The institutional innovation—a Citizens' Information Center—has a growing number of examples in cities across the United States. Our Urban Policy Study strongly implies the need for some such innovation if all the potential members of the People of God are to have the opportunity of identifying themselves to one another and of expressing their identity politically. *Precisely within the split-up, multicentered life of urban society the People of God need a practical method for seeing and encountering one another and their community in all its shifting boundaries—from the locale to the metropolis to the very globe.* The theology of the church has always held that the People of God are not coincidental with the members of particular confessional churches. Some expressions of the ecumenical spirit in recent times proclaim visions of justice and mercy for the whole global village. The size and complexity of the human neighborhood on all its levels demand comprehensive structures of church ministry.

Jefferson clearly envisions the necessity of national and state government; but he insists that all large political structures should be grounded in local public spaces where citizens speak, take responsibility, manifest courage, and win distinction in ways beneficial to others. Such a political order invites the involvement of every person. It encourages mutual respect between citizens and . . . provides a basis for self-respect as well. The early Christian church exemplified these features, and down through history the

church has anticipated in other ways such a political philosophy. That
secular politics should embody its own intercessory prayer "for all sorts
and conditions" of human beings, the Christian church has every reason
to hope. For the nourishing of such a political order and as one of their
basic ministries, the church and the synagogue also have reason to support
Citizens' Information Centers in the Fairmonts of this country. Such
centers could render a richer variety of public service than the tame word
"information" or the scare word "politics" may suggest. In neighborhood
centers citizens can foster art, tell stories, perform drama, make movies,
learn to use a portable television camera, encounter the culture of for-
eigners, listen to music, and hear unfamiliar political ideas in the company
of other persons. Culture, the seedbed of politics, grows more authentically
in quiet human fellowships than in a frantic commercial television studio.
Should not the facility of a television camera be as available to ordinary
citizens as the facility of a television receiver? Our local and world politics
might be more imaginative and human if we engaged more regularly in
sending as well as receiving messages in our urban-global communities.
The economics of buying-and-selling have dominated the first generation
of televiewing in the United States. With imagination, compassion, and
sound political instinct, city churches might turn this medium toward
more humane uses.

An organizational device of the sort suggested here can help deliver
any person or social group from the same tyranny. We cannot be sure
how this stream in his biography will turn, but Charles Najinsky is beginning to experience just such deliverance. His trek toward community
with his urban neighbors began with a specific interest of his own—the
value of his house. This seems psychologically universal for most of us.
Two fundamental principles for the construction of a citizens' information
network peek out here: (1) It must be responsive to the particular conscious
needs of the user, and (2) it must help the user place his or her need in
the context of the needs of other citizens. Such an information network
might be called "contextual." If lopsidedly responsive on either of two
such sides, the system will fail to express a Biblical—or oikodomic—
political ethic: simultaneous service to persons and community.

On the one side, most of us neither expect nor desire to be equally
well informed or equally active on all issues agitating our neighborhoods,
our cities, our nation, or our world. Each of us needs the capacity to get
more information on some issues than on others. How clogged the channels
of information may be on any such issues can be tested if you ask yourself

what three problems worry you most about your own city, and how you would get accurate and action-relevant information on those three problems within the next twenty-four hours. One wonders how long it took Harrisene Little to discover the link between the housing needs of thirty Bronx residents and the possible help of the Fairmont Fair Deal Association. The question required real research, and such research is often unavailable to citizens until long after it might do them concrete good. What good does it do to read in the paper one evening that the construction company has bought out half your block at bargain prices?

But faithfully and ethically speaking, a contextualized information system must be responsive not only to an individual citizen's need but must also relate that need to the need of others. Ordinarily we expect politicians to be "brokers" of the diverse, sometimes conflicting, sometimes overlapping, expressed needs of the public. One can imagine how frustrated the local politician may come to feel in the housing debate in Fairmont. If the Fair Deal Association fails to develop any common cause with its potential neighbors at Foamcut, and if the conflict becomes an issue in the next county election, candidates for office may be tempted to exploit a community conflict which might have been best solved in other, more human ways. *Public officials in Fairmont will have the opportunity to practice justice and mercy, the more just and merciful are their voting constituents.* Some problems beat on the doors of politicians because citizens have failed to engage themselves in those problems, not even to the extent of talking together about them. Citizens should do more talking together: That is one simple conclusion to which this study has led. More stringently put: *Every citizen in a democracy should have opportunity to express his or her selfhood in the public arena; but none should have opportunity to ignore the selfhood of other citizens.* If an information system is to nurture justice, it must serve a plurality of interests. It must help neighbors to hear what they desire to hear and also what they may not desire to hear. It must provide enough information about others to identify the real problems of their mutual relationships. And it must facilitate hope for the solution of those problems. In short, such a system will promote personal fulfillment, build community, and open person and community to as large an *oikoumenē as they both can bear.*

APPENDIX B:

A Compendium of Recent Church Statements

THIS SECTION draws together recent church statements on urban ministry, particularly with reference to public policy. Many churches have not focussed on either the city or issues of urban policy in a thematic way. Those that have, most of which are listed below, manifest an increasing awareness of the need for systemic change and the relevance of involvement in policy issues for bringing that about.

THE FUTURE OF URBAN LIFE IN AMERICA

From: "The Future of Urban Life in America," A Pronouncement of the 13th General Synod, United Church of Christ, 1981.

Theological Background

According to the biblical faith, God's history with the creation begins in the Garden but ends in the City. The salvation of the whole creation does not take place through a return to the beginning but through God's New Creation of everything in the New City without tears and without the forces of evil and death (Rev. 21). In the New Creation the Church will no longer be necessary because "the Lord God the Almighty and the Lamb" will be present in the City (Rev. 21:22). Thus biblical faith claims that the church exists for the future of God's new City and for the formation and transformation of the human city today.

The Bible sees the "city" clearly in all of its ambiguity. The "city" is both a symbol for what destroys the human future and for the divine human cooperation which makes possible a human future.

On the one hand, the city is viewed as the epitome of human rebellion against God. Cain, a murderer, builds the first city. He is unwilling to live in God's creation under the providence of God. So he builds his own "counter-creation," a city with fortified walls, in order to secure himself. The Bible understands the constant human tendency to build "closed cities." The city seems to be born of the compulsion to security and greed in the political, economic, psychological and cultural dimensions of life. Thus the city constantly produces the false religion of worshipping the products of the human mind and hands, segregation among its peoples, exploitation of work, domination and destruction, the arsenals for war and the squalor of poverty. The city, which is intended to secure the human being, instead denies some people adequate food, clean water, shelter, education, jobs and the dignity they need to be human beings. It is no wonder then that the Bible recalls that Israel's first historical appearance is in a city—as slaves building the store cities of Pharaoh. Through the prophets God judges and condemns the city for its inhumanity to the least of God's children, for its destruction of the creation and for its being closed to God's righteousness and justice.

On the other hand, the biblical traditions see the city as part of the human condition. The city, with its memories, languages, communications, sciences, arts, technologies, and large organizations is the means chosen by humanity to fulfill the task of being God's representatives or stewards: the "economists" to God's creation. As a primary center of human power and policy, it is in cities that the impact of humanity on the future of the whole creation is decided. All persons are thus related to the city: positively or negatively, for life or life's destruction. In this sense, rural people more closely connected with the land are also "city" people.

As is clear in the prophets and the New Testament, the city takes on increasing importance in God's history with the creation. *God judges the city.* Because it perverts God's justice and destroys the lives of God's little ones, the city hears the worst threat conceivable for a city—that it will be uninhabited. In our time when people are turning their backs on the city, especially the inner city, as the place of crime, poverty, ignorance and pollution, and when nuclear warheads are aimed at almost all major cities, this judgement of the city is plain.

God calls God's people to love and to suffer with the city and stand in solidarity with it. God commands that we stay and work for the welfare of the city in which we shall find our own welfare (Jer. 29:4-7). Jesus sets his face toward Jerusalem (Lk. 9:51). There seems to be a theological necessity for God's story to find its climax in the city (Lk. 13:33). God's passion for the whole world comes to its fullest expression in the city. Jesus grieves for and suffers with the city (Lk. 13:34; 19:41). Though grief and pathic solidarity with the city look like sheer vulnerability, they are the first signs that we may not dispose of the city but that God's election and redemption of the city will come about through God's own suffering love.

God liberates God's people from the city for the sake of the city. Through the self-giving grace of God in Jesus Christ persons and institutions can be freed from using the city as a means of security, self-justification and greed. Freed by the power of the gospel from the fear of death and from guilt, persons can give their lives in solidarity with the victims of the city. Liberation from the powers of the city does not mean fleeing the city but rather investing oneself fully in it, for "the name of the city henceforth shall be, the LORD is there" (Ezek. 48:35b, cf. Jer. 33:16). The place which the human being wanted to close up for self-protection against God is now opened up by God's own identification with the city's poor and powerless people.

God hopes for the city. The biblical traditions witness that God does not give up hope for the city. Because of that the human being may stay in hope for the city. God promises the new creation of the city, the city in which God will rejoice (Is. 65:17-19). In the coming city "they shall not build and another inhabit; they shall not plant and another eat. No more shall there be in it an infant that lives but a few days, or an old man who does not fill out his days . . ." (Is. 65:22,20). Through the power of the Holy Spirit the Church is called to bring God's New City into our city.

Recommendations on Public Policy

- The churches are called to challenge the maldistribution of economic resources in our society, particularly as this maldistribution manifests itself most visibly in the "core cities" of our nation.
- The churches are called to work with concerned organizations and institutions, public and private, that seek to eliminate: (a) inflation, (b) unemployment and underemployment, (c) inadequate housing, (d) unfair taxation, (e) the financial plight of those incapable of self-support, (f) substandard health care, and (g) environmental and attitudinal barriers to persons with disabilities.
- The churches are called upon to reaffirm support for existing civil rights legislation, including legislation pertaining to disabilities and efforts on the part of the federal government to implement its intentions to achieve integrated quality education, open housing, fair employment, voting rights and equal access to public accom-

modations. We deplore any policy of abrogation or "benign neglect" which may reverse gains thus far achieved in this area and call on the churches vigilantly to support programs that take action to achieve full racial justice and civil rights in our society.

- We believe that the rebuilding of our cities is a major responsibility of all levels of government, the business-industrial community, voluntary associations, the churches and individual citizens. Programs to rebuild our cities should insure that the rights and needs of the poor and powerless living in our cities are both protected and met. All people must have a voice in making decisions affecting their welfare. Therefore, we support the establishment of citizen-based structures to monitor the performance of public and private agencies responsible for the rebuilding of our cities.
- Many problems confronting our cities appear insoluable because of the absence of fiscal and political structures which encompass both the central city and its surrounding suburbs. We recognize the interdependence of city and suburb and the need for cooperative action. We affirm a creative role for state and federal governments in dealing more effectively with urban problems which extend beyond municipal boundaries.
- We believe that the federal budget should reflect a high priority for the restoration of our cities and the well being of the people living there and deplore the current administration's move to reduce further federal support to urban areas.
- In a time of severe economic dislocation, we urge the nation to explore potential alternative economic arrangements which may better solve the problems of people in our cities. Examples might include cooperatives and community based economic development.

URBAN STRATEGY DEVELOPMENT PROGRAM

From "Urban Strategy Development Program," 1977, A Program Situational Analysis of the Board of National Ministries, American Baptist Churches, USA.

Traditional church ministry in urban areas has in a large part been shaped by the equation stated in the beginning. The church has seen the city as a place of sin, as the whore Babylon or the tower of Babel. The city is seen as the place which destroys the faith. But Christ is not dead in the city. The prophetic church stands in the midst of the city trying to understand both the vision and reality of the city. Is it not in the city we see a symbolism that comes out of our faith? The biblical drama begins in a garden, but it ends in a city—the heavenly Jerusalem. The church cannot in and of itself transform the city but it can through its witness say that the city is the decisive locus of incarnation in our day. It seems appropriate, therefore, to rethink our urban ministry and to redirect it in a way that affirms and enables city dwellers to see the promise and possibilities of the city and link this with technical competence to deal with the realities. The church needs to be challenged to develop a clear commitment to the empowerment of people and not a sustaining of the status quo, i.e. keeping people content where they are.

Empowerment—Power. How difficult it is for American Christians to deal theologically with power. In the Lord's Prayer, we profess that all power belongs to God. The power by which humans rule is given by the Lord. This should not be misunderstood to mean the justification for existing power-structures. Equal possession of power is a divine imperative. Powerless people have the right to power. If we understand the right use of power to be the degree to which justice is achieved, then the church must be an advocate of both justice and empowerment.

The main focus of this proposal is empowerment. By empowerment, we mean enabling urban congregations, persons and communities to take responsibility for their own lives. We aim to provide those tools, those models, those information resources which will enable persons to make the city and its institutions work for them, to humanize the system—and if need be, to build a social order in which there is a redistribution of resources and power on a just and equitable basis.

A MESSAGE FROM JOHN S. SPONG, BISHOP OF NEWARK

From: *To Hear and to Heed*, A Report of the Urban Bishops Conference, 1978 The Episcopal Church. Reprinted by permission of Forward Movement Publications, 412 Sycamore St., Cincinnati, OH 45202.

1. The inner city is populated by the victims of our economic system. They are the unemployed, the powerless, the exploited. Many of them

suffer from cultural or linguistic alienation. They are devalued, and the image of God that we Christians believe is in them is violated. A church that will not address the forces that devalue any human life is not an institution that will be taken seriously in the city. We must get beneath symptoms and address systemic causes, and we can do this if we will.

2. The theological principle of Incarnation must be the *modus operandi* of urban church strategy. The church that clings to the style and values of a departed era or social structure will not survive in the city. A fortress church that exists to preserve an outpost of what used to be is doomed. Money that is spent to perpetuate that kind of church life is money that is wasted. If a church is to live in the city, it must develop an indigenous life—and indigenous liturgy. The church must belong to the people it seeks to service. Even the people who never come inside the church building to worship must feel that the church is their ally, friend, co-worker, in the struggle for human justice. Only a church so perceived will live in the city.

3. The ministry of social service may well be important but it is not the appropriate focus for today's church. Social service is something done to or for the recipient. It is not appropriate today for two reasons. First, the church doesn't have the resources to be an effective social service agency. Second, social service finally makes the one served dependent. It ministers to effects—not causes. Time after time, the hearings emphasized the need for the church to identify with the movement for community organization and that funds available for a serving ministry be channelled to indigenous community organization structures, not expended in private church-run social service activities. Our task is to enable the citizens of the city to take charge of their own destiny, to fight their own battles, with the church, for Christ's sake, standing by their side as an enabler and an ally.

THE CHALLENGE FOR EVANGELISM AND MISSION

From: "The Challenge for Evangelism and Mission," A Working Paper of the Urban Bishops Coalition, The Episcopal Church, 1979, pp. 13–15.

The church must ally itself with those public policies and individual initiatives which seek to counter the destruction of the cities and the fabric of communal life caused by opportunistic urban development and by the flight of capital from the cities. Vast areas of the cities have become enclaves of poverty, unemployment and underemployment because self-seeking economics and social policy dictate the abandonment of the city by commerce and industry. The public policy which presently shapes the life of our cities is attached to economic gain, narrowly defined, rather than to a theory of political justice or order. The church must move with those who seek a just and equitable distribution of opportunities and resources through metropolitan planning for the sake of the common good.

In the Biblical witness, the city first symbolizes resistance to God. It is less a symbol of human ingenuity and achievement than it is a sign of arrogance, independence and evil. *Babylon* is the Bible's name for every city. It makes no difference before God: whether ancient Jericho or modern cities of America. They are all under the mark of human sin which leads to their destruction, and clearly that mark is imprinted upon them because they have failed to be the habitation of the God of justice. ("Woe to the bloody city, all full of lies and booty—no end to the plunder." Nahum 3:1)

Yet, the prophet Jeremiah, speaking for that God, urged the people to "seek the welfare of the city where I sent you into exile, and pray to the Lord on its behalf, *for in its welfare you will find your welfare.*" (Jeremiah 29:7) And in Biblical faith the future is envisaged as an eternal city, the New Jerusalem, the city of the living God. The deterioration of the cities of this moment in history is the work of forces, life-draining and life-destroying, which justify the label, "Babylon." But the church is called to recognize that in their welfare the People of God will find their welfare, for cities are places of human habitation in which the fidelity and obedience of the church is tested, and the ultimate transfiguration of life will be wrought by God. The New Jerusalem is not to be confused with cities as they are or even as, through our efforts, they might be. Nonetheless, cities may be either symbols of human greed, cruelty and pride—Babylon—or the anticipated presence (because the Kingdom which is coming is in our midst) of that which God will convert into an eternal habitation.

To that end, the church must coalesce with those who seek to build a new urban economic base and structure, and return participation in economic and urban decision making to the people of the cities. The decentralization of public activity, as well as the dispersion of the planning task and control over services to neighborhoods through the on-going involvement by persons in and decision-making about public policy by groups small enough for real face-to-face discussion, argument, deliberation and consensus formation among those affected by particular policies would restore that degree of responsibility and freedom which is envisaged not only by the political principles of democracy, but also by the Scriptural image of the mature person who possesses both freedom and responsibility in Christ.

In the absence of widespread participation in decisions about the use of a community's productivity, a small minority actually hold the destiny of millions in their hands. The productive earnings of many communities in the form of savings, pensions and real earnings flow out of the cities which produce them. The church must, therefore, work with others in the establishment of cooperative enterprises, community or worker-owned businesses, the scaling down of units of government in order to maximize participation and the molding of all public affairs and private enterprises in the service of the common good.

MINISTRY IN THE NORTH AMERICAN CITY

From: *Lutheran Church in America Ministry in the City: Direction and Guidelines*. Division in Mission in North America, 1977, pp. 6–10.

Dimensions of the City

The North American city is multi-dimensional in nature. To understand the city, is to be able to speak of it in such a way as to see its individual parts while at the same time seeing it as a whole made up of those parts. The dimensions with which we have been most accustomed are those that relate to geography, population, and traffic patterns. In this paper, we shall not abandon those dimensions but rather add others that are important to consider as the DMNA approaches future ministry.

It should be acknowledged that there are various value systems that can be identified within the city. Often, these values underlie the individual and corporate behavior of city dwellers. When seen on a spectrum, the characteristics of city life contain values that may benefit some and harm others. For example, the city allows for anonymity. Some value this greatly as a means to freedom. For others, however, such anonymity may result in loneliness. The attribute of mobility may be valued as a chance for new beginnings. For others, mobility may result in rootlessness and loss of belonging. It is important for the church to understand these values operative in the city and to respond to the various ways they manifest themselves.

A Patchwork of Communities and Neighborhoods:

Most cities can be described in terms of various communities within which there are smaller neighborhoods. The terminology describing these geographical sections of cities may vary from place to place, but generally it is true that one can describe cities in terms of their neighborhoods, which are distinctive for various reasons. These neighborhoods may vary in size and cohesiveness, but it is not unusual for persons to identify their residency by indicating the name of a neighborhood. Every neighborhood has a distinctive image, sometimes widely known. Mention Harlem, Greenwich Village, Haight-Ashbury, Georgetown, the Loop, and people who have never been there can picture a neighborhood. Another way of speaking of neighborhoods in the past may have included such things as primary service areas, parish boundaries, and so on.

Is it worth noting that there is a movement afoot in most major American cities to reinforce and restore neighborhood identities beyond nostalgia. There are many good reasons for this, not the least of which have to do with persons' loyalties and sense of identity, with citizen participation and "ownership" of the environment that affects their lives. If this church is to minister more effectively with city residents, congregations will have to intentionally relate to the neighborhoods in which their facilities are located. The neighborhoods may vary—some being mainly residential, others more commercial—but neighborhood involvement must be primary for congregational ministry in almost every case.

A Network of Systems:

For any city to function and serve its constituents, the existence of a network of systems, both private and public, is a necessity. A system in sociological terms is described as "a continuous, boundary-maintaining, variously related assembly of parts." The systems that operate in the city tie together structures and organizations that may have different locations while related to central policies. The public school system is an example of this. A central school board might determine policy and budget on a citywide basis, but various individual schools located throughout the city implement those policies. The same can be said of neighborhood fire stations, police precincts, welfare offices, political wards or districts, etc. To deal effectively with the systems that affect people's lives for good or ill, it would be advantageous for this church to provide organizational structures within a city that are capable of evaluating and responding to the performance of such systems.

Some of the systems that affect people and shape the city are:

The Political System: The political system pervades the operation of a modern city. The mayor and his administration set policy, choose leadership, regulate many private enterprises, provide services and effect plans for renewal. The political system is made up of formal and informal relationships designed to act on local and citywide issues. Block clubs, neighborhood community organizations, community planning councils and elective offices are all part of the system that determines the operation of a city and apportions its services to citizens.

The Economic System: This system runs the entire spectrum from personal economics—having a job or some other means of financial support (the welfare system)—to public concerns such as taxation, bond issues, costs of services, the maintenance of industry and commerce.

The Cultural System: Many cities make an important contribution through the availability of public institutions and cultural events that enrich the spirit through the arts, music and drama. Theaters, concert halls, museums, art galleries, amateur theatrical groups and even street minstrels are part of this system.

The Mass Media/Public Relations/Advertising System: The press, television, radio and advertising are all part of the system that informs the public and shapes attitudes. Many cities are centers of media activities whose influence extends far beyond city boundaries. This system also has the ability and the opportunity to expose injustice and advocate social change.

The Education System: One of the key systems in drawing persons to or away from a city is the educational system and the quality of its institutions. The educational system may touch people's lives in a number of forms; i.e., local schools; community colleges; educational, cultural and recreational opportunities offered to citizens by high schools or colleges; school taxes; as a means of livelihood.

The Legal Justice System: This system runs all the way from police-community relations to the courts and prisons. Again, this is an example of a system which affects a variety of people in a number of ways. In some sections of St. Paul, Minnesota, for example, it has been estimated that as many as 60 percent of the residents have come into contact with the legal/judicial system through arrest, trial, or imprisonment—often unjustly.

The Professional Sports System: In many cities, professional sports teams become a unifying symbol and may be a common ground for a city's people. These loyalties cross over economic and racial barriers. The Detroit Tigers' winning the World Series in 1968—the summer following the 1967 rebellion—provided a community emphasis that many agree saved the city from additional confrontations. Every city needs common rallying points. The sports system has the potential for meeting some of this need.

Other Systems: We have listed just some of the systems at work within cities. Others, no less important, are health care, housing, transportation and religious systems. As we have said, many of these systems are interrelated, with both centralized and local manifestations.

A JOINT URBAN POLICY

From: "A Joint Urban Policy for the United Presbyterian Church in the
U.S.A. and the Presbyterian Church in the United States," A Preliminary
Statement for their General Assemblies, February, 1981, pp. 7–9.

Biblical/Theological Foundation for Christian Witness in the City.

As Presbyterians we confess that while we have enjoyed the advantages offered by cities, too often we have isolated ourselves from their problems and the opportunities for ministry which urban areas provide. We realize that to effectively minister in urban America we must acknowledge that our area of responsibility is no longer a series of relatively independent suburbs, towns, villages, and rural communities, but is now the whole metropolis. Each unit of ministry must be understood as a part of the one metropolitan effort.

Ministry to the whole city is based on our theological heritage. The early churches arose chiefly in cities. From the book of Hebrews, to John's Revelation, to the writings of Church Fathers, Christians have imagined God's rule as a vision of the New Jerusalem, a city established by God in which peace is the fruit of attentiveness to the claims of justice. Such vision impelled John Calvin to accept a call to Geneva, where he undertook to reform not only the Church but also an economic and urban structure. Seldom have Calvin's expectations been adequately appreciated or appropriated in the Presbyterian Church. It was not from Calvin that we learned to divide the spiritual mission of the Church from secular affairs, or to isolate our ministry to persons from our ministry to institutions and systems. Now, in an increasingly urban civilization, the time is overdue for us to commit ourselves to evangelize the people and redeem the systems of the human city. Nothing less will truly reflect a contemporary faith in the Sovereignty of God, the Lordship of Christ, and the creative work of the Spirit.

We have emerged from a time in which many in the Church declared that the world sets the agenda for our ministry. We believe that our mission must proceed from the Lordship of Christ. Jesus Christ, Himself, sets the agenda for the Church's ministry, and for our work in the world. That agenda has been set forth for us within the Biblical witness.

The Lord's agenda compels us to work for the deliverance of those presently held captive by the "principalities and powers" of this world, to "Bind up the broken-hearted," to "raise up the former devastations," to "give garlands instead of ashes." (Isaiah 61:1-4) We believe that God's agenda compels us to work on behalf of a just community wherein the needs of the poor, the alienated, and the dispossessed are the first priority:

> He has shown strength with his arm,
> he has scattered the proud in the imagination
>   of their hearts,
> he has put down the mighty from their thrones,
> and exalted those of low degree;
> he has filled the hungry with good things,
> and the rich he has sent empty away.
>   Luke 1:51-53

We believe God's agenda compels us to work as agents of His reconciling love, to establish communities responsive to the claims of justice and the principles of peace, and the renewal of the resurrection hope. "All this is from God, who through Christ reconciled us to himself and gave us the ministry of reconciliation [2 Corinthians 5:18]."

We believe that God's agenda compels us to work for the salvation not only of individuals, but for the redemption of the structures and institutions that can make human community possible. It is in the context of community and institution . . . the "New Jerusalem" . . . that the great declaration occurs, "Behold, the dwelling of God is with men. He will dwell with them, and they shall be his people, and God himself will be with them; he will wipe away every tear from their eyes, and death shall be no more . . . [Revelation 21:3-4]."

THE RIGHT TO A DECENT HOME

From: The Right to a Decent Home: A Pastoral Response to the Crisis in Housing. A Statement of the Catholic Bishops of the United States, November 20, 1975, used with permission.

As preachers of the gospel, we proclaim the message of Jesus Christ who identifies Himself with the needs of the least of the brethren. The second great commandment is to love our neighbor. We cannot deny the crying needs for decent housing experienced by the least of the brethren in our society. Effective love of neighbor involves concern for his or her living conditions.

We begin with the recognition that decent housing is a right. Our Catholic tradition, eloquently expressed by Pope John XXIII and Pope Paul VI, insists that shelter is one of the basic rights of the human person. The Second Vatican Council has said with great directness: "There must be made available to all men everything necessary for leading a life truly human, such as food, clothing and shelter. . . ."

As teachers, pastors and leaders, we have the responsibility to articulate the principles and values that govern the Church's concern for housing. We believe that each individual possesses an inherent dignity and priceless worth because he or she is created in the image and likeness of God. We also believe each person should have the opportunity to grow and develop his or her potential to the fullest extent possible. Human dignity and development are threatened whenever social and economic forces imprison or degrade people. We call on Catholics and all citizens to join us in working against these debilitating forces.

Neighborhoods

Housing conditions cannot be separated from the surrounding environment. City services, education, community cohesiveness, safety, government responsiveness, and taxation policies are critical factors in the creation and maintenance of decent housing.

In our view, the key element in the deteriorating urban environment is the decline of neighborhoods. In the past, the neighborhood has played a critical role in the lives of its residents. More recently, neighborhoods have lost some of their influence and importance. Centralized decision-making, suburban migration, deteriorating city services and the loss of ethnic identity have contributed to this decline and resulted in less responsibility for local concerns. A psychological and physical process of abandonment has set in, and fewer resources and people have been available to assist neighborhoods in combating blight and indifference.

Our cities are composites of smaller communities. Strong neighborhoods are the cornerstone of strong cities, and decent housing is a critical factor in the survival and viability of neighborhoods.

We applaud the renewed interest in neighborhoods by those who live in them and govern them. The neighborhood is the most logical basis for a positive housing policy. We hope that recognition of this fact will be translated into policies and provide neighborhoods with the tools and resources necessary to survive. The local parish has a critical role to play in the revitalization of neighborhoods. Effective use of revenue-sharing and community development funds can be a step in promoting neighborhood recovery.

URBAN MINISTRIES

From: The Minutes of General Synod, 1980, Reformed Church in America, © 1980 by Reformed Church Press, New York, NY. Used by permission.

Biblical Mandate

Deeply rooted in the experience and witness of Old Testament people and comprising the central theme of Jesus' preaching in the synoptic gospels, the Kingdom of God is simultaneously past history, current reality, and a vision for the future. The biblical call to the RCA is to proclaim and participate in the Kingdom of God. As participants in the Kingdom of God, the church is commissioned to work for wholeness, justice, and peace (Romans 14:17-19, NEB) in our relationship to God through Jesus Christ, within and among all persons, by transforming persons, institutions and structures which control our lives and society. This biblically-rooted understanding of mission leads us to see ourselves as a denomination called to minister in partnership with persons, communities, and institutions who actively seek wholeness, justice, and peace in urban society.

The Bible further informs our response to this calling by defining the Church as the Body of Christ (Ephesians 4:1-16). The members, individuals, and judicatories of the RCA can thus participate in urban mission through acts of proclamation, advocacy (Isaiah 58:1-12), ministries of service and mercy (Micah 6:8), and corporate sharing and support (Acts 2:44-47).

Since urban settings are contexts in which persons experience many forms of brokenness as a daily part of life, urban ministries is an urgent calling for our entire denomination (Jeremiah 29:7). Further, God has given us a vision of the future, a vision shared with us by Paul, "at the name of Jesus every knee should bow, in heaven and on earth, and under the earth, and every tongue confess that Jesus Christ is Lord, to the glory of God the Father" (Phil. 2:10-11). We are moved to engage in urban ministries by the hope that all people may name Jesus as Savior and Lord, thereby glorifying the name of the Father in heaven who will create a new heaven and a new earth.

Guidelines

The following guidelines will undergird the goals and strategies for the urban ministries of the RCA. These guidelines contain both present realities and future directions. They are statements of "what is" and "what is yet to be."

Urban Ministry and RCA Priorities. Urban ministries will be a continuing high priority among all ministries of the RCA in order that the entire ministry and mission be complete. Further, urban ministries will be affirmed, celebrated, and supported by the entire denomination as integral aspects of RCA mission.

Urban Ministry as an Ongoing Work of the Church. Since an ad hoc or "specialized" connotation of urban work is inadequate, such a ministry will be a normal and regular aspect of the entire church's witness.

Urban Ministry and the Congregation. The primary focus for urban ministry is the urban congregation.

Urban Ministry and the Inner City. Since great opportunities for ministry to human need exist in the inner city, the major focus of RCA urban ministries will be upon the support of inner-city congregations in the utilization of their gifts and resources.

Urban Ministry and Public Policy. Urban ministry is affected by policies and dynamics developed by non-church structures and agencies. Influencing such structures and agencies toward policies and programs conducive to more wholesome life and environment is a needed activity.

Urban Ministry and Inter-Church Cooperation. Systemic and massive issues, problems, and challenges will be addressed at every level in co-operation with partners from other religious bodies.

AN URBAN AGENDA

From: "Urban Agenda," A Report to the Eleventh General Synod of the United Church of Christ, 1978, pp. 6–8.

As our national agenda is an urban agenda, so the urban agenda is the agenda of the United Church of Christ. The theological perspective we bring to the urban agenda combines elements of prophetic fervor normed by humble confession, liberal idealism normed by the awareness of our present realities, and radical hope normed by practical response. We stand in the tension between Babylon and Jerusalem, the biblical images that highlight our potential for good or evil. It is the tension between good and evil that defines our reality as we go about our theological task of addressing the pressing dilemmas facing our contemporary cities.

In keeping with our tradition, we look to the biblical witness to inform our present reality. As we reflect on our present, five biblical themes help to define our reality: 1) Community, 2) Compassion, 3) Justice, 4) Liberation, 5) Hope.

Community

One of the dominant themes in the Bible is the vision of community: the vision of a human community that is inclusive, caring and safe. The prophet Jeremiah addresses the exiles in a strange land: "Seek the welfare of the city where I have sent you, and pray to the Lord on its behalf, for in its welfare you will find your welfare." (Jer. 29:7) The biblical message is consistent in its proclamation that all people of the world are interrelated—bound by the Lordship of Christ to each other, bound in our situation because of God's caring and enduring love. The prophet is absolutely correct: every person's welfare will be found in the welfare of the city because we are brothers and sisters of this earth.

The ideal set before us in the biblical witness is that community is all people living together in mutual respect, caring for each other, and being morally responsible to each other. Our reality, however, in this time lies in one tension between the vision of community and our cultural and social value of individualism.

Compassion

The gospel accounts of the life of Jesus tell us very clearly what the norm for compassion is all about. Jesus spoke and acted compassionately: feeling the pain of the sick, he healed: knowing the pangs of hunger, he provided food: knowing the despair of loneliness, he became a friend. When he approached and saw the city Jerusalem, he wept, for he saw and felt the corruption, violence and despair of the people. We see the corruption, violence, poverty and despair in our modern cities: the reality glares at us, yet we stand in the tension between compassion, the willingness to feel the pain of our brothers and sisters, and apathy and detachment, that urge to avoid pain, the fear of feeling pain, the inability to weep for the afflicted.

Justice

In the biblical story, God demonstrates again and again a special bias toward the poor. God intervenes time and time again in history on behalf of the poor, the oppressed and the exploited. In the Bible, justice is the bottom line, for there is the clear recognition that the poor are poor because they don't have money. Poverty continues to exist because permission is given for those who have to get more, and to those who have not, to stay that way. We stand in tension today between our desire to do justice and our desires to make no sacrifices that would insure justice. Our desires for money and things give permission to those who have to get more, and to those who don't to stay that way. This tension is our reality.

Liberation

The biblical theme of liberation is always addressed to those who are held captive—those who are poor, exploited and oppressed. To be liberated is to have power to influence one's own life and destiny. Liberation affirms God's redeeming activity among the poor and the oppressed; liberation is not the benevolent gift from captors who give only to use people in another way that binds them. The reality of our time, and the tension we feel, is on the one hand our desire to be liberated from the forces that bind us, and on the other hand, our fear of the liberation of others, especially when others are of a different color, of a different culture, of a different sex, or if they are mentally or physically handicapped, or all of the above, and poor. Our tensions can be defined by the problem of "differentness."

Hope

Within the biblical story, the city of Babylon is always condemned. The sins of poverty, hunger, corruption, and violence that mark the city, bring forth the wrath of God. Yet an equally dominant theme is the image of a New Jerusalem—a city in which human beings find goodness in life, a person-oriented city that shows acceptance, friendship, enough money to live freely, and a prevailing justice. Herein lies our hope, and while we do not know (and the Bible does not tell us) what God intends for our modern cities, we know that God calls us to more abundant forms of community. "Hope that is seen is not hope," says Paul. Our reality and one of our most severe tensions is created by our desire to retain what we know, what is or what has been. We want things better than they are, but not if it means changing our values and life styles. Hope in that which is unseen is eminently more difficult.

Urban strategy needs to address a set of interlocking issues that confront American society, and which intersect in the cities, where they are focused and compounded. "It is not a job or an education problem," says Richard Nathan of the Brookings Institution, speaking about minority youth unemployment. "It is all these conditions coming together in cities with huge concentrations of distressed population." Urban strategy, then, needs to speak to employment, housing, health care, Education, Environment, Transportation and Neighborhood development as well as fiscal problems of cities.

CHURCH INVOLVEMENT IN THE CITY

From: "Report to the National United Methodist Church Urban Ministries Network Leaders Meeting," by the Office of Urban Ministries, United Methodist Church, 1979, p. 8.

Church involvement in community development and urban justice advocacy is a crucial component of an effective urban ministries strategy. Even when the issue is church institutional survival, the community context is the critical starting point. And, for the "authentic church," there is no question but that it "exists *in* and *for* the *world*" and that it understands that "the local church is a *strategic base* from which Christians *move out to the structures of society.*"

The work of the Office of Urban Ministries (OUM) is, once again, to enable that church involvement through strategy development, training and consultative services, financial resourcing—and we would add here, especially, networking and coalition-building.

1. *National Urban Policy.* The development of a just national urban policy is a basic priority here. It can provide the framework of possibility or constraint for whatever the church and other groups attempt. . . . There was [in May, 1978] still high hope that the newly announced Carter Urban Policy might furnish a fresh "catalytic occasion" and "general paradigm" for our work in urban community development. Now, we are far less sure, due to the Administration's considerable retreat in commitment. . . . However, the conceptual framework, if not the programmatic implementation, still remains intact—and serves to remind us of the need for a comprehensive and coordinated attack on the crisis of "Balanced National Growth and Economic Development," which is represented in the near-collapse of the central city, urban sprawl, disinvestment, regional conflict, and flight of capital from America. And the concept of "A New Partnership to Conserve America's Communities," with its stress on conservation and revitalization, partnership (of federal, state, and local governments; the private sector, and voluntary and neighborhood associations), and neighborhood development and economic development (as the basic starting points for revitalization), remains eminently valid. Moreover, the concept of an "urban impact analysis" as a key feature serves as a "general paradigm," with implications for the church and all other institutions.

The work of OUM on Urban Policy has centered in strategy development. This has included participation in (1) the National Association of Neighborhoods' Conference on Neighborhoods and Urban Policy (May 21–22, 1978, Washington, D.C.); (2) The White House Briefing for Religious Leaders on National Urban Policy (September 28, 1978) and follow-up meetings of a National Ecumenical Steering Committee; (3) The Churches' Center for Theology and Public Policy—Urban Policy Panel (an 18-month "think-tank" process, involving church, government, voluntary and community organization leaders); (4) the work of the Interfaith Center on Corporate Responsibility's Community Reinvestment Work Group; and (5) efforts to develop an ecumenical partnership, via the JSAC Metropolitan Ministries Task Force, with the National Association of Neighborhoods, and neighborhood and city-wide church and community organizations in ten pilot cities for a "National Anti-displacement Campaign."

A CALL TO COMMITMENT TO THE CITY

From: "A Call to Commitment to the City," A Statement issued by the
National Association of Ecumenical Staff and the Churches' Center for
Theology and Public Policy, July 1978. (The Statement is reproduced
in its entirety.)

This nation's cities are in deep trouble. Many urban residents are
suffering with little or no hope of finding a way out of their misery. The
religious community must share in the blame for this tragic situation.
Although we proclaim our diversity, pointing with pride to an ecumenical
fellowship embracing Whites, Blacks, Hispanics, Native Americans, and
Asians, we have more often than not gone our separate ways when faced
with the reality of urban decay. It is long past time to right this wrong, to
act as one people called into being by God, to follow the Biblical mandate
given by Jeremiah to "seek the welfare of the city . . . for in its welfare
you will find your welfare." Accordingly, we call upon the religious community through its various denominations and movements to commit its
energies and resources to the city, to devise national urban strategies and
policies, and to transform the words of this document into the reality of
God's healing ministry by developing and implementing at the local level
specific agendas for justice.

By issuing this call we do not wish to imply that people of faith have
completely turned their backs on the city. We are not interested in over-
simplification and distortion in order to gain attention. For the urban
religious community does have a long and continuing history of trying to
respond at the most basic levels of human need to those victims of our
chaotic urban condition. Both national and local missions have made
heroic efforts to alleviate some of the hurt our urban crisis has inflicted
on those powerless to defend themselves against the system. We also recognize that not all members of the religious community enjoy the luxury
of being able to challenge the status quo. Many are victimized by it and
are forced to devote their lives to the daily battle for survival. Yet a candid
appraisal can only conclude that efforts to make social and economic justice
a living presence in our cities have been a peripheral concern of most of
the religious community. We issue this call, then, from the perspective
of those, including ourselves, who have been "at ease in Zion" while
others have cried out for help.

We are among the many Christians and Jews, of means and mobility
who profess belief in and commitment to the Biblical God active in the

world on behalf of the poor and oppressed, but have abandoned the cities
in pursuit of a more comfortable and affluent lifestyle. We have benefited
from government highway, tax, mortgage, and development policies which
have created suburban sprawl for the haves and the prison of the ghetto
for the have-nots. We stood idly by and watched the dismantling of the
anti-poverty programs of the 60s. In our own congregational life we have
contributed to and blessed the white exodus from the city, and the resulting
economic disinvestment, by moving our own churches and synagogues to
greener pastures and by looking "beyond the Beltway" for the location of
new houses of worship. Even those middle-class congregations which have
remained in the city have, with far too few exceptions, exhibited a greater
concern for protecting their own real estate and searching out larger and
more convenient parking lots than in risking a commitment to the poorest
of the poor who live at their doorsteps. More than ten years ago the Kerner
Commission warned us that we were becoming two societies, one poor
and Black and the other White and rich. Today, we must acknowledge
the even starker reality that other minorities are also part of that poor
society, not only in the secular world but in our religious community as
well. In short, God's all-consuming passion for justice has become an
optional activity for many of those who call themselves his people. We
must confess our disgraceful and sinful behavior toward his children trap-
ped in the vicious circle of urban poverty and despair. We must accept
his judgment upon us and repent. We must renew our life together.

In calling Christians and Jews to repentance and renewal we think
not primarily of prayer and resolutions, although pray and pass resolutions
we must; not simply of holding our heads in shame, although guilt is part
of any authentic prophetic religion; not principally in terms of bigger and
more frequent charitable offerings, although the need for charity will not
disappear; instead we commit ourselves to the Biblical concept of repentance as radical change. We are required to turn around, face in a new
direction, change our whole way of thinking and acting. We are called to
take seriously God's liberating work in the world and to follow where he
leads. We believe the Lord of history and all creation is active in our
nation's cities, redeeming them as fit places to live.

For too long the religious community has preferred to ignore God's
redemptive activity. We have conformed to this world instead of committing ourselves to transform our society into his kingdom. For too long
we have played secular macro-economic games concerned with a statistical
analysis of the "health of the economy" while the lives of individual human
beings have wasted away. While many cities continue to cut vitally needed

services, we try hard to be convinced by those "experts" who argue that it really isn't correct to speak of an "urban crisis." We continue to congratulate ourselves on the "success" of the civil rights movement and do not combat the institutional and personal racism still rampant in our congregations and in the nation as a whole. Although forty percent of our Black inner-city youth cannot find work, we tend to celebrate the slowly declining national unemployment figures. Our response to crime is largely technological: more police, better equipment, stronger locks. More often than not rats outnumber human beings in decayed housing and yet we do not challenge an economic system which every month is pricing more and more people out of the private, and even subsidized, housing market, whether as renters or owners. We worry about inflation, and rightly so, but do not hear the cries of those who tell us that inflated dollars are better than no dollars at all. We complain about the high cost of food, yet we forget about those in the inner city who not only pay more for food but have difficulty finding a grocery store in the first place. We wring our hands that cities are becoming "wards" of the federal government, yet we do not make it possible for our urban areas to compete on an equal basis for private economic investment. And even when reinvestment does take place, we do not question the market-place mentality which seeks new opportunities at the expense of the poor and powerless, who are often displaced from neighborhoods and residences they have called home for years.

These few examples by no means exhaust the agenda for justice which God lays before us, but they do condemn our indifference and inaction; they do call us to repentance, renewal, and commitment. For the first time in many years the moment is ripe for the religious community to make the revitalization of the cities a major national goal. The urban neighborhood movement has taken on a new vitality. The sons and daughters of those who fled the cities not too many years ago are looking toward our urban centers to make their homes. A number of cities, large and small, continue to thrive and have much to teach their less fortunate neighbors. Other cities as well, although victims of urban decay, are facing their problems creatively and courageously.

On March 27, 1978, President Carter announced his long-awaited and long-promised urban policy: the first time an American President has attempted to put forward a comprehensive and coherent national policy for cities. The religious community made no serious organized attempt to influence the direction of this policy as it was being formulated. Although there is much in the administration's urban policy to commend, there is also cause for concern. Both the resources it makes available and the uses to which it plans to put them do not adequately reflect Biblical norms of economic and social justice for the poorest of the poor. We cannot be satisfied with anything less than a policy committed to that vision of the city, indeed of all of society, which is set forth in the Jewish and Christian traditions. The vision to which God calls us is one of opportunity for all of his children within the context of an inclusive and caring community. It is a vision of the city which extends beyond municipal boundaries to express the inter-dependence of urban, suburban, and rural communities. It is a vision which defines the health of our society by the health of its most problem-ridden central cities, which makes our own self-interest inseparable from the welfare of the weakest and poorest among us. It is the vision of *shalom*.

We have no adequate translation for *shalom*. Our word "peace" captures one side of it, but *shalom* is more than the absence of war. It is justice and love, wholeness, order, and harmony. *Shalom* puts people first and calls us back to life on a human scale, to city living which can embrace the creative rhythm of work, rest, and play. But it can only break into our midst when the whole of society accepts responsibility for the spiritual and physical well-being of all of its members. The prophet Isaiah brings *shalom* to life when he tells us that "the wolf shall dwell with the lamb and the leopard lie down with the kid . . ." For Christians the culmination of this vision of *shalom* is found in Christ as the Prince of Peace inaugurating the Kingdom of God on earth. The concreteness of the images in the Hebrew Scriptures and the incarnation in the Christian both run counter to our tendency to push the Kingdom of God entirely beyond history and make of it a totally spiritual concept demanding little or no commitment to *shalom* here and now.

With regard to the well-being of cities, the Biblical message is clear. There *is* continuity between the *terrestrial* Jerusalem and the heavenly city. The vision of "the City of the Lord, the Zion of the Holy One of Israel" *must* be reflected in our nation's urban policy. The path we are to take to move toward this vision, the "plumb line" against which we are to measure our actions, is that of distributive justice; justice seen as a special bias toward the poor and oppressed. In the Biblical story God again and again demonstrates his special bias. In fact, it is difficult to find any theme more clearly stated in the Scriptures than that of God's intervention in history for the poor and oppressed. In the Jewish and Christian traditions the bottom line is always justice, not economic theory and political strategy. Yet far too often the religious community has been co-opted by the political process in seeking to accommodate justice to what appears feasible, rather than committing ourselves to change what is feasible so that it conforms to justice.

If we are to be faithful to the prophetic Biblical imperative to pursue justice for "the least of these," we had best re-examine our traditional "trickle-down" approach of aiding people in distress. It is time that our search for innovative urban policies led us more in the direction of "filter-up." And what this means in a time of ever-increasing scarcity are hard decisions in favor of distributive justice, not easy-to-live-with programs which tend to perpetuate the status quo. In short, our religious tradition will not permit us to deal with cities without confronting those values which motivate our economic and political decisions.

We are under no illusions that a commitment to the city which is based on the vision of *shalom* and the reality of distributive justice will be an easy one to make, but our faith demands no less. Urban policy and urban ministry must be given top priority at the national and local levels and include:

1. substantial and continuing action by our institutions, congregations, and people, with major allocations of staff time and financial resources.

2. sustained theological study and reflection on the meaning of the city and God's redeeming activity on behalf of the poor and oppressed.

3. renewed emphasis on ministries of service, nurture, and celebration open to all urban residents.

4. support of lasting national, regional, and local inter-faith coalitions to engage in a long-term struggle to influence public policy through the processes of economic and political analysis, lobbying, monitoring of governmental and private sector activities, and evaluation of current programs and policies.

There are no instant solutions to the problems of the cities. But the vision of *shalom* tells us that our hopes are grounded in the reality of the Lord of history. What the future holds for urban America depends in no small measure on the commitment of the religious community to seek the welfare of the city. We believe God is calling us to this commitment.

APPENDIX C:

Governmental and

Non-governmental Organizations

THIS APPENDIX gives a sampling of federal agencies and public interest organizations which deal with urban policy on one or both of these two levels: (1) the formation of urban policy (2) the implementation of public policy. This list is intended to serve as a first step in helping readers to find sources of information and support. The particular strengths or weaknesses of an organization will become apparent as the reader deals with each. This list is limited to a sampling that has proved particularly helpful to the public.

URBAN-ORIENTED FEDERAL GOVERNMENT DEPARTMENTS AND AGENCIES

Department of Housing and Urban Development
451 7th St., S.W.
Washington, D.C. 20410
(202) 755-5111

The Department of Housing and Urban Development (HUD) is the principal federal agency responsible for programs concerned with housing needs and improving and developing the nation's communities.

Community Development Block Grants

Local governments in cities over 50,000 and urban counties with populations over 200,000 receive Community Development Block Grants, through HUD, for community development projects that can include property acquisition, housing rehabilitation and rehabilitation loans, public improvements, etc. Small cities compete for CDBG discretionary funds.

Many neighborhood projects have been funded; and block grants can be made available through the local government to private non-profit entities, neighborhood based groups, local development corporations and small business investment companies.

Housing Consumer Services Program

Provides support services and a limited program of grants to more than 550 HUD-approved counseling agencies; this program also helps bring community services to subsidized housing projects.

Urban Development Action Grants

Provides grants channeled through HUD area offices to distressed urban areas to stimulate private investment and spur economic development; can be used for neighborhood-based revitalization of jobs, housing and business; community groups can serve as subgrantees.

Rental Assistance

Section 8 program provides subsidies to pay the difference between market rates for housing units and what lower income families can afford (no more than 25% of household's adjusted income). Can be used for existing apartments, as well as moderate and substantial rehabilitation and new construction. Funds flow through local public housing authorities.

Direct Loans for Housing Elderly and Handicapped

Section 202 program provides direct, long-term loans to private non-profit organizations and consumer cooperatives, to finance rental or co-operative housing for elderly and handicapped persons.

Mortgage Insurance Programs

HUD's Federal Housing Administration provides insurance on single- and multifamily mortgages and on home improvement loans and mobile home loans. The insurance on multifamily mortgages includes that on cooperative housing, condominiums, and elderly projects. Applications are processed through HUD Area Offices.

Department of Justice
10th and Constitution Avenue, N.W.
Washington, D.C. 20530
(202) 737-8200

Plays a key role in protection against criminals and subversion, in anti-trust law enforcement, and in enforcing drug, immigration, and naturalization laws.

Community Anti-Crime Program
Provides funds and technical assistance directly to neighborhood groups
and organizations for community-based anti-crime activities.

National Consumer Cooperative Bank
2001 S St., N.W.
Washington, D.C. 20009
(202) 673-4300

The National Consumer Cooperative makes loans and provides technical assistance to consumer co-ops and to employee-owned producer co-
ops. Loans from the Bank Fund are made at prevailing interest rates and
loans from the smaller Self Help Fund to co-ops whose members are low
income persons or to beginning co-ops can be made at less than market
rates. The Co-op Bank has regional offices in eight cities: Boston, New
York, Charleston (S.C.), Detroit, Minneapolis, Fort Worth, Oakland and
Seattle. Loans have been made by the Co-op Bank to food co-ops, housing
co-ops, health care co-ops, co-op child care centers, farmworker co-ops,
a co-op bookstore, handicraft co-ops and others. A co-op may be formed
by an existing group such as a neighborhood association, church or labor
union to meet the needs of its members.

National Credit Union Administration
Washington, D.C. 20456
(202) 254-9800

The NCUA is the regulatory agency for federal credit unions. It
provides technical assistance for groups seeking a Federal Credit Union
Charter. It also provides guidance to federal credit unions in recordkeeping,
management, auditing, loan collection, credit union membership, etc.
The agency administers the National Credit Union Share Insurance Fund
which insures members accounts in federally and state chartered credit
unions.

Neighborhood Reinvestment Corporation
1120 19th St., N.W.
Washington, D.C. 20036
(202) 634-1900

Neighborhood Housing Services Program
NHS is designed to reverse neighborhood decline by promoting reinvestment in neighborhoods. NHS programs are private, locally-controlled,
locally-funded corporations. They offer financial and rehabilitation services

to residents of the locally-selected NHS neighborhood. Each NHS is based on a working partnership of neighborhood residents, representatives of local financial institutions and representatives of local government. Lenders commit themselves to offer mortgages and loans to the neighborhood. Cities promise to provide public improvement, residents promise to improve their housing.

Small Business Administration
1411 L Street, N.W.
Washington, D.C. 20416
(202) 653-6365

Aids, counsels, assists, and protects the interest of small business.

Economic Opportunity Loans

Provides loans and loan guarantees through SBA district offices as well as management and technical assistance to disadvantaged individuals who have the resources and desire to own their own businesses. This loan can be applied to both established and prospective small businesses.

Small Business Administration Section 7(a) Loan Program

Provides direct and guarantee loans to small business to cover costs of constructing, converting, and expanding business facilities (including purchase of land, buildings, machinery and equipment) and for working capital. SBA may guarantee up to 90% of a bank loan amount not to exceed $500,000.

Section 502 Local Development Company Program

Provides long term financing through intermediary organizations called Local Development Companies which may either be a profit or nonprofit type provided the company has the furtherance of economic development as its principal purpose. This program requires that ownership and control be vested in those who reside or do business in the specified locality. 502 loans may be used to finance construction, modernization or conversion of plants.

PRIVATE, NON-PROFIT AND URBAN-ORIENTED ORGANIZATIONS

ACORN (Arkansas Community Organization for Reform Now)
523 West 15th Street
Little Rock, Ark. 72202
(501) 376-7151

A multi-state network of community associations providing technical assistance to neighborhood groups on social service delivery and neighborhood improvement through a community organizer training program conducted by its Institute for Social Justice.

Center for Community Change
1000 Wisconsin Ave., N.W.
Washington, D.C. 20005
(202) 338-6310
    A non-profit organization which provides technical assistance to community-based organizations and their low-income constituents in support of local economic development and neighborhood revitalization. The technical assistance comes in the form of workshops, publications, and consultation focusing on topics such as crime prevention and the use of CETA programs. Information is provided for both rural and urban areas.

Center for Community Economic Development (CCED)
639 Massachusetts Ave.
Cambridge, MA 02139
(617) 547-9695
    Provides research and publications to local cooperatives, community development corporations, joint ventures and other community-based economic development organizations conducting local development activities.

Center for Neighborhood Technology
527 W. Randolph St.
Chicago, Il. 60606
(312) 454-0126
    This center provides technical assistance to neighborhood-based organizations to help groups to plan, design and secure funding for alternative neighborhood-scale technology programs, such as energy conservation, urban gardening, and housing rehabilitation. Publishes biweekly newsletter, "The Neighborhood Works."

Institute for Local Self Reliance
1717 18th St., N.W.
Washington, D.C. 20009
(202) 232-4108
    Provides direct technical assistance to neighborhoods and cities in the

areas of urban food production, urban energy and technological resources including energy conservation, community economics and government, waste utilization, and food co-ops and access to information. Publishes monthly newsletter, "Self Reliance."

Jubilee Housing, Inc.
1750 Columbia Road, N.W.
Washington, D.C. 20009
(202) 332-4020
 Provides technical assistance in housing rehabilitation for multi-unit apartment buildings for tenant owned and managed, low-income people's cooperatives.

Low Income Housing Information Service
215 8th St., N.E.
Washington, D.C. 20002
(202) 554-2544
 Provides information on low-income housing issues.

National Association for the Advancement of Colored People (NAACP)
1790 Broadway
New York, N.Y. 10019
(212) 245-2100
 Through its 2700 branches, the NAACP Housing Division operates programs to combat housing discrimination, monitor local housing and community development activities, run information centers and sponsor non-profit housing. NAACP's Economic Development Division, through the branches, focuses on community action to develop jobs and stabilize local economic bases. Local community groups can link up with the NAACP branches to coordinate revitalization strategies.

National Association of Neighborhoods (NAN)
1612 20th St., N.W.
Washington, D.C. 20009
(202) 332-7766
 NAN provides technical assistance through conferences, workshops and publications to its members. There are 14 citizen-controlled task forces which deal with issues such as: crime, housing and community development, energy and volunteerism.

National Center for Economic Alternatives
2000 P Street, N.W.
Washington, D.C. 20036
(202) 833-3208
    Provides technical assistance to groups seeking alternative avenues to
local economic development such as cooperative ownership, work-your-
own-farms, capital reallocation and job stabilization.

National Council of LaRaza
1725 Eye Street, N.W. Suite 201
Washington, D.C. 20036
(202) 659-1251
    Provides technical assistance on economic development and social
service delivery to towns of 5,000 and under, concerned with Hispanic
social, economic, and community development.

National People's Action
115 West Washington St.
Chicago, IL 60607
(312) 243-3038
    A coalition of grassroots and community based organizations united
to halt neighborhood deterioration and provide technical assistance on
urban reinvestment, zoning, real estate lending practices and community
organizing.

National Training and Information Center
1123 W. Washington Blvd.
Chicago, IL 60607
(312) 243-3035
    Aids in planning and developing national, regional and local con-
ferences with technical assistance in media coverage and public relations.
They also provide on-site consulting and training to developing organizations with developing neighborhood power bases.

National Urban Coalition
1201 Connecticut Avenue, N.W.
Washington, D.C. 20036
(202) 331-2400

A coalition of minority groups. Conducts local model urban programs, neighborhood revitalization programs, neighborhood housing services.

The National Urban League
500 E. 62nd Street
New York, N.Y. 10021
(212) 664-5262
Provides technical assistance in economic development through efforts of community programs, housing counseling, and planning advocacy in disadvantaged black and other minority communities.

Neighborhood Development Collaborative
First Maryland Savings and Loan Building
Suite 200
Crofton, MD 21114
(301) 261-3939/3932
Works with non-profit community organizations and for-profit corporations in physical, economic and human service development projects. Conducts research, develops policy and provides training and technical assistance in these areas.

BIBLIOGRAPHY

Berger, Peter. *Pyramids of Sacrifice*. New York: Basic Books, 1974.

Carlisi, John, and Carol Conroy. *Attracting Resources for Community Development: A Guide for Neighborhood Development Organization*. Washington, D.C.: Neighborhood Development Collaborative, 1980.

Coats, William. *God in Public: Political Theology Beyond Niebuhr*. Grand Rapids, Michigan: Eerdmans, 1947.

Committee on Banking, Finance and Urban Affairs, Subcommittee on Housing and Community Development, U.S. House of Representatives, *Urban Policy*. 95th Congress, 2nd Session, 1978.

Committee on Banking, Finance and Urban Affairs, Subcommittee on the City, U.S. House of Representatives, *To Save a City*. 95th Congress, 1st Session, 1977.

Committee on Banking, Finance and Urban Affairs, Subcommittee on the City, U.S. House of Representatives, *Toward a National Urban Policy*. 96th Congress, 1st Session, 1977.

Committee on Governmental Affairs, Subcommittee on Intergovernmental Relations, U.S. Senate, *Urban Policy in America*. 95th Congress, 2nd Session, 1978.

Cross, Robert D. (ed.). *The Church and the City*. 1865–1910. New York: Bobbs-Merrill, 1967.

"Eirene," *Theological Wordbook of the New Testament*, Vol. 2, edited by Gerhard Kittel and Gerhard Friedrich. Grand Rapids, Michigan: Eerdmans, 1964.

Frick, Frank. *The City in Ancient Israel*. Missoula, Montana: Scholars Press, 1977.

Garn, Harvey, et al. *A Framework for National Urban Policy: Urban Distress, Decline and Growth*. Washington, D.C.: The Urban Institute, 1978.

Greeley, Andrew M. and Gregory Baum. *Ethnicity*. New York: Seabury Press, 1977.

Harman, Willis. *An Incomplete Guide to the Future*. San Francisco: San Francisco Book Co., 1976.

Linn, Johannes F. *Policies for Efficient and Equitable Growth of Cities in Developing Countries.* World Bank Stall Working Paper No. 342. Washington, D.C.: The World Bank, 1979.

Kane, Margaret. *Gospel in Industrial Society.* London: SCM Press, 1980.

Mackensie, R.A.F. "The City and Israelite Religion," *Catholic Biblical Quarterly,* 25 (65), 60–70.

MacPherson, C.B. *The Political Theory of Possessive Individualism.* New York: Oxford University Press, 1962.

Martin, Keith D. *Perspectives on an Urban Theology. Shalom Papers,* 3. Washington, D.C.: Churches' Center for Theology and Public Policy, 1977.

Nathan, Richard and Charles Adam. *Understanding Central City Hardship.* Washington, D.C.: Brookings Institution, 1976.

The National Commission on Neighborhoods. *People, Building Neighborhoods.* Washington, D.C., 1979.

The President's Commission for a National Agenda for the Eighties. *A National Agenda for the Eighties.* Washington, D.C., 1980.

The President's Urban and Regional Policy Group Report. *A New Partnership to Conserve America's Communities: A National Urban Policy.* Washington, D.C., 1978.

Shriver, Donald W., Jr. and Karl A. Ostrom. *Is There Hope for the City?* Philadelphia: The Westminster Press, 1977.

Soloman, Arthur, (ed.). *The Prospective City.* Cambridge, Mass.: MIT Press, 1979.

Stackhouse, Max L. *Ethics and the Urban Ethos.* Boston: Beacon Press, 1974.

Stanfield, Rochelle L. "Federal Policy Makers Now Must Ask: Will It Hurt the Cities?" *National Journal.* 11 (1979), 1203–1206.

Stanfield, Rochelle L. "The Neighborhood—Getting a Piece of the Urban Policy Pie." *National Journal.* 10 (1978), 624–629.

Stanfield, Rochelle L. "Two Views of Carter's National Urban Policy." *National Journal.* 10 (1978), 1389–1391.

U.S. Department of Housing and Urban Development. *A Survey of Citizen Views and Concerns About Urban Life.* Washington, D.C., 1978.

U.S. Department of Housing and Urban Development. *The President's 1978 National Urban Policy Report.* Washington, D.C., 1978.

U.S. Office of Consumer Affairs. *People Power: What Communities Are Doing to Counter Inflation.* Washington, D.C., 1980.

Urban Policy: A Black Perspective.—Urban League Review. 3 (1978), entire issue.

Walsh, Annmarie Hauck. *The Public's Business: The Politics and Practices of the Government Corporations.* Cambridge, Mass.: MIT Press, 1978.

Ward, Barbara. *The Home of Man.* New York: W. W. Norton, 1976.

Warner, Sam Bass. *The Urban Wilderness.* New York: Harper and Row, 1972.

The World Bank. *World Development Report, 1979.* Washington, D.C.: The World Bank, 1979.